To Laura

Journey Through Darkness

Howard Brown

Best Wishes

Howard B. x

checked

ROMULUS PUBLISHING
Newark • England

Published 2008 by Romulus Publishing

A catalogue record for this book is available
from the British Library.
ISBN 978-095565-910-2

Romulus Publishing
PO Box 9419   Newark   NG24 9FH   England

E-mail: howardbrown@romuluspublishing.com

Typeset in 11pt Sabon by
Free Thinking Design Peterborough England

Printed and bound in Great Britain through
SS Media Limited Wallington Surrey England

Papers used by SS Media Limited are natural, recyclable
products made from wood grown in sustainable forests.
The manufacturing processes conform to the environmental
regulations of the country of origin.

In Dedication to
Nick, Chris, Kelis, and Mom,
without whose existence my life
would have taken an entirely different path

Speak the truth and speak it ever
Cost it what it will
For they who hide the wrongs they do
Will do them ever still
– Anon

The following have saved me much embarrassment
with their advice and assistance in the compilation
and proofing of this book:

Anne, Bekah, Razor, Lyndsey, Lynn, Matt, Nick, Sam

Many Thanks

1

I know the rule, try not to get out of bed until it's time to get up. Interrupting your sleep during the night makes your brain start a fresh rest cycle so when you get up in the morning you feel like you've hardly had any slumber. Couldn't help it though, had to take a leak, courtesy of a late-night tipple and things on my mind. So when Nia nudged me to answer the door at 7.15am I felt like a zombie. She said it was the postman. That was all I needed. I'm not in the habit of answering the door to strangers in my dressing gown. Makes me feel vulnerable. So I dragged on a pair of jeans and a T-shirt as I stumbled out of the bedroom. The knocking was incessant, 'Postman, knocking like that it had better be something special!' It seems I have a penchant for understatement. The racket must have made Nia look out of the window because as I reached the top of the stairs I half-heard her voice, *'Howard, it's the police!'*

I paused, 'What do they want?' was my first thought, maybe someone I know must have messed up, which is pretty much standard for someone involved in the fight game, but as far as I know had nothing to do with me. When I opened the door I was met with a reasonable enough question, *'Howard Brown?'*, I replied in the affirmative while thinking, I know policemen are big guys, but this is ridiculous, this fellow, and the goliaths I clocked standing behind him were as big as WWE wrestlers. *'We have a warrant to search these premises on suspi-*

cion of drug trafficking', *'sure'* I said after pretending to read the piece of paper that was held to my face. They marched authoritatively past me into the through-lounge, so I followed, and it was only when I opened the blinds to the rear of the house that I saw umpteen guys in my back garden, and another couple scrambling over my garage roof. It's amazing how non-plussed you can be in a situation like that. I think it's the numbness you feel when you're caught in a whirlwind.

Before I could sensibly collect my thoughts, my diaries, telephone books, and other paperwork were on my dining room table, with me sat down and being questioned, oh so politely, by two detectives from The National Crime Squad. Don't know how I noticed, but one of the officers searching the house opened the patio doors, and Pepe was in. That was all I needed. Pepe was the family pet, a brown-and-white coloured Lop-eared rabbit, whose only interest when he came into the house was to chew whatever furniture or wiring he came across, because of this I made sure that he spent most of his time outside in his hutch unless one of the family were prepared to baby-sit him. He was so keen to come inside that if you opened the patio doors he would barge into your legs in a bid to get past. I stood up sharply, *'He'll bite through the wiring!'* Well, you've never seen anything so surreal in your life, as four of those gargantuan police officers tried to catch that rabbit in what seemed like an excerpt from the Keystone Cops, and yet by all accounts was supposed to be a serious crime procedure. The image will stay with me for the rest of my life.

This episode and the politeness of the arresting officers made it difficult for me to comprehend the gravity of the situation. They even asked my wife, if she and the children were 'decent' before venturing upstairs to continue their search. Nia, bless her, kept her composure, was her usual demure self, and took our two younger children, Chris and Kelis to school in as apparently unruffled a manner as one could wish. She was to break down woefully later on. Thankfully our older son, Nick, was away on a degree course in Bedford and was spared this onslaught on the family home.

The kid-gloves attitude of the officers was unexpected as I know from chats with various friends and associates that one of the psychological ploys of the police is to handcuff your partner and march her out of the door to the police station in front of you. That sight certainly puts the pressure on. But thankfully, none of that for me and for whatever reason that I was arrested in such a dignified manner, I'm very grateful.

Having some knowledge of the legal system and feeling that this was all one big misunderstanding, I chose what I felt was the best course of action when under interview at the police station, I replied with the same answer to every question. '*No comment, no comment, no comment.*'

2

It was eight weeks earlier that I bumped into Lex up on Broad Street. I was standing outside the Sports Café when he sidled up to me and whispered *'small world, isn't it!'* The last time I'd seen him was about eight months prior at a World Championship Kickboxing event in Amsterdam. He was a good friend of Michel's, an up-and-coming Dutch promoter that I'd become friendly with, and was clearly a popular guy who I took to that weekend because of his affable and self-deprecating style. He was with another familiar face, Gunther, a tall blonde haired rock star type who also frequented the Dutch kickboxing fraternity. Lex said they were on business together for the weekend and were taking in the sights for the afternoon.

As a promoter myself I was familiar with most of the big hotels in Birmingham city centre, as I used them to accommodate incoming international fighters, so when Lex told me that he and Gunther were staying at The Swallow, one of the most prestigious hotels in Birmingham, and one that I had never booked, how could I refuse his invitation to join them for a look around the place. You never know, I might decide to use it on my next show.

Lex speaks broken English, and although admirably fluent, (considering that I don't speak Dutch), he often searches for the correct words to express himself more clearly, so naturally you frequently help him out when in conversation. This little hiccup didn't make conversation with him anything less enjoyable, quite the opposite in fact, as he's such an effervescent and engaging guy.

Lex had many questions for me about English guys that he knew, especially in the Birmingham area, and without betraying any confidences, and I held many, I obliged him with what he needed to know.

No one likes to think of themselves as naïve, and I had a good idea of the 'business' that Lex was in town for even before heading back to the hotel, but his affairs were nothing to do with me so I was unconcerned about getting wrapped up in them myself. The business, was cannabis importation from Holland to England, and this subject formed the basis of much of our conversation.

This kind of talk was something that I was used to. My first trip to Amsterdam was in 1978 when I flew over on my own as a novice fighter to face Jean Coopmans, the Dutch Featherweight champion, in my first Muay Thai kickboxing bout. It was a baptism by fire for me as I wasn't trained in Thai Boxing, I practised Shotokan Karate and was a keen amateur boxer. I fought my heart out and lost narrowly on points. Coopman dropped me with a kick to the thigh in the third round, I wasn't used to the technique so found it difficult to block. I got up and stamped the canvas with my foot to get rid of the numbness while the referee gave an eight count. When we resumed action I tore into Coopman. The crowd loved it and I became a kind of adopted son to the fighters at the Chakuriki gym where I was training that week. I learned a lot from the trainers and fighters there, much of it gave me a big head start on the fledgling English kickboxing scene when I got back home.

As the afternoon wore on Lex became confident enough to discuss people and matters that he was normally too guarded to mention. It was exciting and eye-opening chatter, as most of the people that he mentioned, not only did I know, but I knew very well. I joined in with relish, and felt obliged to impart information that was divulged to me in secrecy but without mentioning specific names. That's the thing about grown men that are involved in serious crime, they've got some wicked stories to tell. Because it was the middle of the afternoon, I declined the alcohol that the guys offered me from the hotel mini-bar. It made little difference anyway, we had such a good time, that I still got tipsy with the euphoria of it all and felt fully charged when I headed back to my car.

When the police played the tape of that afternoon's conversation to me I was well and truly dumbstruck and the phrase 'another fine mess....' ran repeatedly through my mind. It's up to the Police Station Duty Sergeant to decide whether to hold a suspect in custody or not, and with the names of some of the individuals mentioned on that tape I knew for sure that I was going nowhere. I was charged with conspiracy to supply cannabis and held overnight in the cells at Rose Road police station.

The duty solicitor who sat in during my interview ferried information to me about the emotional state of my wife and children, and my brother-in-law, Steve, drove Nia over in a bid to see me but it was declined. I was allowed the Kentucky Fried Chicken meal that they brought me though, and I won't deny that I thoroughly enjoyed it.

Later that evening the officers at the station asked me if I wanted to telephone my family and allowed me out to the reception area. Nia was understandably very upset. Thankfully Nick had come home from university to help lend support and I have to say, it's rare that I've ever felt so helpless. It was a feeling that I was going to get used to.

I was escorted back to my cell by a very friendly senior police detective who stood to chat with me outside my cell door. He said that it had caused quite a stir that I was held at the station as I was a local celebrity in Birmingham due to my success in the ring and that I seemed too nice to be seriously caught up in such nonsense. All he wanted was more information about some of the characters mentioned during the hotel conversation, and specifically about the Dutch figurehead that was constantly referred to on the tape as 'Breitling'. I told him that I had no real idea, as most of the chat was hearsay and bravado. He insisted that if I cooperated then I would in all probability be released to go home that very night. What a relief from this nightmare that would have been, but I genuinely couldn't help him. He wasn't even looking at me when he closed the cell door. It can be quite jolting when someone switches from hot to cold that fast.

In the morning I was ferried by prison van to Birmingham Magistrates Court were I was formally charged. Nia, Nick, and a few friends were present and it must have been quite a shock for them to see me being led up from the cells in handcuffs. The duty solicitor was still acting for me and he felt sure that getting bail so that we could sort this mess out would be a matter of course. He was wrong. The Crown Prosecution Service scared the magistrates to death with a picture of me as an extremely successful criminal who lived in luxury and who had the 'means and the contacts' with which to flee the country, alleging that I had transacted drug deals in the region of 30 million pounds. I wondered which movie it was that they thought they were watching. Bail was denied.

I was taken back down the stairs with that same non-plussed feeling again, even though it was clear to me, I was going to spend some time in jail.

Birmingham Prison is known as 'The Green', simply because it is located in the Winson Green area of the city. It's an old Victorian building and at the time was desperately in need of modernisation, and whether you are a prison officer, visitor, or inmate, it can adequately be summed up in one word, 'daunt-ing'. Its look was in keeping with its reputation, it has housed some very notorious, and some very hard men during its history and deserved its notoriety as one of Britain's toughest jails. If you wanted to act the fool, the Green wasn't the place to do it.

Anyone that has experienced it will tell you the same thing, prison processing is a de-humanizing experience. The worst part of it is the bureaucracy. The waiting around for transport, the handcuffing process, disembarkation at the court or prison, the wait for the strip search, clothing, toiletries, and cell allocation, all of them are interminable. The handcuffing did give me a chuckle though. I always had to wait until last because of the note on my file. As a retired world kickboxing champion I was double-cuffed to officers for entry and exit to the prison van, even though my background and personality were well documented and it was common knowledge that I was a very placid guy. The officers always apologised for the inconvenience but I didn't mind, it was pretty cool really.

I shared my first night in jail with a guy called Martin, an unshaven and unkempt fellow who I placed at about fifty years of age and assumed to be a vagrant. He was already in the cell when I arrived and had positioned himself in the top bunk. My heart sank a little when I saw him. I'm a stickler for hygiene so I wasn't too impressed.

Prison cells are not the biggest of spaces, and are particularly sparse, this one comprised a double-bunk, a sink, a toilet, a table, and two chairs. There was no television, so you had to provide your own entertainment. Thankfully Martin was quite amiable. I gathered this wasn't his first spell inside and he confirmed as much during the course of our habitation. As an ex-fighter, I should apply the old adage more than most, 'never judge a book by its cover'. I re-learned it again that night. Martin was as educated and eloquent as anyone that I've ever met, and when, for whatever reason, we started talking about English literature, he recited Rudyard Kipling's popular verse 'If' from beginning to end. It's my favourite poem. I was blown away and figured that the best thing that I could do while in custody was gain access to the library and use the time wisely to catch up on some reading.

That night was the first time that I'd gotten a good night's sleep since my arrest so when the cell door was loudly unlocked and flung open it was pretty startling. It was real early too, morning, but not breakfast time. Martin had started to rise when he heard the keys in the door and was hopping down out of his bunk when a voice boomed, *'Get outside!'* He wisely obliged and I thought, 'Well, they've come to put you in your place kid, just block what you can and take your beating like a man.' I figured that if I fought back matters would only escalate. It was quite simply a no-win situation.

By the time the prison officer stood in the doorway, I was in a sitting position by the side of the lower bunk and feeling just how I don't like to, vulnerable, mainly because all I had on was a pair of shorts. I was ready for anything though, or so I thought. The voice erupted again, *'What the hell are you doing here?'* 'Me', I replied *'What are YOU doing here?'*

It had to have been twenty years since I had seen Mark Page. My last recollection was in 1979 when we were both being awarded our first degree Blackbelts in Shotokan Karate. I stopped practising that art then, it wasn't practical for the sporting career that I wanted to forge as a kickboxer, but it suited Mark, and he was still actively training which was admirable as many of the guys from that period had stopped working out long ago. Mark was 'old school' in his attitude to martial arts, he wasn't so much interested in the competition aspect, but more so in the street-defence applications, the throat-clutching and eye-gouging techniques etc. Now I knew why. He'd been in the prison service for years and was well known as one of the no-nonsense officers. Mark does have that Clint Eastwood type aura about him. He doesn't smile or talk much and is an 'honourable' prison officer, in other words, he would take off his radio, belt, and his keys and lock himself in a cell with the inmates that 'fancied it'. No matter who came out on top, which was invariably Mark, the matter would rest there and go no further. With the advent of the politically correct brigade, he's part of a dying breed, but he's definitely got the respect of inmates and staff alike.

We didn't speak for long, but I was assured that if I needed anything within reason, it would be provided. I don't think my requests shocked him too much. Access to the payphones, library, and gym. Mark nodded, told me to ask for him person-ally if I encountered any type of problem and said that there were a few other officers who wanted to meet me.

What later became apparent is the amount of prison staff that practice martial arts, and some to a very high degree. I spent seventy days at The Green before obtaining bail and was treated with respect throughout the length of it. I didn't take advantage either, so long as I got plenty of access to the three facilities I treasured I was as happy as anyone could be in that predicament. And throughout it all I never once imagined that I would be found guilty of anything.

That same day I was told 'the Dutch guy' that was on 'C' block wanted to see me and was seeking permission to come over to my wing. It was said with such reverence that I figured Lex had made quite some impact in the jail. I hadn't really given it much thought that he would be there, but it should have been obvious. He was arrested as part of a police surveillance operation just two days after our meeting at The Swallow Hotel in a swoop that saw another seven men, all from Birmingham, also taken into custody for cannabis importation. Gunther, fortunately for him, had already headed home. The police had then put me under scrutiny for a further two months in the hope of uncovering even more criminal activity, and after finding zero, decided to pick me up on the strength of the tape alone. Lex filled in the gaps.

I kept a low profile throughout my time on remand, which wasn't difficult as it's pretty easy to keep out of trouble if you don't take drugs. I never have and never will. I don't even take aspirins. I'd never been more grateful for that stance until then as the drug scene in jail is horrendous, and forms a sub-culture that trades in millions of pounds of contraband a year. The drug of choice for many is heroin, a truly abominable addiction, the pandemic of which in British jails is a legacy of government stupidity.

Not that many years ago cannabis was the most popular drug in the prison community and prison officers would turn a blind eye to discreet use as it made their job easier. People stoned on cannabis are usually as chilled as you can get and just want to eat and sleep. If they cannot get hold of the drug for a period of time, they normally accept that fact with no apparent psychological or physical misbehaviour. 'Brown', as heroin is known, is a different matter.

Mandatory random drug testing for inmates was made fully operational within Her Majesty's Prison Service in March 1996 with a view to curbing drug abuse and punishing both users and suppliers. Prison officers quite wisely lobbied that cannabis should be made exempt from this and be either legalised within the prison system or detected and punished in a less severe manner. They knew what they were saying and foresaw the dangers that the think-tank groups did not.

Drug tests consist of taking a sample of urine from the subject and screening it for abnormal levels of either cannabis or opiates (heroin), with traces of either drug rendering the offender liable to punishment such as loss of sentence remission days, loss of privileges, or solitary confinement in the prison segregation unit, affectionately referred to as 'the block'. Opiates can be clear of the body's urine within a day or so, cannabis takes almost a month to pass through, the upshot of which is that a night smoking 'a spliff' of weed would leave the participant susceptible to a positive drug test for two to three weeks, whereas a boost of heroin could be flushed from the system within a day or two. The upshot? Heroin abuse explosion.

This was bad enough, but the ripple effect, was much worse. Many inmates that were normally just occasional pot smokers, a drug low on the addiction scale, became heroin addicts, a substance that is extremely addictive and far more damaging physiologically. These new converts, who only began to take brown because of spending time in jail, then took this addiction with them out onto the street when their jail term was over. And with increasing demand, guess what happens to supply? Its simple economics, it shot through the roof and the problem perpetuated itself both inside and outside the prison walls.

Different types of drug use can be related to particular crimes, crack cocaine tends to make users, and indeed dealers, prone to violence, and they become loud, aggressive, and impossible to reason with. Heroin addicts, become equally desperate when they run out of funds to obtain their pick-me-up, and although less violent, are certainly more plentiful. Their crimes of choice are burglary and mugging, choices which are often a first and not a last resort.

Although not directly responsible for the heroin trade, the introduction of random MDT's within the prison system was a major catalyst in its boom and has added considerably to the rising crime rate in Great Britain. The mind-boggles at how teams of government experts did not forsee the effects of such an ill-thought out policy and neglected the advice of the people at the front-line, the prison officers.

What surprised me was that a lot of black guys were also hooked on this abomination. I, quite naively, thought that such a situation could never exist. Black people smoke weed, some are of course addicted to crack cocaine, but heroin was predominantly used by whites and Asians. It was a culture shock for me, and one that introduced itself in the most disgusting manner. I was asked to clean a cell in which the incumbent inmate, one of the 'brothers', had been violently sick after snorting a contaminated batch of brown. I wondered what type of a sickness it was that could yield such filth. I have never had to perform such a revolting task in my life. I was to become aware, and once in quite tragic circumstances that this was not a rarity.

Still, none of this was my problem, and users don't have time to mingle with guys like me who don't give a hoot about either supplying or taking the drug. All I did during those two and a half months on remand was read and work-out in the gym, and the only grief I ever came across was over something really trivial, a postage stamp.

Canteen days were every Wednesday, the busiest day in the jail. Guys would load up on tobacco, which is jail's number one currency, phone cards, chocolate, biscuits, and any of the other available goodies from the prison canteen that they could afford. Top of the list for me were phone cards, so that I could speak to Nia and the children on a daily basis, and postage stamps so that I could write to my new solicitors, to my mother, brothers, and my sister in America, and reply to the numerous letters of support that I was receiving from all corners.

I guess my demeanour gave away the fact that I was a literary kind of guy, that plus the fact that I used to order the Sunday Times every week when every one else was reading the News of the World or Sunday Sport. I was obviously a kind of sore thumb walking away from the newspaper collection desk with that broadsheet every Sunday morning. So I wasn't at all surprised when I was accosted by one of a Jamaican 'yardie' crew and asked if I had a postage stamp that he could borrow. I'd seen that crew around but never spoken to them, I had brief chats with lots of guys, but never associated with anyone in particular so I guess I came across as a loner type figure. I'm of Jamaican descent too, and was born and raised in the Handsworth area of Birmingham, and even when I moved to a more prosperous location at the height of my fighting career, I was introduced in pre-fight build-ups as hailing from that inner city area. I was too proud of it not to be.

I was only too pleased to help out by lending to someone in need and asked him to hang on while I fetched a stamp from my pad. He told me that he'd give it back to me the next week, I didn't believe him for a second, and I had stamps coming out of my ears, but as I didn't know him I didn't tell him that I didn't want it back. Jail isn't the place to give guys an inch. I figured that I'd just let the issue slide without any fuss.

A few days later I was on my way out to the exercise yard when I walked past the guy I lent the stamp to and his buddies, I smiled, as I always do, and looked to nod a greeting to him. He saw me, kept his head straight and walked past me as if I didn't exist. Fancy that, slighting me when I'd just helped him out and I didn't even know him from Adam. Pissed me off. I made my mind up right there and then, he was going to give me that stamp back.

I waited until the day after the next canteen and made a point of going for a walk in the exercise yard that Thursday morning. The yard area was a large concrete playground that you were allowed to walk around in an anti-clockwise direction, or alternatively find yourself a spot to stand in and relax. Fresh air is a valuable commodity in jail, and while going out into the yard wasn't freedom, it felt like you were being let out of your cage for a while. The only person that I would regularly walk the perimeter of the yard with was Lex, and we'd spend the time discussing our cases, legal precedents, family, and of course, the fight game. Other than that I'd march around on my own and just take in the air. I'd get approached from time to time by guys that had heard of my fighting career, they quizzed me with martial arts and boxing queries or more usually knew someone that was a blackbelt in karate or something similar and wondered if I had heard of them. Invariably I hadn't, but I'd always accommodate them, I've never seen the point in being rude or offish with other people. It's just plain bad manners.

The guy that I lent the stamp to used to stand on a rock mound in one corner of the yard with his friends and I guess they looked quite intimidating standing there everyday with arms folded and in serious discussion. They didn't know that I was a fighter, all they saw was this little guy who didn't even look like he should be in jail, as everybody used to constantly tell me, so I figured they'd all be in for a shock when I walked up to him. The way I saw it there were only four of them, and if I felt there was going to be any action I'd just have a world championship flashback. Most guys can't fight anyway, and the mood I was in I fancied a tear-up. As for any disciplinary action I knew that the officers in the jail had my back and any incident would in all probability be swept under the carpet.

'*Got my stamp?*' was all I said to him, they all looked at me as if they didn't have to answer and I'd slink away. They were wrong, I didn't budge, I was just clocking which two I was going to wallop first. Human instinct is a funny thing. I could sense they weren't up to a ruckus in a prison yard and I'd never seen any of them in the gym either, if we were on the 'outside' I've no doubt that they would have shot me. But there aren't any guns in prison so bravado is only going to take you so far. The guy I lent the stamp to folded almost straight away and started stuttering, just like the pig in the old Walt Disney cartoons, that he'd have the stamp for me the next day. I didn't say a word, I just stepped down and continued my walk around the yard. They stared daggers at me throughout, but who cares, they had no bottle and we all knew it.

As far as I was concerned the matter was over, I didn't care about a postage stamp, I just wanted to let those guys know that I wasn't some punk that could be disrespected, especially in jail. So it took me by surprise the next day as I was doing my usual solo marathon around the yard when my 'debtor' marched towards me with an outstretched hand. I could see even from a distance that he was holding a postage stamp, and as he got closer, I could also see that it wasn't a new one. It looked as if it had been carefully torn from a used envelope. I'd done the same thing many a time when the post office stamping machine had missed a stamp, it could simply be re-used, and I'd pull it off and glue it to a fresh letter. I pressed his hand down and told him that I'd never wanted the stamp back, just the offer. He said *'So that's the way you run things?'* I said *'Yep, that's how I run things'*. He clasped my hand as 'brothers' do, nodded, spun on his heels and bounded off like the happiest soul in the prison. I thought to myself, 'Now why in the hell did we have to go through all of that?' Well, that's jail.

Back in the real world I was encountering a different type of problem. I'd made a fresh application for release to a Crown Court Judge, and bail had been granted in the sum of fifty thousand pounds surety. I wasn't allowed to put up the guarantee myself, as it was ruled that it had to be secured with a third party. The logic being that if I was going to skip bail, I'd think twice about allowing a friend or relative to lose money or property. But no matter what security was offered, the police found an excuse to decline it. They refused offers of security bonds, property, and other solid funds. For some reason, they did not want me to be allowed outside at all. I can only think that it was because anyone's chances of beating their charges if they are on the outside are greatly increased with the extra freedom to access legal information and gather witnesses. There is also the chance of course that they could do a bunk but I think all concerned knew that was never on the cards for a family man like me.

Nia worked her socks off trying to juggle suitable security for the bail required and we would spend much of the time on her weekday visits racking our brains to decide on the best course of action.

Throughout this time I was reading a book every day or two and although the prison library had a fair selection, I was soon to run out of titles that interested me. I'd taken in some great material though, my favourite was Nelson Mandela's life-story *Long Walk to Freedom*, it's gripping, funny, informative, and truly inspiring, reading that book was the only time that I'd ever shed a tear throughout my entire time in prison. Mandela was recounting a series of tragic events in his life that included the deaths of his son, and the wife of a close family friend. Nelson Mandela is the spitting image of my own father who had passed away just two years before, and not only that, they shared similar mannerisms too, so when he was describing his reaction to being passed the letter informing him of the death of his child, I could picture it vividly. His story strengthened my resolve to never feel any self-pity for my own personal plight, no matter what the outcome of my situation, it was just another of life's tests, and it measured very low in the scale of human injustice.

I also took great pleasure from reading ex-World Boxing Champion Barry McGuigan's autobiography. Barry and I are old acquaintances having co-commentated at a kickboxing event in Dublin many years previously where he was special guest. His phone number and address, were in my telephone book, the one that so interested the police, along with certain other celebrities, mostly from the boxing world, and even a few police superintendents that I was friendly with. During that trip to Dublin, one of the youngsters that was helping out with the promotion nervously told Barry that his father idolised him and that he couldn't wait to tell him that they'd met. Barry told him there was only one thing to do then, go and see his father, he looked at me expectantly, and did not have to ask twice, *'Howard, you coming?'* I was more than game.

By the time we got to his home I was excited for the lad, what a treat for his father, they certainly wouldn't forget this day in a hurry. We entered the house and Barry stopped short of going into the sitting room, so we stood in the corridor while the youngster told his dad that someone had come to see him. We could hear his father's gruff response, he wasn't keen on seeing anyone, but the lad insisted. I was chuckling away in the corridor as Barry pulled me and we walked through the door. The look on his father's face. Sheer magic! Barry, class act that he is, introduced me as a friend of his, Howard Brown, World Kickboxing Champion and explained that we were in town for the kickboxing show at The National Stadium. We spent about half an hour chatting before having to head back to our hotels to prepare for the show, but for me it was perhaps the most memorable part of that particular trip. Moments like that in peoples lives are priceless, and Barry impressed me no end on that day.

The most disturbing tome that I read while on remand was *Biko* the biography of the South African anti-apartheid activist, it's a harrowing document, and once again rammed home how fortunate I was in spite of my predicament. It also made me consider what I would do to improve my lot if I was to fail in my bid to beat the charges against me. It's par for the course for ambitious convicts to obtain a university degree if serving a long enough sentence, but what to study? Law and Medicine were out of the question as far as I was concerned as those two careers do not allow ex-felons to practice them. I rattled my brain as I thought it might be wise to prepare for every eventuality, but couldn't settle on anything that struck my fancy, so I thought I'd leave the issue alone until a later date.

Mark Page and quite a few different officers, nearly all martial artists of course, would pop by my cell regularly for a chat to discuss mutual acquaintances and see how I was getting on. I was asked if I'd read Sun Tzu's famous military treatise, *The Art of War*, I hadn't as it wasn't in the library, but it sounded like a must read. The next day when I'd finished my duties as a landing cleaner, I went back to my cell to find it on my bed. I lapped it up, not just because it's a great read, but also because its strategies can be used as great analogies for everyday life. I gave it back to the officer it belonged to the very next day. It wasn't much later that Mark came around smiling and said that he had a few books himself that might interest me. I told him to decide what to bring as I'm as broad-minded a reader as you're going to get, it could be *Mein Kampf* by Adolf Hitler for all I cared. He told me he had just the thing.

He opened my cell door the next day, passed me a neat looking paperback, and looking sternly at my cell mate said, *'It's not for anyone else Howard, give it me back as soon as you've finished. I think you'll really enjoy it!'* The book was called *The Templar Revelation* and began with a chapter entitled *The Secret Code of Leonardo Da Vinci*. Once again I swallowed it up. The tales of the warrior monks known as the Knights Templar, and threads of secrecy running down through the ages amongst the cognoscenti, was like boys own stuff and intrigued me no end. Little did I know how much further I was to pursue this new interest.

Back then my quest for freedom seemed like an endless battle, at this stage I'd already been refused bail twice by the magistrates courts, then also had the aforementioned surety acceptance problems with the police, so when I got the letter telling me that my application was now before a Crown Court Judge, my expectation levels were not at their highest. I was told to be prepared to attend court on the stated date as release on bail was a possibility.

Nia and a family friend, one of my sureties, attended the court hearing which was held in the Judge's Chambers. The Judge reduced the bail to forty thousand pounds and accepted the security offered with the minimum of fuss. He must have been impressed by these two polite and well-presented ladies because common sense prevailed and at last, I was out.

3

It's funny how much your perception can change over such a short period of time. When I arrived back at the family home I should have taken my first impressions as an omen of things to come. The house that I had spent the last five years in seemed like somewhere else entirely, it looked completely alien. Its size, colours, and the shape of the rooms seemed to have changed somehow, in actuality they hadn't, it was me, I had new eyes. And I wasn't the only one, so had Nia. Any displays of affection from me were met with a coldness, and firmness, that I had rarely seen her demonstrate. It wasn't the welcome home that I was expecting, or even appreciated at the time, but I have to admit, in a sense it was impressive.

For the first time in twenty years she had to handle all of the affairs of the family without my presence, and she did it glowingly. I wasn't the only one that had bags of time to do some soul-searching, she had too, and her conclusion was quite simple. My arrest and imprisonment were the straw that broke the camel's back. She'd had enough.

Over the years, although I'm a quite doting father, I'd neglected her on the emotional front. She always complained about how much I horsed around with the children, but never with her, and it was a valid argument. It's one of those female statements that guys can think are petty, but on reflection, they're far from it. I was to learn another valuable lesson over the coming months, and any guys out there that have experienced it will tell you the same. When a woman has seriously made up her mind to end a relationship, it's over. No amount of logic and 'too little, too late' hugs and kisses is going to change that fact. Just take it on the chin and move on. Better to end the relationship on a mature and amicable note than to leave it in hostility, especially if you value the emotional welfare of your children.

The truth, as Nia continually pointed out, was that any distress that we'd experienced as a couple during our relationship was invariably my fault. If I'd listened to her more often, some of the problems that we'd encountered in life could have been avoided. It's true. I'm as stubborn as a mule at the best of times, so what could I say? Not a lot. Nevertheless, we stayed together as a couple over the coming months and she remained supportive while I prepared to do battle with the Crown Prosecution Service.

The taped conversation with Lex and Gunther in the Swallow Hotel was my main problem, and the crux of the government case against me. The reason for this in legal terms was because the conspiracy laws in Great Britain are quite sweeping. If any person has knowledge of criminal activity, whether participating in it or not, they can be indicted with the charge of being 'knowingly concerned' in its implementation. The sentence for conviction of this offence is the same as if you are found guilty of the conspiracy to carry out the alleged crime itself, and is a legacy of the Guy Fawkes gunpowder plot to blow up the houses of Parliament in 1605. These laws have since been used and updated to combat terrorist threats and offences, and are a large part of Britain's legal armoury in the war against illegal drugs.

My charge was 'conspiracy to supply' a slight variation from being 'knowingly concerned', which was surprising, but in light of the scope of the conspiracy laws this oddity made little difference, I was up against it. My problem was that I was seen to be condemning myself with my own big mouth. I was to use this argument myself on a completely different topic over the coming years, and to good effect.

I had learned whilst incarcerated that to rely totally upon your legal defence team was a negative stance, and a risky one, far better to assist by researching the details of your case yourself to make sure that all possible avenues of defence are explored. The way I see it the onus is on the defendant to pursue this in order to ensure that every aspect of their case is dissected with a fine tooth comb. The police and Crown Prosecution Service often make the silliest mistakes while carrying out their investigative and administrative procedures with the end result being that if uncovered, resultant charges are often either dismissed by the Judge or dropped before they even come to trial. In this respect I had one very promising avenue of defence to explore, a technicality, but a realistic one.

To install surveillance equipment in a third party property and spy on its visitors, the permission of the property's owner is normally required. In my case the permission of the Swallow Hotel would have to have been gained for the recorded tape to be admissible in court as evidence. My task now was to research the police procedure in this matter and if there was even the tiniest of clinical errors in the process of gaining permission then the charges would have to be dropped. This was imperative for me as the most important thing at that point was damage limitation. My family had been embarrassed enough already as news of my arrest had spread like wildfire in family, business, and social circles. There's nothing as juicy as scandal, and it would have been great for those that I cared about to have the whole matter put to bed as groundless, as one big misconstrued mistake.

My solicitors arranged a capable barrister to handle my case, and assured me that all the possible technicalities that I brought up would be analysed, and all precedents in similar cases researched and compared to my own before we even thought about having to defend the case in court. This was a ray of light and I felt optimistic.

Prior to my arrest I was running classes in my profession as a kickboxing instructor and also having building work done on a disused building which I planned to open as a full-time fitness and martial arts gymnasium. I had already obtained the necessary planning permissions from the city council and the refurbishment was on schedule. Before my arrest that is. The one weakness of being a sole trading business is that if you are not present to operate it then everything comes to a standstill. You can insure against illness, as I always do even though I'm very rarely ill, but the 'holiday' I'd just taken was what you might call an unforeseen occurrence. Not only had I to now reorganise a new workforce, as the previous builders and decorators had nearly all found new work, but my classes were decimated.

The reason that I was so keen to open my own gym was to use it as a specialised headquarters for my kickboxing classes. I previously rented hall space in various sports and recreation centres, which was expensive and limited, lacking the opportunity to develop the flexibility and ambience required to be a true professional in an increasingly more competitive business. I would also have been able to make extra income from renting time slots to other martial arts, sports and social groups, and could then run national and international training courses for both instructors and less experienced students alike. Part of my lease agreement also stated that I had the option to buy the freehold of the premises for a stated price within a certain time period. It was a sensible and exciting proposition.

It took me a few weeks to contact my students and get my classes back to some semblance of normality, and to try and compensate for my loss of earnings while away I centralised them at the new gym thus alleviating the expense of hall rental fees. Although the bulk of the building was not ready to be officially opened yet, the main training hall was comfortable enough to work out in. Changing space was a problem, but most of my students arrived for class changed and ready to train anyway so we got around it. They were as excited about the prospect of their own 'training home' as I was, they were also quite touchingly concerned about my situation and the charges against me. People can be discreet though, and they were respectful enough not to ask me any details about the alleged offence or my time inside.

My other headache now was timescales. The refurbishment work had lost impetus with my absence and I was struggling to reassemble a solid workforce, I could get the odd electrician here, the odd plasterer and tiler there, but it was extremely difficult to coordinate with any flow, which left me both frustrated and with a lot of time on my hands as I chased around and waited for skilled workmen to finish existing jobs and be free to restart mine. I decided on the most obvious course of action to pass any spare time, especially as my literary taste buds had been reawakened. I decided to do more reading. It was as if fate was playing me into a corner.

Almost all black people believe in the bible to some extent, it's a legacy of slavery and colonialism, I was no exception. My father, already a successful businessman arrived from Jamaica in 1951 on the British government promise of opportunity for all immigrant workers who were willing to help rebuild Britain after the wartime setbacks and labour shortage. A man of vision, integrity, and impressive ambition, he had buried his own father at the age of seventeen and as the youngest of seven brothers, had assumed the role of financial head of the family from that day on. He was truly a remarkable man. His older brothers resented his ability to make money out of the minimal of opportunity and it was a situation that haunted him throughout my childhood, because while they learned to loathe him, he cared very deeply about them.

His family had been raised as Roman Catholics, and as a devout adherent to that religion he sought to pursue it when he came to England. The difficulties in doing this were one of the many realities of the wider world that he was to face up to. White people did not want black people in their churches, the church was as much a hub of social gathering as it was one of worship and as far as many Caucasians were concerned black people did not have souls anyway, they were viewed as lesser mortals, and 'wogs' and 'niggers' were not made to feel welcome in their pews. To get a grip on my father's reaction to this attitude you have to understand his background and the social standing that he was used to as I will mention in a moment.

In spite of this barrier, he was keen for us to have a healthy respect for God, and for our religious education he made do by sending us to the local protestant Sunday school, which was a lot of fun as we used to enjoy mixing with the other children on our street that also had to attend the classes. Junior, Edge, and I, the three youngest of seven brothers, were born in England. Our four elder siblings had a different mother, and Dad brought them over to England from Jamaica in the late nineteen-fifties. They helped tend to us as toddlers and despite the age gaps, we all loved each others company. Depressingly for him, Dad's control over them had waned due to his departure to forge an even more successful life abroad, and they had no interest, or time, for any form of church. We, the 'new' family, had no choice.

I was about ten years old when the Jehovah's witnesses came calling, how opportune for them. With his yearning for a spiritual home and their academically based approach to the bible and circular logic, Dad was a blank canvas waiting for an artist. This wasn't just a window of susceptibility in his life, it was a canyon, and they leapt in. I remember my parents telling us one evening to get ready as we were going out. It was to a meeting held in a school hall in a district not too far from where we lived. We hadn't a clue what was going on and did as we were trained to do, which was quite simple, whatever our parents told us. This religious meeting was my first glimpse at the power of indoctrination, where groups of people would suspend the use of their independent minds, and begin nodding wholeheartedly at what an eloquent speaker had to say. Religion and politics, not so strange bedfellows!

We got dragged along to these meetings for years and this experience is one of the many reasons I state that parents do not have the moral right to attempt to indoctrinate their children into any religious or political system. In fact, the opposite is true. Their duty is to inculcate open-mindedness and examination of other points of view in a bid to teach tolerance, ethics, and logic. (The parents might also learn a thing or two while on this path!) When their charges are adults they can decide for themselves with minds unburdened by fear and repression what, if any, theological or political avenue they wish to follow.

The indoctrination of the innocent is an abominable instilling of phobias that can cause much psychological anguish in later life and I am grateful that I have always been a strong-willed and logical thinker. There are many who are not so fortunate, but more of that later.

Due to his abrupt childhood my father wasn't trained at length in academics and was extremely embarrassed about his inability to read fluently, a situation that he took pains to rectify throughout the years. (Because of this he was a soft touch for any encyclopaedia salesmen that passed our way and he created a library of books for our consumption from infant school upward. One way or the other, he made sure that we regularly read them all). His business strengths lay in well grounded common sense, recognition of opportunity, and basic mathematics, all coupled with an ardent work ethic, one that I am grateful that he, and my mother, passed on to their children.

Born and bred in Jamaica's second 'city', Spanish Town, he accrued an impressive portfolio of property and livestock and was held in the highest regard within the local community. He was quite the dandy too, and used to conduct travel between his various freeholds on the back of a white horse, relishing in the reverence of the local townsfolk that used to doff their caps to him as he rode past. Life in England was quite a comeuppance. I remember on one occasion, I couldn't have been more than five or six years of age, he was bringing me home one evening from visiting friends when a group of teenagers bumped into him while running down the road we lived on, and quite naturally he reprimanded them. They waited until they were about twenty yards or so away before shouting the usual racial obscenities, I can't say I blame them for getting to a safe distance first, Dad was only five feet seven, but he was as wide as he was tall and didn't look like a pushover. It was my first brush with racism, and also one of the very rare occasions that I saw anyone dare to take umbrage with my father, only in retrospect can I imagine the change in his existence that his travels had brought him. I admire his strength, because throughout it all he only had one goal in mind, a better life for his family and opportunity for his children.

By the early sixties he had already bought three properties in England, and I was born while we were resident in the second, a large Victorian dwelling that in former times was the main house on Boulton Road, belonging to the family of the famous eighteenth Century English industrialist, Matthew Boulton. The house was actually two properties in one as it extended to the street that ran behind and our garage actually had a separate street address. Dad converted the second floor of the garage into a boxing gym for my older brothers and professional boxers such as British and Empire champion Jack Bodell used to turn up on occasion for sparring sessions.

As infants Junior, Edge, and myself would often scuff the skin off our knuckles on the sand-filled punch bags in 'who could punch the hardest' competitions. Tears would flow when the stinging set in.

My elder brothers were Sid, Bibs, Willie, and Manley. Sid, Manley, and a cousin, Larry, were the pugilists and made quite a mark on the British professional boxing scene. Sid was the tough-nut and appeared on television in a couple of contests, eventually punching it out with the public on the fairground circuit in his post-career years, but Manley was the hot prospect, having the curse of both inherent talent and the lack of commitment that is often allied to it. He's left-handed and was a natural southpaw with scintillating punch power in both hands. Sid berated him once for not training often enough to which he replied, *'Tell all the boys I've knocked out to train.'*

He fought future boxing great and world champion Ken Buchanan on the Scotsman's way to the top and floored him before being stopped by Buchanan when he regained his feet. Manley always complained that Ken should have been counted out and he was cheated. Apparently, he stood arrogantly over his foe after knocking him down instead of retreating to a neutral corner, the referee, Wally Thom, then walked Manley to a designated post, and started the count from the number one instead of four or five when he returned to Buchanan.

Whether this is an accurate account of what happened I do not know as I was only a schoolboy at the time, but my brothers used to tell it with great relish. My adult opinion is different, Manley should have trained harder instead of partying all the time.

On a positive note for the sport Dad never tired of telling us that Larry was the real champion, he settled the mortgage on his house early on in life with the extra money he used to make from his boxing career and retired from the game with something to show for it. Because of this he and Dad had a heightened respect for each other which continued on the other side of the pond when many of my family emigrated to America in the nineteen eighties.

By the mid-sixties my elder brothers had all left home after various fall-outs with Dad about their lifestyle in England. They loved the night-life and he thought they should concentrate more on their education. As a result the gym became an unnecessary appendage and Dad decided that he would use the space to start a business. He was already working in the local factory, Avery's, the scale-makers, in a regular nine-to-five day job, and also traded as both an English estate agent and Jamaican realty broker, conducting the buying and selling of land and properties in both Handsworth and Jamaica, and now also thought he would use his weekends to provide a butcher service for West Indians and Asians in the area. To give you a glimpse of the energy of the man, he used to conduct both his estate agency and real estate businesses from an office at home and the phone box outside Avery's during his work and lunch breaks.

The new gap that he had spotted was typical of him. English butchers used to strangle their chickens and display them on hooks in butcher shops with their wrung necks dangling full of congealed blue blood. Immigrants were not used to this and thought it unhealthy, they preferred their livestock decapitated so that the blood would run out and not contaminate the poultry. Because of this and the convenience of an immigrant butcher within the locality, business thrived, and before we knew it the service was in full swing with our large back garden a menagerie of chickens, ducks, and the odd goat, a speciality at Jamaican weddings.

I used to grab a couple of Dad's many carving knives and try to assist him every Saturday, the main day on which the business operated. Being only eight years old, I was at first a nuisance, but he never shouted at me or chased me away, and I was so determined to help out that I would see him give the odd wry smile when I used to catch a chicken or struggle to disjoint one of the slaughtered ones. My brothers were not too interested. Edge was too young, (or as usual pretended to be), and Junior had a natural aversion to the grisly nature of it all. I was a born slayer and loved it. It wasn't long before Dad bought and presented me with my own set of knives and took me through the whole process, I was so excited. He taught me how to weigh the chickens in the scale and calculate the prices as well as the physical end of the business. When I tell my children that I was working from the time I was eight years old it is a literal truth. To all intents and purposes I was Dad's business partner. It was great bonding but still didn't save me from the whackings though.

Dad, like many immigrant parents, was a serious disciplinarian, and when we played up or didn't fulfil our household chores, boy, did we get it! Mom was the opposite and the worst she would ever do was take off one her shoes and throw it at us as we ran away laughing. Only a brave soul would have laughed when the old man was on his way.

As the eldest of the group, Junior nearly always got the worst of things, this was a natural phenomena, I suppose Dad felt that not only should he know better, but that he should also have kept Edge and I in line. This was extremely unfair, but I know of eldest children from many families who had to endure the same burden and suffer the emotional scars this treatment invariably inflicts. Dad's pragmatic approach to discipline was so bad sometimes that we used to be in fear of what mood would take him when he came home from his day job. The effects of this treatment became clear when I started school and got into a few fights, I used to feel sorry for some of the other boys if that was the best that they could do when they hit me. After the onslaughts at home I felt they were just tapping me. Needless to say, my brothers and I soon built up a fearsome reputation as an alpha-male family.

On reflection, and in fairness to Dad, he was overloaded with the burden of trying to regain his former status in this new land as well as the responsibility of providing sustenance and opportunity for what was a sizeable family. I was married with my own children before I fully appreciated what it must have been like for him. Nevertheless, as our school behaviour indicated, it is certainly true, violence breeds violence.

My very eldest brother, Sid, told me that we younger children never really knew Dad, because when he was in Jamaica and they were children, he was a barrel of laughs, and fun was the order of the day. They couldn't wait for him to come home to play with them. This was part of the problem when they arrived in England, this new and more serious fellow was a stranger and they couldn't understand why he was often so morose. It was to eventually drive them apart and was another of those situations that became a source of constant regret to my father, a man whose stern exterior was equally matched by a huge heart. Cancer eventually claimed Dad and he left this planet just how anyone might wish to, surrounded by his wife, children, grandchildren, extended family, and many friends. I miss him, but boy, was I glad that he couldn't see what I was going through now.

Again, it was not until I reached my adult years that I realised the real backbone of the family was my mother. She met my father when she came to England in 1954 and he was bowled over by her beauty, intelligence, and reserved character. He was already doing quite well and she had her heart set on a nursing career. When Junior, Edge, and I were infants he forbade her from working and made it clear that he wanted her to be a housewife for the rest of her days. Many heated arguments ensued, but the little lady won out and as soon as Edge started school mom enrolled to become a nurse. In later years it was one battle that Dad was glad he did not win.

My mother is extremely academic, and it is clear that had she the benefit of an English education at an earlier age she would not have been a nurse, but a doctor. She relished in taking and passing every exam on offer and made steady progress through the nursing ranks to become more than a match in terms of financial income to my father. To his credit he accepted this situation, and mom's ambitious nature with great pride.

When they moved to America mom's credentials saw her earn so well that together they were able to assemble a portfolio of property worth well in excess of one million dollars within a decade. Dad even admitted to me that if he had listened to her opinions a little more when they were in England he would have been even more successful. That old Victorian spirit is a bitch and I have to say my father was unashamedly chauvinist. Still, they made a great team and mom still calls him 'that man' when recounting his stubbornness. Naturally, she misses him more than anyone else.

By the time I hit my teen years I had already decided that religion was not for me, stories of talking snakes and decent people being killed by a God because they didn't believe in the Bible made less and less sense, aside from that a gentleman called Bruce Lee arrived on the scene and his religion, martial arts, appealed a lot more to a kid that was athletic and came from a boxing background than attending religious meetings.

I was always proud of the fact that two of my elder brothers were well respected professional boxers. What boy wouldn't be? I remember the head gym teacher during my first years at senior school, Mr Gilliver, asking me during a maths lesson if it was my brothers that he had read about in *Boxing News*. I replied *'Yes sir'* real quick. Boy, did that set the tone for me amongst my peers. Pugilism tends to run in the genes, so it was no surprise that Bruce had me both transfixed and devoted.

With his unparalleled charisma and prowess, he was another Muhammad Ali, this because of the way that he transcended the art that he advertised so well, he was a one man phenomenon. Nevertheless, even though I had no interest in religion, like a lot of people, I always wondered about how man came to be on this planet, and was happy to accept that in large part the Bible might well be true.

After reading *The Templar Revelation* I was not so sure. Using comparative analysis it presented some intriguing insights and hypotheses into the gospel stories of Jesus, eye-openers that could never dare to be mentioned by any religious establishment. It is a brilliant book for anyone with an open mind, and so I decided to see if I could find any similar reading material to pass my time. My first trip to a city centre bookstore was a success. I bought a book written by a little known author named Alan Alford entitled *When The Gods Came Down*. This well presented work discussed the ancient origin of the gods and backed up its arguments with solid research and logic. It punched even harder than Bruce and I lapped it up while continuing to accrue as much material on this subject as time would allow.

There was still a very important distraction however, my upcoming trial. Repeated meetings with my solicitors were not yielding too much success in the finding of a precedent by which my charges could be dismissed. I spent a lot of time researching the matter myself but came up with nothing, while all the time being assured by my solicitors and barrister that they were doing the same. My trust in them was waning and so was my confidence in remaining a free man. I had more faith in Lex who was in a similar predicament as the tape of our conversation was also crucial to his case, which in all probability would likewise have to be ejected if the recording was deemed inadmissible. Because of this I used to visit him at the Green every two weeks or so to discuss developments and exchange information. Our conversations ran through the usual emotional gamut's, from energised optimism to monotone not-so-promising debate, these moods seemed to alternate from one visit to the other, and although nothing dampened our resolve, the possibility of failure was ever present.

It was about one month before the trial date that the reality began to sink in that I would have to face a judge and jury, as my barrister explained to me the situation regarding the legality of the taped conversation. It turned out that in a similar criminal case just a few years previously precedent had already been set governing the legal stance of dubious covert surveillance and it ran thus. If the end product of such an operation yielded details of criminal activity then the recorded information would be allowed to be used as courtroom evidence. The reasoning for this was that although such surveillance might well be technically 'illegal' it uncovered a 'greater evil' and was therefore deemed justifiable. I was stuck, and my choices were now considerably narrower.

If I ran a trial in a bid to prove my innocence and was subsequently found guilty, then the full weight of the law would be thrown against me in sentencing. Maximum sentence for conspiring to supply the then class B substance of cannabis and its related varieties was fourteen years imprisonment. Added to this was the fact that the local daily newspaper, The Birmingham Evening Mail and its sister publication, The Birmingham Post, would also have featured my trial as front page news on every day of its sitting. Goodness knows that they had enough pictures of me from my sporting success over the years to cause adequate sensation. This is without taking into account that regional television had plenty of footage too. How would my family have dealt with the scale of such a scandal? It was a horrendous proposition.

On the other hand I could plead guilty and agree a much lesser sentence with the Crown Prosecution Service, maybe even five or six years. This still seemed a lot but with good behaviour I would have to serve only half of this and probably only a year to eighteen months under closed conditions, the rest of the time would be spent in open jail where I would be allowed to find employment outside the prison and spend time with my children at weekends. The added attraction, if one can use such a word in a situation like this, would be the vastly reduced amount of publicity if no trial were to take place because I accepted the charges made against me.

I discussed the situation with my barrister and of course with Nia, and the latter course of action seemed the most prudent. I was a man of previously good and unblemished character and a pillar of the local community where I regularly organised and took part in charity functions, so a sympathetic sentence seemed quite plausible. It was not an ideal situation, but seemed the obvious choice to make.

It was clear now that short of a miracle, I would be unable to spend any quality time with my children for a year or two, so I decided to allocate them as much time as possible during evenings and weekends. It was the most important item on my agenda, sorting out my business affairs was easily second place. What I feared the most was that I had to tell them of the fate that awaited me. Informing Nick and Chris was not too difficult, they were upset, but old enough and strong enough at twenty and fourteen years old respectively, to deal with it. Nia helped out substantially by counselling and reassuring them that everything would be okay. Telling my seven year old baby girl, Kelis, was another matter. I was petrified.

Females are a rarity in my family. I have one sister, Patsy, who I love dearly, even though, like my four eldest brothers she was not raised with us. My mother had given birth to her from a previous relationship before coming to England, and Patsy was brought up by both her father and my mother's parents. Dad wanted to adopt her and bring her to England but her natural father would not allow it, and so I did not even meet her until I was seventeen years old. It was a shame in some respects but a blessing in others as she grew up to be of great assistance to my maternal grandparents. She is well educated and was a secretary at the Supreme Court in Jamaica's capital city, Kingston, before making a new life for herself and her children in America, living just a few miles away from mom.

There were several girls among my cousins but not many, the Brown family is overwhelmingly male, and as a result what

I understand about women is miniscule at best. So, all things considered this was not the best preparation to deal with the new number one woman in my life.

All three of my children were born by caesarean section, and for Nick and Chris I simply sat in the hospital waiting room while Nia gave birth. With Kelis, Nia maintained that she wanted to be awake while the delivery took place, so I decided that I would sit in with her. The reason for this was the diagnosis that took place during the pre-natal check ups. The ultra sound scans had revealed an abnormality in the foetus and the doctors had advised us that it might be wise to terminate the pregnancy as the unborn child was likely to be born with a deformity. We decided against that option and figured that if this were to be the case we would simply shower the child with extra love and protection. As it turned out, thankfully, the doctor's fears were ungrounded. Kelis was born perfectly healthy, and I was over the moon. A baby girl, I couldn't wait to spread the news.

Parents get better as they get older and more used to parenthood, I was no exception, and so Kelis got the best of me. Nick used to get a whacking at the slightest move, not just because he was male and I was an inexperienced parent, but also because he usually deserved it. That boy used to walk into a room and say *'it wasn't me'*, when I wasn't even aware that something had gone wrong. He was like 'the mummy' from the Hammer horror movies because he had to walk towards me with his hands outstretched for a slapping so often. He was so mischievous that his uncle Edge nick-named him 'Scamp', a moniker that has stuck with him to this day. Chris was the opposite, like most kids in the middle are. He had noted the recklessness of his brother from an early age and figured things out. Don't rile the old man when you've done something wrong. I remember once shouting at him for some misdemeanour or the other for at least two or three minutes and he never said a word while I lectured him on why he should know better at the top of my voice. He waited until I had finished my rant before stating quite calmly that it wasn't him responsible.

I felt such an idiot that I then told him off for not sticking up for himself. He just looked at me without saying a word and went about his business. Chris very rarely got smacked. Kelis was something else entirely.

My problem with Kelis was the obvious one, how do you discipline a girl? With the lads I just spoke to them sternly or gave them a wallop, which usually decided matters real quick, that's how I was brought up and it seemed to work quite well, but I just couldn't bring myself to treat Kelis so roughly, and if it were not for the fact that her mother had no such problem, Nia is a stern and intelligent disciplinarian with her children, Kelis would have been spoilt rotten. A case in point is the fact that she is the only one of my children ever to have said the word 'no' to me and she wasn't even at school yet. I took the ever so brave route of calling her mother to complain and that issue was soon sorted out.

I spent a great deal of time with her as an infant, even more than I did with the lads, she was like a little doll as little girls are, and so dainty with it, that is apart from one thing, her temper, which I figured must have been the defect the doctors spotted on the ultra-sound scan. Sagittarians tend to be that way, and the other one in the family, her uncle and my younger brother, Edge, was also just as quick-tempered as a child. If you ever beat him at a game, it was unwise to gloat, not unless you were ready to start running. Fortunately he outgrew this trait, I hoped that his niece would do the same. The only times that I did bring myself to give her the odd slap on the hand or bottom was when she lost it uncontrollably. I don't tolerate tantrums from either children or adults, and neither did Nia, the children all learned this quite quickly and would rarely 'perform' in front of friends or in the local supermarket. They knew they'd get a smacking no matter where they were. Kelis took the longest to appreciate this. She was fine when in company but had a fearsome temper when playing with her brothers, to the point where every other member of the family used to chant to her in unison the line from the Disney movie, Beauty and the Beast, *'Kelis... you must control your temper'*. Everybody but

Kelis found it quite amusing.

As the boys were a lot older than her they had their own friends and activities so next to her mother I was her best friend, we used to play together and went swimming religiously every Sunday morning. It was on such an occasion that I told her that daddy was going away for a while. She was only seven, and asked me a stream of questions about when I would be back, could she come too, how long would I be gone, and why was I going away? We both broke down and cried in the car as we hugged each other. I dread to think of how she coped, especially on Sundays, when I was finally 'taken away'.

I relish the company of my children, and from day one all three of them were what you would term jolly babies. They were up for a laugh as soon as you smiled at them, which made it difficult to get any rest on some nights, as after early morning feeds when they had progressed to the bottle I could rarely get them back to sleep, I'd look at them and say a few words, they'd smile widely, and then start giggling, so nodding back off clearly wasn't on the agenda. This ambience perpetuated itself throughout our household which was always full of fun. I encouraged this in the light of my own childhood because it's always great for anyone to have a merry house to come home to, and dad is the person that usually sets the standard, how sad would it be if my own children did not get excited about me coming home from work? I invariably took them to school each morning which was one of the great points about being self-employed and collected them too whenever I could. It was great bonding, and at this point I was thankful that I'd had the chance to invest in my relationship with them as much as I had, all the while wishing that I had done so even more.

My mother flew over from America to lend moral support during the week of my trial and Nia and I had acknowledged that no matter what the outcome, it was the end of the road for our marriage. Yet we both still hoped that in light of the ambiguous evidence against me, my guilty plea, and flawless background, that the judge would take a sympathetic view and pass a lenient sentence.

When he said ten years imprisonment I was tempted to take a look around and see who he was talking to as he obviously had the wrong case details in front of him. He didn't. The attempted consolations of the court usher's as I was led down the stairs made little impact, although to my own surprise I was as calm as I have ever been, only in retrospect can I acknowledge that this is a common reaction to shock. The best way that I can describe that day in court is to equate it to a Hollywood dream sequence, the only difference was, no one yelled 'cut'.

4

Lex had made a nice little niche for himself as reception desk clerk at the Green and was responsible for organising the initial aspects of new inmate processing such as reception registration and wing allocation. He was in this capacity informed of what sentences had been passed at Birmingham's Crown and Magistrates Court each day and how many inmates were expected, he was not however, made privy to the identity of incoming prisoners.

Knowing that it was the day of my trial he checked the lists for how many people had received sentences in the five to seven year range to see how I had fared. He knew someone had received a double figure special but not for one moment did he contemplate that it was me. When I walked into reception and told him the good news he burst out laughing, so did I. Well, it was either that or a good cry.

By the time I got to C wing a couple of dozen or so inmates had assembled and were standing outside their cells waiting to greet the new arrivals. As I walked through they burst into applause, convicts appreciate guys who are doing long sentences, and I was the star of the show.

One of the men that had been arrested with Lex in the cannabis swoop was Rick, a very experienced and successful local businessman with a demeanour much like my own who had been given the job as wing roll-board administrator. We got to know each other when I was on remand and he got the nod from the attendant prison officers to organise a phone call for me so that I could talk to Nia. She was at the gym informing the landlord of the result of my trial when I called and we both wanted to know how each other were faring. I think I managed to cheer her up somewhat with my upbeat chat and she did the same for me.

I was allocated a cell and spent the evening in discussion with my cell-mate, a younger lad, who was serving five months for an affray charge. I didn't sleep much that night, my head was awash with how I would tackle my avenues of appeal against the length of my sentence. It was my main concern. I spent the following morning talking to Rick in the special cell-cum-office he occupied that was reserved for the roll board orderly, he speeded me to the front of the employment list and I was told that I would start work after the weekend, as it was now a Friday, as a cell painter. I was also brought a radio by one of the officers, and wrote separate letters to Nia, Mom, and each of the children during the day.

I appreciated the visit that I got from Tim Murphy, one of the most pleasant senior officers in Winson Green. Tim is both intelligent and a gentleman and we shared a natural affinity aided by the fact that he used to practice Muay Thai Kickboxing, an art that I was well versed in. We discussed how I might progress through the prison system as I would, if avenues of appeal failed, have to spend approximately three years in closed conditions. It wasn't what I wanted to hear but was a reality and I don't like my ears tickled, much preferring to know exactly what I'm up against so that I can make realistic preparations. Tim assured me that with my mode of conduct all the best avenues in terms of work and prison transfer would become available to me as soon as possible.

After the research that I had conducted while on bail I had already made up my mind that I was going to spend my time in prison writing a book about the origin of organised religion, its reliance on earlier belief systems, and the political scenarios that influenced its development. I was sure that I had recognised many points that were not mentioned in the books that I had read, and that there was plenty of scope for original material. It was obvious that such a venture would be immense and that I could never have dreamed of undertaking it had I not been incarcerated. I was equally sure that I would find it quite fulfilling whether my work was a commercial success or not. The completion of any such work is invariably left to posterity and is almost as much a testament to someone's existence as having children. It seems that there is often a plus side to adversity.

One of the points of interest for me concerned the authenticity of both the Bible and the Koran as the authorised and infallible words of a supreme being. If such a claim were true then the information in both books would be flawless and original. I learned very early on in my reading that they most positively were not. Most people are familiar with the biblical story of creation where God created the first human couple Adam and Eve in a paradise location and how in disobeying his edicts they were expelled from the Garden of Eden and sentenced to mortality. The Old Testament then relates how upon becoming grossly disappointed with man's behaviour God then decided to get rid of mankind and start his experiment again with the new 'Adam', a righteous individual named Noah, who he would allow to survive a world-wide flood so that he and his family could repopulate the earth. The dating of this deluge was what interested me the most, according to the Bible it was approximately 2400 B.C. and it is this chronology that in my mind presented an insurmountable hurdle to any claim of validity.

Common sense would dictate that for the many different peoples and cultures of the human race to have evolved from this one family in what must have been just a few hundred years, was from many viewpoints a logistical impossibility. Notwithstanding the fact, that there is no geological or documentary proof of such a deluge in the records of the nearby civilisations that existed during this period. Egypt and Sumer to name but two, were in full flight during this time and such an event would have decimated them, it did not, and there was something even more revealing, factual evidence that is far from common knowledge.

The producers of the first section of the Bible, the Old Testament, were people known as the Hebrews, or Israelites, who were neighbours to the two most advanced world cultures of their time, namely Egypt and Sumer (Sumer, the site of the biblical Garden of Eden, is modern-day Iraq and the area came to be regarded by a variety of historical names including Mesopotamia and Babylon). Even by modern standards the people of Sumer were extremely well progressed in terms of social structure and government. They built walled cities with efficient irrigation, are credited with inventing the art of writing, used a silver standard for business transactions, developed a system of letting money at interest, had schools, teachers, and a postal service, and as they used to write on clay tablets they also used clay envelopes. The evolution of their literature was expansive enough to comprise memorandums, and devise the arts of poetry and theatre. While the Bible portrays the people that lived near the Israelites as immoral and savage heathens, this evidence is somewhat at odds with such an accusation. To make matters worse, the Sumerians had their own version of the Noah and the ark story which not only pre-dates the Old Testament writings by at least a couple of thousand years, but also precedes the dating for the biblical flood itself.

In the original Sumerian version, the protected human was named Ziusudra, who being warned of a world-wide flood that was being sent to destroy mankind, was likewise instructed by a god to build a large boat, and take aboard representatives from the animal kingdom to save them from death. This tale and its esoteric details proved so popular in the ancient world that when the Sumerians were conquered by the Akkadian people circa 2400 B.C., (the period in which the Bible states that the deluge took place), the victors kept the tale and changed the hero's name from Ziusudra to Atra-Hasis. Remarkably, this happened again when Sumer became known as Mesopotamia, the tale survived and Atra-Hasis became

Utanapishtim and continued in this guise throughout the dominion of the Babylonian Empire. In the first millennium B.C. the Babylonians took the Israelites captive for some seventy years, and when they were set free, they penned their own version of the same story, and renamed the flood hero as Noah. Thus it is a matter of record that the biblical version of the Great Flood was the fourth twist of an intriguing tale that has meanings far deeper than many would suspect.

I know that many biblical believers would reject such information, but the truth is that it is factual and irrefutable. What surprised me upon acquiring this knowledge and double-checking its sources, was not the fact that the Hebrew leaders, like many before them, had plagiarised this divine saga, but that the earlier versions were not common knowledge. Why was this information not taught at school? It certainly fell under the realm of historic academic study. The answer to this would take a while to sink in.

What I found equally intriguing is that the Bible depends largely upon its genealogical detail to sustain its claims to authenticity, but with Noah now a proven fabrication, where did this leave the rest of the Old Testament? As the second Adam he is a major lynchpin in the biblical bloodlines, from the 'original' couple Adam and Eve right through to Jesus the Christ. Again, to me this was a major obstacle to any fundamental belief in the biblical canon. Upon researching the truth of the Great Flood legend I knew things would become truly interesting, hence my decision to delve deeper and see what else was to my mind deliberately hidden under the covers.

I received the first letter of my sentence on that first Saturday morning. It was from the head solicitor of the defending firm, he wrote to commiserate and said that he could only describe my sentence as 'savage'. This seemed the general consensus of opinion but was of little comfort to me, which is why I had already determined to make the best of a bad situation, one that if I were of lesser resolve would have been crushing. I was pleased to note that my stoic nature had been taken on board by many of the officers that I had to interact with. Anyone that is given a large sentence is immediately put on 'watch' just in case they decide to commit suicide and the cell occupant card which is displayed outside their 'pad' door is coded to state this. I was standing outside my cell on the Saturday when an officer looking for a particular inmate stopped to read my card and asked *'Is this you Brownie?'* I told him it was and he took a pen from his pocket and scribbled over the code muttering *'Lets not be silly!'* before continuing with his duties.

The post I was to begin as a cell painter was a temporary one to get me on the prison work ladder. This was a crucial step as there are always long waiting lists to get certain jobs which are much sought after because of the perks associated with them. In prison terms the Green is known as a 'local', which meant that its infrastructure was not designed to deal with too many long-term prisoners, instead processing them through to more suitable venues. Because of this most prisoners were 'locked down' in their cells for up to twenty-three hours per day with no television or radio. So any jobs that entailed long periods outside of your cell were much valued and could range from wing cleaner right up to the top positions such as reception orderly, visits orderly, block orderly, and officer tea-boy. Everyone knew when one of these positions was to become available simply because of the release or transfer date of the current holder. There was also of course the surprise vacancy if the incumbent holder failed a drug test and was sacked. This left plenty of room for sabotage and once in such a position you would have to be careful who you entrusted. For a loner like me this was never going to be a problem.

I was told that very weekend that the block orderly position would become vacant in January and that it was mine if I wanted it. The thought of working down in the 'dungeon' appealed to me due to the opportunity to read that it yielded, much of the time in this job was spent waiting around to collect meals for the inmates held in solitary confinement and keeping a relatively small area clean. I set my heart on it and politely declined the other posts that I was offered.

My first few weeks at the Green, now as a convicted prisoner, shot by and Christmas was now only six weeks away, I both looked forward to and dreaded it simultaneously, I knew it would be a time when my absence from home would be hard on the children but their Christmas visit here would be better than expected. I'd already planned to get lots of presents for them all. It was mostly chocolate, but lots of it, and would certainly make for a nice surprise. I valued the privilege of being able to do this and thought how someone like Nelson Mandela would have relished it. During his incarceration on Robben Island he wasn't allowed to see his wife for months on end, and when the visit was allowed, it was just her, no children. And even then the couple were separated by a glass partition, only able to view each other from the neck up. This kind of comparative thinking was to keep me in good spirits throughout the entire length of my sentence.

I was inside less than a month before I was asked to do my first 'babysit'. This simply meant having to move to problem cells, which in one dedicated unit were specially padded for any prisoners that were considered a self-harm risk. Inmates that were normally required to perform this task were specially trained as 'listeners', I wasn't a listener but was asked anyway and did it on a regular basis. In this particular instance an inmate had tried to hang himself and was moved to the prison hospital wing. This had left his cell-mate, a lad that suffered with schizophrenia in shock and with guilt-pangs as he felt that he might in some way have been responsible. I was asked to spend the night with him. He was given medication by the hospital staff and slept like a baby after we had talked for a couple of hours. He told me that he was serving ninety-one days for stealing CD's from a Virgin record store and also had charges pending for a domestic burglary. I collected his breakfast for him in the morning as he struggled to rise in time to get it for himself and gave him a cake and a few other extra tit-bits from my groceries before being moved back to my own cell.

That same evening I was asked to baby-sit again, this time with a guy named Adrian who had slashed his wrists, more in an effort to gain sympathy than anything else it seemed to me, so I tried to raise his spirits as much as I could, he had a monopoly on self-pity though and it was hard work. In the end a doctor had to come to the cell and sternly tell him to pull himself together as his attitude would not lead to early release, which I think he believed it might, but only further distress. It seemed to work and at least got me out of there. I didn't get back to my wing until late afternoon and so missed the mid-morning gym session which was most annoying.

I received another letter that day from my solicitors informing me of the date and venue of my confiscation order hearing. Once convicted of a drug supplying offence the courts then decide how much you might have financially benefited from your activities and set a figure that you must repay under the legislation known as the Drug Trafficking Act. They do this by assessing your current realisable assets such as your house, car, bank balance, savings, and jewellery etc., and 'ask' you to pay a sum equivalent to their total. You are set a time limit within which to do this and if you do not then you must serve an extra period in prison consecutive to your sentence in lieu of non-payment. In my case the total benefits figure bandied around the court was originally thirty million pounds which was later reduced by the Crown Prosecution Service to fourteen and a half million. This court appearance was for a final figure to be decided upon by the sentencing judge, and I was told that I was to be taken to Hereford Crown Court on the outskirts of Wales for the hearing.

When I arrived I was informed by the barrister selected to represent me, as my original advocate was at another trial, that he had good news, the CPS had agreed to reduce the benefits figure from fourteen and a half million to four and a half million. How this was good news I will never know, maybe he felt that I could write the court a cheque for that amount there and then. He also told me the Judge had settled upon a realisable payment figure of just under fifteen thousand pounds which comprised of the equity in the marital home, sale of Nia's car, and encashment of a joint insurance policy. I argued that half of the equity in the house belonged to Nia, she had bought her car herself with a bank loan which could be verified with documentation, that half of the insurance policy also belonged to her, and that the house and insurance policy should not fall within the calculations anyway as we had possessed them outside of the time-frame in which I was accused of dealing drugs. He agreed but advised me that it would be wise not to contest what was a generously low figure in view of the total amount of benefit that the Crown had ordered against me. This he stated was because the Judge had the authority to declare without needing substantiation that I had hidden assets, and that he had the power to pull a figure out of thin air to the tune of hundreds of thousands or maybe even a million pounds that I would have no chance of repaying which would in effect double the servable time of my sentence.

Unlike normal charges, in confiscation hearings the burden of proof lies with the accused to disprove prosecution allegations, in other words you are guilty until proven innocent, there is also no jury so you are at the sole mercy of the trial Judge. This was a man who had just given me a ten year sentence that even made the attendant police gasp at my trial. I had little choice but to grudgingly sign the documentation of acceptance that effectively waived my rights to appeal this injustice. I got the impression that the Judge in question wasn't too pleased during the hearing that I wasn't cock-a-hoop at his apparent generosity as he also allowed me a twelve month time period in which to make payment. I nodded politely when he outlined the details of the order but I didn't smile. In effect he was ordering me to make my wife and children homeless. I was truly pissed off.

To take my mind off the day's events I started work on the structural layout of my book that very evening and came up with what I considered a suitable working title considering the mood that I was in, *'Rulers & Lies – Religion Unfolded'*. I was exactly one month into my sentence.

My next family visit was more down-to-earth as the strain of the situation was starting to show. Nia laid into me vehemently about the mess I'd gotten us all into and its effect on the children. She was livid and really let rip, the shock had worn off and she stated things as they were. It was genuine and justifiable anger. I sat silently and took it. I couldn't retort, I couldn't encourage, I just sat there ashamedly as it was all so very true. The whole situation was a disaster and it was all my fault, promises of any future success would have been well out of place. There was no immediate solution and I was uncharacteristically dejected.

The gym in the Green is pretty well equipped with free weights and a variety of weight training and jogging machines, there was also a boxing punch bag which the guys used to queue around to use for a few minutes at a time each. I used to smile at the inability of any of them to even stand up correctly let alone put together anything seriously menacing, but it would have been perceived as big-headedness to start giving tips, especially as I hadn't shown my hand myself, so I didn't pay too much attention. I couldn't be bothered with the fifteen minutes or so in total that I'd get on the bag either, to me it was a waste of a work-out so I just stuck to a weights and fitness routine that I'd devised for myself.

It's not unusual for me to not even bother with the normal three minute rounds with a minute break in between when I do bag work. I generally punch the bag relentlessly for one hour straight while working on a variety of different techniques and strategies as well as my speed and power. After the mauling Nia gave me and the looks of despair on the faces of the children I was in the mood for a serious work-out. It was fortunate that Mark Page had popped by to see me that week and threw a package on the bed. He said, 'Howard I think you'll need these'. It was a pair of boxing bandages with which to wrap your hands. He must be psychic.

I took them to the gym on the very next session and as soon as the bag became free, I started punching. When someone who is trained in the art hits the bag the sound is distinctly different to that of a novice. The gym came to a standstill and a small group of the guys stopped their work-out to come and watch me as I laid into that equipment. There was about forty minutes of the gym session left, which for me was barely enough to unload as much as I really wanted to. Boy was I stressed. I don't think anyone in the gym that day paid full attention to their own workout while I flailed away. A few guys started asking me for tips on footwork and how they could develop stamina like mine, as usual I accommodated them, but the truth was that I was still so pissed off I could have punched through walls. I didn't get the chance to use the punch bag again. I'm told that on the following gym session the chain that it hung from snapped when the very first guy hit it. The gym officers didn't bother to get a new one.

Lex, Rick, and the other guys that were arrested in connection with the hotel surveillance had all been sentenced by now. Lex got seven and a half years and Rick got eight. I felt sorry for them both even though their sentences were less than mine. Rick was a family man so I knew what he was going through, so was Lex, whose story was in a sense just as ill-fated as my own.

The story runs that a Dutch world kickboxing champion, who I know of but have never met, was exporting shipments of ecstasy tablets to a contact in England, and often used to fly over himself to collect his profit when the contraband was sold. His English contact had fallen behind with payment on one particularly large consignment and they agreed to meet in a hotel room in London to resolve the situation. The meeting erupted into an argument and a fist fight broke out in which the English lad was beaten to death. It was this tragedy that led to the police surveillance that was placed on the English group Lex met with prior to his arrest, they also received shipments, albeit cannabis, from the same Dutch fighter. The reason Lex travelled to England is that the kickboxer in question had a world title contest to prepare for and did not want to interrupt his training to make the trip himself. He asked Lex to come over for him and Lex jumped at the chance, the way he saw it, not only was he being paid for a relatively simple task, but it was also a free holiday to boot. It's the longest holiday he's ever had.

Sentenced prisoners are categorised into different security brackets which break down from 'A' to 'D'. 'A' category inmates automatically include murderers, three-strike lifers, dangerous and violent offenders, terrorists, and anyone serving an extraordinarily long sentence. This of course is subject to review and to some extent the discretion of the prison authorities. These inmates are held in the 'A' category section or maximum security wings of selected prisons under the close scrutiny of experienced prison officers. 'B' category consists of convicts serving eight years plus but usually not considered violent or maximum security risks and they are held in medium security closed facilities. Anyone serving seven years or less is normally categorised as level 'C' and held in low security closed prisons. The lowest category is of course 'D', which is reserved for people given sentences of less than four years, or longer serving inmates that have been de-categorised down the scale as their sentences draw to a close and they are being prepared for release into the community. Anyone serving double figures, i.e. ten years or more, is automatically registered as 'A' category, but is de-categorised according to the latter criteria within the first week or so of their sentence if eligible. I fell into this bracket. Lex was issued with a 'C' category and Rick with 'B' and within a week or so of our convictions we all had some idea, pending appeals, of what modes of progress through the prison system were open to us.

I kept myself busy and Christmas week came and went in a hurry as I constantly gorged myself on reading material. I re-read *The Templar Revelation* and made notes on it as well as on another interesting book titled *The Sirius Mystery* by Robert Temple. I also drafted a preface for 'Rulers & Lies', one that I would later discard as too bland and amateurish.

I began my apprenticeship as block orderly the first week in January which was a good start to the New Year with the added bonus that I could now get a shower every day as segregation was a self-contained unit. Normally inmates would only be granted access to the showers two or three times a week while resident on their wing and of course after any gym session, if they were lucky enough to be allowed one. Gym allocation was a lottery and in many ways restricted, due to shortage of space, to 'familiar' faces. Like many British jails, the Green was way overcrowded and exceeded its safety limits by a considerable margin, so to get the post that I did meant that I was a very lucky man.

My joy at my new vocation however was to be short-lived, I was told that I was due to be transferred to a different facility before the incumbent orderly could complete his hand-over and that I should immediately pre-prepare my belongings. It's an understatement to say that I wasn't happy about this sudden turn of events but you know what they say about the best laid plans of mice and men. I gathered together what little I had and readied myself for the move. It was the last one that I would make for quite some time.

5

HMP Rye Hill was a brand new six hundred and sixty inmate private jail that had come in over budget and over schedule. It was operated by Group Four Security who had lobbied for and won the contract from the British government. When I arrived there I was one of a total of only twenty-eight convicts and the facility was like a ghost town. We had the run of the place and were allowed to choose our own cells once we were allocated to our 'units', as the wings there were called. It was the commercial face of independently managed British prisons, with the heads of staff known as 'directors' and not by the usual term of governors. It was all pretty snazzy, we were even called by our first names and encouraged to respond similarly to the officers in a bid to keep a human face on things. Even as a novice inmate I could see the difficulties that this more lax approach might yield.

Erosion of what in government run facilities was a distinct division between inmates and 'screws', as prison officers are often referred to, proved unpopular with hard-core convicts, they were used to matters being more clear cut. This was not the case at Rye Hill, and was exacerbated by the fact that the unit officers were all new recruits who underwent a mere six-week training programme before being allowed, unsupervised, onto active duty. Group Four foresaw this shortfall to some extent because they hand-picked the first six months intake of inmates from the 'best behaved' records of other British prisons, they soon ran out of those however, especially with the overriding problem of a jail to fill.

Prisons are a commercial enterprise and the government pays a yearly fee for every inmate held resident, and with Group Four shareholders demanding returns on their investment, the pressure was on to maximise profits. Influx soon changed from 'best behaved' to 'all-aboard'. The result, the turnover of burnt out and abused staff at Rye Hill was phenomenal. Staff recruitment took the form of advertising in local and regional newspapers, so not only were inmates privy to what members of staff were earning, but very soon we also discovered their backgrounds, which ranged from supermarket checkout girls to building site labourers and pub managers. The only professionally trained and experienced prison staff were members of the upper management. It was a farce.

This as usual did not concern me as I had devised a time-consuming agenda for myself which would take me through my custody whether my appeal against the length of my sentence was successful or not. I had no time to be confrontational or involved in any other way with either officers or inmates especially as we were all now privileged with the privacy of single cells that consisted of a bed, a toilet, a sink basin, a cupboard, shelf space, and a colour television. There was also the chance to work full-time in the industries department and almost unlimited access to the gym. It was as good as a bad situation can get.

As far as my project was concerned I was beginning to analyse what is termed the esoteric nature of the holy books, that is to say their hidden messages. It was plain to me that any surface reading of these texts could be very misleading for the simple reason that the people who wrote them did not think as we do, so to scrutinise them from a modern perspective would be erroneous. The writer that I have to thank for pointing this out is Alan Alford. He illustrated in what was to me undeniable fashion that some of the 'little' details in the biblical manuscripts were of profound importance.

For example, the second chapter of the book of Genesis details how after creating Adam from the dust of the ground, God then placed him in the garden he planted that was 'eastwards' in Eden. The 'eastern' location at first seems like inconspicuous detail until you realise that it is one of the most important points of the story, for the 'east' was none other than heaven itself, information that is both profound and extremely revealing.

To the ancient mind, the two main directional points in theological terms were 'east' and 'west', a point borne out on many occasions in all of the biblical texts and many other culture holy books. The 'west' was the domain known as the 'underworld', the place that later came to be regarded as hell, and henceforth pictured as a solely dark and fiery location reserved for torture and punishment. This horrifying image was not always the case however, in ancient terms the lower region, like heaven was a spirit world to which all the dead, whether deemed good or bad, would have to travel for judgement by the gods. Those that were judged favourably could then ascend to heaven, but this did not apply to everybody, and indeed there were also paradise locations in the lower realm reserved for the good souls of the lower social classes. Evildoers would not necessarily be doomed to everlasting torment, as death at the hands of various underworld monsters, later to become known as demons, was the most common option. The bulk of ill-judged souls were usually eaten.

Both of these realms, the east and the west, consisted of two kingdoms, the 'north' and the 'south', and it is here we see the ancient theology reflecting the real life northern and southern kingdoms of both the Egyptian Empire and the lands of the Hebrews. It is also because of the east/west axiom that the temples of the Egyptians, early church buildings, and the mosques of Islam all face the 'east'. It was not originally borne out a literal geographical reverence, but a spiritual one, they were designed to symbolically face heaven.

What Alford's work made clear was that when the thought

patterns of the ancients were applied to the ancient texts they took on another aspect entirely. It also became obvious that biblical translators, whether deviously or not, intentionally mistranslated many apparently insignificant details when they could not make sense of them. In the famous story of Moses and the exodus of the Israelites from Egypt we have a prime example. It is accepted in almost all biblical translations that the refugees crossed a waterway known as the Red Sea, when the Hebrew narrative relates that they crossed the 'Yam Suph', which translates as 'Reed Sea', another mystical term that is laden with important esoteric meaning.

In ancient Egyptian culture they acknowledged the existence of a mystical waterway that stretched from the under-world to heaven that was called the 'Sea of Reeds', this because one of the most popular modes of travel across it was on boats made of reeds. Gods that travelled from heaven often came down in such crafts to be reborn in the underworld before ascending to the earth. To assume that this sea was full of reed plants or was a marshland, as a literal interpretation of its title might imply, is a gross misunderstanding of the texts.

In one of the earlier versions of the Noah's Ark story, the hero then known as Utanapishtim was told by the gods to tear down his dwelling, a 'reed' hut, and to use the material to build the vessel that would save mankind and the animals. Similarly, in the birth legend of Moses he was placed in a 'river' amongst the 'reeds' in an 'ark' made of bulrushes before finding safety. The clues pile up to show that the tale was not a literal event but another reworking of the Great Flood story depicting travel between supernatural realms. The numerical details and appar-ently nonsensical wording, confirm the true nature of the message that the ancients were trying to convey, and yet organ-ised religion has eroded them by simplifying important coding into a literal reality.

Nevertheless, many occulted themes, such as the Reed Sea and the east/west geography, were a constant in the tales of all of the Middle Eastern belief systems, a fact which could never be coincidence. I continued to read and gather as much information as I could, from as wide a source base as possible, in a bid to cross-reference them all. Goodness knows I had the time.

Having determined that I was going to make the most of every second that I spent in prison I decided to enrol for full-time education so that I could research and write 'Rulers & Lies' as a self-study project. I soon learned that such an option was not available, and was told that I would have to use my own time to pursue such a venture. Either a recognised educational course would have to be followed or I would have to go to work. I didn't muse long over the answer and decided to join the prison workshop so that I could purchase the many books that I would need from my wages instead of having to ask Nia to get them for me all the time. With full time work, training in the gym every day, and studying and writing at night I knew that time would fly in positive fashion and that this simple routine would leave me exhausted almost every night. Every inmate wants their 'bird' to fly by as quickly as possible and I was not about to succumb to drug use, like so many others, to achieve this effect.

I spent my first day in industries packing tea, coffee, milk, and sugar sachets for the ministry of defence. I turned it into a logistics exercise and devised a collating system that saw me finish in ultra quick time with the minimum of effort. It was enjoyable from that perspective and I don't think I could have handled it any other way, my brain would have fried. The workshop prison officers took note and I was discreetly taken to one side and asked if I wanted to be a supervisor when the more lucrative and interesting contracts began. Why not I thought, after all I wasn't sure how long I could have made teabag packing a fun proposition.

The other project that kept me occupied was helping to set up a boxing programme in the gym. The government were at this time phasing out the use of punch-bags in British jails but I managed to convince the gym and senior staff at Rye Hill that if boxing sessions were held in a controlled manner it would be good for the prison and actually lead to less violence and not more. They conceded that the stress release and physical exertion of those allowed to train in the noble art would in all probability be a positive for the gym curriculum, but that if there were any breaches of discipline by anyone taking part then the classes would be halted. What also helped was that a group of the officers also wanted me to run martial arts classes for them which to be honest I was not averse to doing. In an old style jail it would have been a no-no as my fellow inmates would have been furious. But at Rye Hill no such boundaries applied. Inmates even played pool and table tennis with prison staff, who were usually bored stiff, as a matter of course. The officers' classes were refused but the boxing programme was set up with gusto and once the gym budget was negotiated I was called in to select what equipment would be needed.

They bought everything that I suggested and more, and although we were not allowed to engage in full-fledged head sparring as none of us possessed head-guards or gum-shields, we got away with what we could in addition to using the punch-bags, speedball, focus pads, and skipping ropes to our hearts content. During my time at Rye Hill some really talented boxers and kickboxers passed through the doors and we enjoyed some classic sparring sessions in both sports to which the gym officers turned a blind eye which was pretty sporting of them.

On the education front I was still getting some resistance to gaining evening and weekend computer access so that I could type out my notes and assemble them on floppy disc. They were piling up now and needed cataloguing especially as my hand-writing is so dreadful. The notes that I made when I was tired or something dawned on me in the middle of the night and I leaned out of bed to my paperwork to ensure I wouldn't forget the point to be made, were either nonsensical in the cold light of day or looked like a spider had stepped in ink and crawled across the page. It was a frustrating time, but I ploughed ahead regardless, never losing faith that I would succeed in complet-ing my work no matter what hurdles had to be overcome.

With this pragmatic and philosophical mindset, very few things got my goat at Rye Hill, but one that did was the treatment of visitors. Inmates are convicted felons and expect to be degraded to some extent as part of the punishment for their crimes. Visitors however, are not, they have not been accused, tried, or convicted of any offence, and for the large part are decent and law abiding citizens who through no fault of their own find themselves in the position of offering moral support to the wretched. This view is not shared by the prison system.

It is understandable that preventative measures have to be in place to ensure against possible breaches of security, so the use of proven methods of weapon and contraband detection such as scanners and x-ray machines cannot be derided. There was however one device, known as the Baringer Machine, which was used to conduct an ion test on the hands of most visitors. The machine proved so inaccurate that government run prisons no longer use it. It allegedly measures the amount of drugs in someone's system from analysis of a hand swab in supposedly unerring fashion. In practicality the claim was ludicrous. Nia failed it almost every time in one period of visits and was from one swab declared to have opiates, marijuana, and cocaine simultaneously present in her system. This would have been laughable if it were not so upsetting. Nia is as law-abiding and health-conscious a person as one can get. She wasn't the only clearly innocent victim either. There were many other partners, wives, fathers, mothers and grandparents who also fell foul of this nonsense and were made to feel like common criminals by the prison staff. It got to the point where inmates were advising visitors to wear polythene gloves when they filled their petrol tanks, wear gloves while driving, and let the children turn any door handles once they arrived at the prison building.

To rub salt in the wounds of such victims, those inmates that knew that their visitors were active drug users used to brag about how they easily passed the Baringer Test after 'blazing' marijuana in their cars on the way to the visit. To them it was highly amusing and in a way their own middle finger salute to the ineptitude of the prison system. To guys like me it was the opposite.

Visits were scheduled for either one and a half hours for 'standard' prisoners, or two hours for 'enhanced' cons who had model records. If your visitors failed the Baringer Test this privilege was taken away. Either the visitor in question would not be allowed into the visits room if you demanded your full time-slot allowance, or your visit would be reduced to half an hour and take place behind a glass screen via intercom. This stance was both embarrassing and unnecessary as there were special visit tables with cameras above them so that your entire visit could be scrutinized by the security staff. This would ensure that there was no smuggling of contraband which was the whole point of the exercise anyway and no rule abiding inmate would have minded such a minor intrusion. Yet it was only after a barrage of complaints from well respected model prisoners and the subsequent threats of legal action from family hired solicitors that use of this infernal security device was curtailed and applied with selective discretion. I for one asked one of the deputy directors to subject his own staff and their families to a Baringer Test so that he could gauge its efficiency first hand for himself. He declined, and with good reason.

Prison morale is one of the most important issues in any lock-up. If the inmates are in depressed mood, particularly upset or united over a sensitive issue then governors, or in Rye Hill's case, directors, wisely take note. No one in their right mind really wants a prison riot, or even any lesser form of protest such as hunger strikes or refusal to 'bang up', the term used for getting behind your cell door at lunch, dinner, and night-times or upon request.

The morale of the prison staff is also of major importance. It cannot be overlooked that they spend lengthy periods of time with men, or women, who display a variety of moods, and in the main have only a grudging respect for the people that are prepared to turn the key on them at night, ask them to strip naked, and in some cases treat them as lesser members of the human race. One has to remember that prisoners come from a variety of backgrounds. Not all are uneducated or without an exterior support system. Indeed the looks of disdain on the faces of some prison staff when they realise after witnessing prison visits just how much more advanced financially and socially some of their charges are than they, are at best pitiful, and at worst, ugly and vindictive.

The other problem at Rye Hill was that the bulk of the general staff were so young. It never bodes well when relative youngsters are instructed to patronise and advise people with the equivalent life experience of their parents on personal and social issues, especially when the inmates are aware that but a few months ago the 'officer' in charge was employed in a dead end job. It was unfair on both parties and the looks of embarrassment on the faces of some of the staff when they were 'advising' world experienced inmates during rehabilitation courses and sentence planning made for uncomfortable viewing. Stuttering and red faces were the order of the day. If convicts had any brains though they acted in subservient fashion and nodded like the toy-dogs people put in the back of their cars. These embryonic 'assessors' had a large say in how well you would proceed through your sentence and could assist or hinder your release with the stroke of a pen.

I remember on one occasion that I was being escorted back to my unit after a particularly pleasant night-time visit by Nia and the children when I got into conversation with the officer that was accompanying me. He was a young fellow with a particularly meek demeanour and couldn't have been more than twenty-seven or twenty-eight years old, who told me that I didn't know how lucky I was. I could hardly believe my ears but the statement was so odd that I thought it best to listen rather than argue. I asked him to elaborate and he said that sometimes he didn't even want to go home. I didn't ask him why and just allowed him to unload as much as he wanted in that short walk. I only saw him a couple of more times, obviously he left the job. As I said, the turnover of the general staff at Rye Hill was phenomenal. The only time I have ever witnessed anything similar was in the British insurance industry during its recruitment drive in the seventies and eighties.

The truth is, that prison officers are in a lot of respects serving a sentence along with the prisoners. The only difference being that the officer sleeps elsewhere. Some 'screws' are so keen on their job, presumably because of overtime pay, that not only are they there to lock you up at night, but are the same faces that unlock you in the morning for five or six days a week. I wondered upon witnessing this whether things had become so tough on the outside that people would voluntarily opt for such an existence. Inmates were there because they were being physically held captive and for no other reason. What excuse did the officers have? Even in government run prisons, where the staff support and social network systems were far advanced to the one that existed for Rye Hill staff, the worst statement that a con could make to an officer in heated argument was 'at least I've got a release date!' It has led to many a prisoner being knocked cold on the spot. It is an extremely accurate maxim that the truth hurts, and in the latter cases, it hurt everybody.

As the deputy director that I debated the practicality of the Baringer Test with was well aware, any obvious lapses in the morale of his inadequately trained staff could lead to breaches in security, and sure enough, they did. Not all staff left the establishment because they could not take the intense mood of prison life, some were simply fired, and this in a situation where Group Four were struggling to recruit reliable personnel.

Although infrequent, once or twice a year an inmate would be caught in a compromising situation with a female member of staff. She would be dismissed from her post, and he would be shipped to a higher security facility, which would also be a setback to the inmate's proposed date of release. In one situation, one clinching couple got engaged to be married as soon as the female half exited the prison service. I thought that particular state of affairs was quite romantic to be honest. Shit happens. But the over-riding reason for staff dismissal, and one that on occasion saw police attend the premises and criminal charges brought against the officers concerned, was supplying drugs. Prison is a hotbed for corruption.

The average weekly take home pay of the staff at Rye Hill was in the region of two and a half hundred pounds, so one can only imagine how they felt when they saw prisoners visitors roll up in executive saloons, convertible sports cars and four wheel drive vehicles on a weekly basis. When you factor in the predatory business nature of many cons, and the intimate relationships that were developed because of the close proximity and endless hours that inmates and warders spent together, then it was inevitable that the weaker willed staff would become susceptible to the opportunity to double their wages with little effort and apparently minimal risk.

In most cases all they were required to do was meet with an outside contact provided by the inmate and bring a small amount of contraband through the, for them, lapse prison security, and pass it on to their new 'employer'. The amount of money made by supplying drugs in prison is truly mind-boggling, and for some inmates to have made their fortune while incarcerated was not unusual, some intentionally failing to obtain early release until they had feathered their nest to the required extent. From a strictly commercial point of view I could see their point as many businessmen would give their eye-teeth to monopolise a captive market, and for the jail drug barons this was exactly the opportunity that presented itself.

Officers would earn a commission that was meagre in comparison, but one that doubled their weekly take home pay for just a few minutes work. In many cases these were not creatures of the highest ambition, or intellect. As a result the obvious increase in their disposable income would often be on display to their colleagues who having put two and two together would sooner or later inform. They were not the only ones to do this and jealous inmates would often do the same. Loose lips sink ships, and prison is nothing if not an ocean of ego and gossip. There are no fictional soap operas to compare, and for a guy that thought that he knew a lot about life, I quickly learned that in this world I was a novice.

6

It is said that the people who cope with prison life the best, other than career criminals, are former members of the armed forces and ex-public school students. The reason for this is that they are used to the discipline, confinement, and petty rules that form part and parcel of the penal system.

There are timetables for almost everything, getting up in the morning, collecting your breakfast, and going to work or education, with each and every part of the day broken down into segments which are rigidly adhered to. Then there are the issues which one felt could have been dealt with differently such as the wearing of a sports bib over your upper garments on visits. This was supposedly because it would make inmates more visible and prevent them swapping places with a visitor and exiting the building. Such a rule would make sense in the case of identical twins if the twin brother wore the same garments on a visit as his sibling. Other than that, why not just make sure that before visitors were allowed out convicts were checked-in and identified. In retrospect I imagine that this type of measure was implemented because of the susceptibility to bribery of some of the staff, I knew that they could be incompetent but that particular legislation seemed plain silly. Still, as a disciplined ex-athlete I found it easy to acclimatise to all of these regulations.

I married young, as most sports people do. I was twenty-two years old when Nia and I tied the knot at the city register office. We were already co-habiting and it seemed the natural thing to do as Nick was six months old and we had both committed to making a go of life together. This suited me as training for contests in both boxing and kickboxing, as well as working full-time in a major high street bank, was demanding, and the support of a partner in such a routine is almost essential to success.

The key to achievement in any field is discipline and dedication, these are difficult tenets to keep if you lead a single life, as talent alone doesn't always sustain success, and without a suitable support system it is easy to lapse. There are many examples of this philosophy in the sporting world and it was a lesson driven home to me as an adolescent.

My brothers and our friends were in our early teens when we started to venture out to Birmingham central for extra excitement, as it was only natural that we began to outgrow the local youth clubs. The cinema was always, and still is a regular pastime for us, but it wasn't time-consuming enough so we also started to visit the city ice rink which was a huge meeting place for teenagers from all over the region, there was much fun to be had and new friends to be made from both sexes. It was an exciting time.

Junior did not take to ice skating with the fervour that Edge and I did, we were like twins growing up, and shared to a large extent the same group of friends right up until his departure to America with my parents in the early nineteen-eighties. By our very nature we leapt to the head of the alpha-male fraternity that existed at the Silver Blades Ice Rink, the main group of lads were excellent hockey skaters and all of them were handy with their fists. So it was just the skating that we had to catch up on. We attended and practised six or seven times a week even during the afternoon figure skating sessions that would allow it, and with the assistance and training tips passed on by our new friends we soon became more than adept on the ice.

We would go skating three or four weekday evenings a week, catching the bus from the main road in Handsworth to the city centre. The same number bus in the other direction would take you to the city of Wolverhampton via an area called West Bromwich. This little town was next door to Handsworth, so to speak, and home to one of England's most famous soccer teams, West Bromwich Albion. The club was established in 1878 and has a successful history, taking pride of place for many years in English football's illustrious First Division. In the late seventies it attracted a lot of extra attention because three of the country's top black soccer players, affectionately known as the 'three degrees' in replication of the famous singing trio, all featured in its first team, namely, Laurie Cunningham, Cyril Regis, and Brendan Batson, when players of colour were only just starting to get prominence in the English game. One of our friends was on his way to joining them.

Bob Hazel, was big for his age and like lots of us, pretty handy at playing soccer, he was very good, but none of us regarded him as outstanding enough to make the professional grade. When Edge and I were waiting for the bus to go into town, we would pass Bob with his training gear in hand as he caught the same number bus from its stop over the road to the West Bromwich Albion training ground to practice as an apprentice. We thought that we were so cool, all dressed up and heading for fun into the city centre, and that Bob was pursuing an intangible dream, that we never gave it a second thought about the seriousness and dedication that he was putting into his efforts. To us Bob was just another local guy our age that was getting his fun in his own way.

When the news spread that Bob had been officially signed by the Albion and that he was playing in the reserve team, it was the talk of Handsworth. He wasn't just 'good' like everybody else anymore. He was outstanding. Everyone was so proud, especially those of us that knew him, and when he made his first team debut it hit me like a right cross that he was the smart one and we were the dummies. Well, almost. Fortunately for me I had already begun to take my martial arts quite seriously but boy did I step up the pace. Bob Hazel had led by example and showed us all what could be done if you isolated and dedicated yourself to a cause. I started doing the same and Edge followed suit. We joined a boxing club to complement our growing martial arts skills, and gradually phased ice skating out of our agenda, playtime was over.

In 1975 I was mesmerised by an American kickboxing contest that featured a fighter known as Benny 'The Jet' Urquidez which was shown on a British Television programme called World of Sport. Benny could box, unlike most western kickboxers back then, he was also teak-tough, fit, and a great karateka. I thought straight away, that's for me. I'd been raised on boxing and it is still my favourite spectator sport. The layman may never understand the technical and strategic intricacies of the fight game, and may think that being tough and a lunatic are the essential ingredients. I'm the first to admit that taking part in contests is not good for the grey matter, but it is a remarkable tool for the discovery of your own character. I can only describe it as physical chess with a marathon and a mugging thrown in for good measure, and you soon learn about the depths of your own resolve. It is also rewarding from a psychological standpoint, for when you master its technique and its discipline, your ego is sated, your confidence is boosted, even in other walks of life, and you feel self-fulfilled, with the added bonus that it is one of the most proven and effective training systems for keeping in shape. That's why, thirty years later, I still work out, hard. I'm not ready for golf just yet.

When I enrolled at the Haichi-Shin Kai Budo Academy, I told the owner, a judo instructor named Tom Ryan who asked me why I wanted to join, that I was going to become a kickboxing world champion and needed to learn karate to do this. He said that they could provide all the facility for me to do just that. I felt that he was patronising me but joined anyway. The only person that ever needs to be convinced of your intent and aware of your limitations is yourself, and I knew that I had the will to win. It didn't help that I lost my very first contest, albeit by a close points decision, and I guess some of the people that I knew thought that mini-setback would dampen my ire a little bit. It did the opposite. I could hardly wait to get back in the ring and won my next contest by a second round knock-out at Birmingham's Digbeth Civic Hall. Accolades flowed and pretty soon I wasn't the only kickboxer at the Haichi-Shin Kai. My career would go from strength to strength and I travelled the world as a fighter and coach for the next twenty years. I have many inspirational sources to thank for this. Bob Hazel is one of them.

There was another factor that also helped in my passage through this dark period of my life, and that was the academic discipline that was instilled into me at school. One of the premier Grammar schools in England, Handsworth Grammar, was situated just fifteen minutes walk from where I lived. It was part owned by the state and part private, and had a history and tradition for sending its premier students onto degree courses at the country's top Universities, including Oxford and Cambridge. When I passed what was effectively the Grammar school entrance examination, known then as the eleven-plus, as that was the age at which you took it, and was accepted into this faculty, my parents were cock-a-hoop. So was I. What I didn't know was that it would take me years to settle.

There were only two boys that passed the eleven-plus at Boulton Road Junior School. That was myself and John Morgan, who used to come to play at our house sometimes after school. He, my brothers and I, would try to ride the nanny goat around the garden like cowboys when dad wasn't around. She wasn't too impressed. John decided to go to Lordswood Technical School, while I went on to 'the Grammar'. So when I got there I had no friends, I vaguely knew a couple of other lads from having played inter-school junior football matches against them, but not in any social fashion.

The scenario was not the same for the other boys that attended, they seemed to all have arrived in bunches from academically more successful schools which were predominantly in the much more upmarket area known as Handsworth Wood. While they ran around playing I stood in the playground as it seemed to spin around me. I went from alpha-male to zeta in a heartbeat. It didn't help that my parents went overboard kitting me out in the compulsory school uniform that was required, and mom bought me a satchel that was so big on my small frame that Junior and Edge used to tease me that it looked like the satchel was walking up the road on its own as I left the house every morning.

To make things worse, the cultural differences between the pupils at Handsworth Grammar and those at my former school, Boulton Road, were huge. The children at the grammar were in the main well prepared for what lay ahead. Many came from middle-class backgrounds and were ready for the disciplined regime of a semi-private institution. I was clueless. There was no such thing as homework at Boulton Road, as far as I was concerned once the bell rang, school was over until the next day, and current affairs, what the hell was that? It was all too much change and too rapid for me to merely take it in my stride. Fortunately I excelled at reading and found the English based subjects fairly easy. I still rarely did my homework on time though and was always in the bottom portion of the class. I tried to prove myself in other ways.

In my first month, I was involved in at least one fist fight a week which led to an encounter with a teacher that I will never forget. As I walked through the school playground on a mid-morning play-break I kicked a football that came across my path and it flew over the school wall and into the street. I didn't mean for that to happen and it was a little bit of a predicament as we were not allowed to step outside the school perimeter during school hours, but it was obvious that I would have to go and collect it. At that moment one of the lads that was playing with that particular ball pushed me and ordered me to go and get it, I changed my mind instantly, told him to go and get it himself and continued my walk towards the main school building. I couldn't have got more than 20 yards or so when I was pushed again and started slugging it out with the same lad who had quickly collected the ball and decided to teach me a lesson. He and I were to meet years later as he got a terrific job with the same bank that I did and was a genuinely nice guy, but he made a mistake that day and was fortunate that the metalwork teacher, Mr Jones, came and pulled me off him. I couldn't believe it when he was told to *'Get to your class!'* while my instruction was *'Brown, come with me!'* I thought here we go, favouritism for the posh white boy as Mr Jones ushered me to the metalwork shop. He was livid. He didn't allow any of the waiting pupils inside and made sure the door was fully closed before taking me to task. He asked me bluntly and firmly, *'Are you going to fight every-one in the school?'* I was mystified, his question was one of genuine concern and not what I was expecting, I anticipated some form of detention or corporal punishment, but not this. It got worse.

He proceeded to tell me how my parents must have been very proud that I had gained entrance to one of the best schools in the country and that I really had a chance to make something of myself. He then reeled off the details of most of the playground fights that I had been involved in and how he had been paying close attention and hoped that it was just a phase of adjustment, but had sadly noted that the situation was not improving. Even at that early stage my first response to any confrontation with another student was 'See you at four o'clock!' Mr Jones was having none of it and put forward the golden question, calling me by my first name he said *'Howard, are you going to settle down, stop the fighting, and do what you are here to do?'* Normally in situations like this I was used to raised voices, an ass-whipping, the cane, or something similar. Mr Jones had played a master stroke. He talked to me as if I was an intelligent adult and any bravado on my part was a non-starter. It was my first encounter with this approach and when I felt the warmth on my face I knew it was tears that were trick-ling down. It was a wake-up call and I was forced to recognise that I felt ashamed. It was ages before I had another fight, at school anyway.

That was lesson one but I was to learn a lot more from the real tour de force at Handsworth Grammar and the man that kept the institution on track, Peter Guggenheim, the school headmaster. Mr Guggenheim was a six-footer who walked bolt-upright and had a booming and authoritative voice which was aptly allied to an awe-inspiring presence. Even the teachers tip-toed and stuttered when he was around and no pupil, no matter how confident or how tough, and there were one or two real macho lads at the grammar, dared confront him.

When the bell rang to signal the close of playground breaks, crowds of lads used to try to get through the double doors at the various entrance points, all seemingly at once. The prefects on duty never could control the situation and it was usually fun pushing and shoving as we tried to get through a two-person space four or five at a time, that is unless Guggenheim's voice was heard even remotely in the vicinity. It was like magic. One moment there were thirty or forty guys bulldozing their way in, the next, it was like a ghost town. When you heard even a whisper of that man's baritone rumblings, you made yourself scarce, and sharpish. I was special though and he and I had a very close relationship. That man gave me six of the best with the cane so often that it had Guggenheim and Brown on the Headmaster's study plaque.

This chastisement was for a variety of misdemeanours, such as horsing around, fighting, and consistently failing to complete my homework on time. Guggenheim used to cane us on the palms of our hands, which were ordered to be extended out in front of us as he drew the weapon out of that secretive black gown of his and brought it above his head to deliver three strokes on each hand. The man was like Zorro. What used to piss me off was that no matter how much you tried to bend your thumb back so that the bamboo would only strike the fleshy part of your palm he always managed to whack the joint of your thumb, and boy that not only hurt, but it made the joint turn blue. It would take about half an hour before you could fully make a fist again.

Once he caught me goofing around at the end of a class with one of my pals, Pete Scullion, we were play fighting with chairs raised above our heads, and it was just our luck that at that moment he walked past the open classroom door. He told the two of us that if we wanted to exercise so much that we should get down to his office and he would warm us up. We stood outside his door polishing our shoes on the back of our trousers and adjusting our ties as we were hoping that we might only get four strokes of the cane if we at least looked presentable, Guggenheim was a stickler for clean, tidy, and correct school uniform. It didn't work as he was obviously in a frivolous mood that day. Pete was ordered in first. The only thing that kept me from crying when I got back to the classroom was the sight of Pete writhing in pain with his head buried in his folded arms as he slumped across his desk, it was pretty funny. Still, I was to get my revenge in the best way possible.

In my first four years at this prestigious school, the only thing I excelled at was sport. I was in every team going, soccer, basketball, table-tennis, cross-country, athletics, I was in them all, I even played chess for the school on occasion. My efforts went into everything but the academic curriculum. But when things got serious, and people started talking about careers and what we were going to do after school, I started to pay attention. Your work options largely depended upon how good your exam results were. What career I chose didn't particularly bother me, what did was the thought of the one man that I feared even more than Headmaster Guggenheim, Dad. I decided to salvage the situation and worked out a timetable of study that would allow me to cram as much information as possible before the due date of each exam.

For a solid month before my GCSE 'O' Level examinations I got down to some serious work. I would go home, lock myself into our front room so that no one would disturb me and in effect teach myself from text books much of the information that I was too stupid to pay attention to in class. I'd often mentally kick myself as I realised how easy a lot of the material was to learn and used to think 'Is this it? Is this what was taking so long to teach in class? No wonder I got bored and played the fool so much!' I actually started to enjoy myself. It got to the point where I could hardly wait to sit some of the exams. During this period even Dad tip-toed around me and helped not only to make sure that I was not disturbed, but also that mom and my brothers brought me my dinner and collected the plate. That was unheard of in our family. We lads always took turns to do the washing up, it was a house rule.

When the exam results came in that year I couldn't wait to get back to school to collect the necessary paperwork. I knew that a lot of my teachers had written me off or had a low expectation of success, on my previous form if I had passed two or three exams it would have been a good result, and even so this would still have put me in the running for an executive type job. Such was the reputation of going to Handsworth Grammar. Well, I didn't pass two or three 'O' levels, I passed seven, and did not just scrape through but passed many with flying colours. I'll never forget my mathematics teacher, Johnny Proctor, who was also one of the school football coaches, who despaired at my efforts in his class even though we had a great affinity. He ran through a crowd of lads, grabbed and hugged me and laughed and laughed at how easily I'd passed every one of the maths modules. I felt good too. The teachers that had no success with me in exams from my earlier years largely ignored me, it was as if I had cocked a snoot at them. I was to discover later that it wasn't because they did not like me, but because I did not try when in their classes, and all the while clearly had the ability to do better.

With the current situation that I was now in I remembered how I had squandered those first four years at senior school and it occurred to me what I could have achieved if I had knuckled down earlier. There was no way I was going to repeat that error now, as far as I was concerned if I did, particularly while in jail, it would be akin to doing time twice, and there was no way I was going to waste that most valuable of commodities again.

I was by now very deep into my project and at this point considering the physical nature of the gods, the reason for this was that someone had pointed out a description of Jesus to me as painted in the final biblical book called Revelation. In this text he was called, as he often is in the gospels, the 'Son of Man', and the scripture foretold of his return to the earth on Judgement Day. He is portrayed in that text as a being with hair as white as snow, feet of brass, and a voice that sounds like 'many waters', and cuts a truly formidable figure. It was further stressed to me that this proved that he was a black man and that the 'gods' were negro, just like original man who they had made 'in their own image'.

On the face of it such an argument sounded convincing and I thought, 'So this is what white academics have been hiding all these years?' What scoundrels! Heavenly Jesus was an aged black man with hair like sheep's wool that was as white as snow, flaming eyes, brass coloured feet, and a Paul Robeson voice. This scenario would certainly be embarrassing for white supremacists on Judgement Day! The argument got me thinking that it could indeed be a possibility, but the only problem was that I had never seen a black man with brass feet and flaming eyes.

Intriguingly enough there was a counter argument to this, which indicated that the 'gods' were Caucasian. It is based upon an episode cited in the Book of Enoch, an extraneous text that was not included in the Old Testament but one that is well respected as a work of early Hebrew religious literature. The relevant passage describes the birth of the baby Noah, who is revealed as having white skin, golden hair, and eyes so bright that when he opened them they 'lit up the whole house like the sun'. So in this case the divine infant that God eventually chose to save the inhabitants of the earth was a blond-haired white man with radioactive eyes.

Both arguments are clearly ludicrous, but the very fact that they find wanton believers in this day and age who are more than willing to propagate them as valid proofs of a selective ethnic superiority are as disturbing as they are comical. There are a wealth of other descriptive passages of the gods in the works of many of the ancient cultures, and to my mind their physical qualities posed a riddle that could surely be solvable and make some kind of scientific sense.

The writers of these early works were far from foolish and numbered among the most advanced brains of their time. With this respect alone it should be obvious that it would be irresponsible to sideline their work as mere religious myth. There had to be more to it. What I needed to keep in mind was that the authors were bound by oaths of secrecy and rarely, if ever, penned anything in overt fashion. Everything was obscured by imagery and metaphor, and to them, if you could not begin to fathom their coding then you were not worthy enough to comprehend or receive its true meaning. It is this mode of thought that separated the public at large from the rulers of society, the men that belonged to the most secretive of clubs and wielded much of their power from hidden bases. Theirs was the power behind the throne, the one that has spanned the ages and as I was to realise, still holds sway today.

To begin this analysis it was necessary to collate the various peculiarities of the divine beings as well as take on board the thoughts of the more sensible authors who had previously examined similar data. The common denominators in the vision of Jesus and the Noah story were their light coloured hair and flaming eyes. In the Egyptian texts the sun-god Re also had fire in his eyes, and another of their principal gods, Osiris, had metal limbs of iron and gold, reminiscent of Jesus' brass feet. The description of the Hebrew supreme God Yahweh, or as he is more commonly referred to nowadays, Jehovah, was also of interest. Both he and Jesus descended or were prophesied to land on the earth amidst thunder, lightning, smoke, quaking terrain, and the sound of 'trumpets'. Once again there are parallels in the earlier Egyptian texts, where upon rising from the earth back up to heaven, the sky thundered and the earth quaked for the god Osiris.

There is another mysterious and powerful being mentioned in the Old Testament, a creature known as Leviathan, who the church try to pass of as a literal earthly animal such as a crocodile, whale, or hippopotamus, which is odd as the creature is described as having multiple 'heads' and is clearly based upon the mythical Hydra of Greek legend, which was a many headed dragon that breathed fire. What is significant here is that Leviathan is described in exactly the same terms as Yahweh.

The book of Psalms tells us that smoke billowed from God's nostrils, he 'bowed' the heavens, was surrounded by darkness and yet had brightness around him, he was accompanied by thick clouds and passed by with hailstones and coals of fire, before revealing the channels of the sea and the foundations of the world. This riddle is compatible with the description of the Leviathan in the Old Testament book of Job. The monster also issued smoke from his nostrils, his sneezing flashed forth light, and burning lights and fire shot out of his mouth. But even more revealing is that he is described as a sea creature. This because he is associated with water, made the 'deep' boil like a pot, and left a shining wake behind him so that 'one would think the deep had 'white hair'. In a literal framework these descriptions are most puzzling, especially if you do not bear in mind that all is not what it seems.

The 'deep' and the 'sea' were not necessarily earthly bodies of water in ancient theology, and in these references could refer to either the 'celestial ocean' which we call outer space, or indeed the physical oceans that form much of the earth's surface. The 'celestial' version was the one through which the gods travelled, part of which was the portal the Egyptians referred to as the Duat, and is referred to in the story of Moses as the 'Reed Sea'.

So, what then were these divine creatures, that had 'white hair', 'flaming eyes', roared like thunder, were surrounded by darkness, thick clouds, and smoke, had the ability to penetrate the earth, were made up of metal, whose 'glory' mere mortals were afraid to approach, flew through the celestial oceans of outer space and parted the seas?

To answer this we only have to place ourselves in the shoes of the ancients as they witnessed such flaming objects roar through the sky with such force and brilliance that they could turn 'night' to 'day' and vice-versa, and descend into the earth with the power of a standard nuclear explosion, while at the same time fulfilling every description of the gods as portrayed in the holy books. To them they were gods descending from heaven. To us they are meteorites.

Even to modern man, with the advantage of our knowledge of this phenomenon as relayed to us via Hollywood, the television, and science books, to actually behold such a spectacle would be truly humbling, and to make sense of such a natural occurrence without the scientific knowledge that we have today would be impossible. Even a mere two hundred years ago, American President Thomas Jefferson stated, *'I would sooner believe that two Yankee professors lied, than that stones fell from the sky.'* The French Academy of Sciences debunked reports of such sightings as superstition, and other authorities claimed that these blazing boulders were normal rocks that had been struck by lightning. Yet there is clear geological evidence that at some stage in our history there was a spate of meteor showers that damaged the earth, changed its climate considerably, and wiped out entire species of wildlife. It also seems clear from the ancient tales that unless the divine descriptions are one huge coincidence that man was also around to witness his fair share of them.

Meteors vary broadly in both their composition and reaction to entering the earth's atmosphere. In essence they are extra-terrestrial bodies known as meteoroids that survive impact with the Earth's protective layers and enter its inner space. The ensuing air resistance causes the object to heat up and emit light forming a fireball which can rival the sun in intensity and travel at speeds ranging from 25 to 45,000 miles an hour landing with the force of a medium atomic bomb. It has been estimated that some of the older meteor damage on the Earth's surface, such as Arizona's Barringer Meteor Crater were caused by 'space rocks' that landed with the force of approximately 150 Hiroshima bombs.

In terms of structure about 8% of meteorites that fall to the earth are similar to terrestrial rocks, while another 5% are iron, with intergrowths of iron-nickel alloys, such as kamacite and taenite. As they travel through the atmosphere, some smaller meteorites are less compact and thus barely noticeable during the daytime, disintegrating to emit flashes of various colours including yellow, green, and red, which to the human eye and psyche must appear truly remarkable, unsurprisingly some of their sightings have been considered 'proof' of divine intervention, and even, as is more common nowadays, evidence of alien humanoid activity. In the broadsheet written by German 'student of the holy scripture and the free arts' Samuel Coccius in 1566 he reported that many large black globes were seen in the air, moving before the sun with great speed, and turning against each other as if fighting. Some of them became red and fiery and afterwards faded and went out.' This miraculous event was unsurprisingly ascribed to a divine interlude, no doubt today it would be credited to UFO's.

As well as the visual impact of this phenomenon, meteorite falls are also accompanied by the explosions, detonations, and rumblings caused by the sonic booms created by their speed of travel and the shock waves resulting from their continued fragmentation. These sounds are so loud that they can be heard over areas many thousands of kilometres wide. Just to add to their mystique and what must be the inevitable confusion of anybody witnessing their passage, they are sometimes also supplemented with whistling and hissing sounds, with fireballs leaving dust trails in their wake for some time.

Naturally, large iron meteorites are unapproachable when they land on Earth, as they are often still white hot and susceptible to explosion, making sense of the depictions of them (the gods) having voices like thunder, making the earth quake, being inclined to 'break out' in anger against the people, having 'hair as white as wool', 'flaming eyes' like the sun, being 'girded with brass bands', or having 'feet like brass'.

The comparisons continue to be glaring, from the penetration of the Egyptian Gods Osiris and Isis into the 'middle of the earth', the thunderous landing of the Hebrew God, Yahweh on Mount Sinai in the book of Exodus, the impervious and fire snorting Hydra Leviathan with the 'many heads' of a meteorite shower, and the predicted arrival of Jesus on the clouds amidst the sound of trumpets on Judgement Day. It seems almost certain that the fire-breathing dragons that flew through the air in ancient tales, the brightly coloured Phoenix bird of Egyptian lore, the original angels of Mesopotamian legend, and the notion of fiery locations within the earth, e.g. Hell, were also founded upon the then barely credible phenomenon of the meteor.

To be fair to ancient man, before the advent of modern science what would any of us have made of these roaring missiles of fire that either turned night into day, or darkened the skies, and left a flaming rock residue around an entrance into the earth?

I pondered this for some time because to jump to the conclusion that it was the definite solution to the mysterious origin of the gods was way too simple. The issue of man's need for an explanation of his origin seemed far more complex than that, there was much more evidence to gather, analyse and cross-reference before any such deduction could be positively reached. I was excited though, for most of the metaphorical descriptions of the gods as related in the works of many different ancient cultures could be ascribed to these mysterious heavenly bodies. This feeling was compounded when I discovered that not only had the earliest religious records from the land of Sumer assumed that 'heaven had exploded' to become united with the Earth, but also that this theme was continued in the holy books, it was in hidden form in Genesis chapter one, and blatantly reproduced in the Koran.

The logic of the ancient thought patterns here seemed obvious. Flaming rocks falling from the sky must have been caused by a huge explosion from above, but one too far away for man to witness it. In the mind of earlier cultures the rocks that did not penetrate the earth's surface were pieces of this superior planet, and the ones that impacted with enough force to create craters were the gods themselves who had descended into the earth, a theory that was to become part and parcel of every major religion on earth.

It was hard for me to believe that I was in jail and yet having such a fulfilling time with this project, especially as I missed my children more than anyone that has never been through this type of experience can imagine. It would be fair to say that from a psychological point of view the writing of this book was the only way I could give myself any release from the guilt of causing them such pain. It was my therapy.

7

While I was adjusting to my new surroundings, Nia and the children were doing exactly the same with their lives 'on the outside'. What shone through clearly was the strength of a family unit, as what surely helped them to cope with this new situation was that they all had to rely upon each other. Being aware of this was a unique experience, and one of the few plus points of being in jail is being able to see how your loved ones would have fared had you passed away. It is surprising who steps up to the base to be supportive, and who does not.

From my experience anyone that gets a considerable sentence will see those close to them experience marked changes in their social circles, and make no bones about it, things will never be the same again. I remember asking Nia constantly to tell me who had made contact to offer her moral support throughout my time away and when I ran through a list of names I thought she would have heard from her reply was invariably the same. She hadn't heard a dicky-bird. Yet on the other end of the scale, people who I hadn't expected to give a hoot would either telephone or pop around unexpectedly for a chat with her. It just goes to show that you can never second guess anyone and don't really know the people you interact with until the chips are down.

It was a different matter on the inside. I was never short of people that wanted to visit me, but the truth was that visits were awkward. Sessions took place twice a day from Tuesdays through to Saturdays, once in the afternoon and once in the evening. Prisoners were issued with three, four, or five visiting order forms per month, depending upon their prison status, which they had the option of sending out to prospective visitors for completion. Visitors were then required to submit these documents by post or alternatively telephone with the order details for confirmation of date and time slot allocation. In certain cases, space permitting, they could ring the jail at short notice, bring the visiting order form with them and still get allocated a spot. I was careful who I sent my visiting orders to. The last thing I needed with my stringent timetable was being visited out of the blue. I was a supervisor at work and whether I'm working for pennies or for diamonds, I take my responsibilities seriously. I can't help it, it's my nature. What really pissed me off though, unless it was someone really special like my mom, sister, or brothers who regularly flew over from America, was if someone turned up unexpectedly on a Saturday evening. That is because my schedule went something like this.

I worked in industries from nine to five Monday to Fridays and when I eventually got through the bureaucracy, I also attended computer classes on Monday and Thursday evenings. While there I would be allowed to type out my work as a word document and save it to floppy disk. Every other evening was spent in the gym, either boxing, lifting weights or playing basketball, my all time favourite participator sport. Nia and the children would visit me once every two weeks on a weekday evening and occasionally on a daytime slot when the children were on holiday or a close friend wanted to see how I was doing. At lunchtimes, roll-call lock-ups, and evening shut down, I would be immersed in study unless there was a television programme or movie that I really liked and I would treat myself to some time off. As a result I looked forward to my weekends as much as someone would on the outside. Saturdays and Sundays gave me plenty of time to study and still get the chance to relax at the same time, and of course being a movie buff made weekends a special treat.

Movies of our choice were rented from the local video store and screened twice a day on Saturdays and Sundays and we made it our own cinema experience by drawing the curtains in our cells and escaping the reality of our confinement. I attended an extra session of computer class on Saturday mornings and taught a boxing class in the gym during the afternoon, so from my point of view visits were strictly forbidden during that time as the class would have to be cancelled and I don't like letting people down. It was a simple and well-balanced schedule, after such a hectic week, and with my age-old penchant for movies, how I looked forward to Saturday nights after I had washed and dried my laundry. I figured I had earned the treat. With this in mind you can imagine how I felt on the odd occasion that a visiting order had gone astray and I saw my name on the evening visits list. I was not a happy fellow.

When I told people that I was busy so they should inform me well in advance when they wanted to visit, they must have thought I was being awkward. To them I imagine it was nonsensical that someone in prison could be pressed for time, maybe they thought I was becoming mentally disoriented, or even depressed and unfocused, and that in reality they were doing me a favour. Well, if they wondered why I kept checking the time during their visit I can assure them it wasn't because I thought it was going quickly.

With some visitors I distinctly got the impression that coming to see me could be equated with a trip to the zoo. It certainly is true that a visit to someone in jail is an abnormal experience, it must indeed be odd observing society's notorious being held captive. I found that nearly all visitors enjoyed spending some of their time scanning the visits room and analysing the many fascinating characters that shared space with their friends or loved ones. The most popular question was 'What is he in for?' It was entertaining watching them try to guess. As I stated earlier prison is not entirely full of dead-beats, and confines many intelligent and aspiring men, media stereotypes are not as common as one might think, there were guys from so many different walks of life it was an eye opener even for many of us on the inside. New inmates would come in and you would think, just like your visitors, 'What the hell is he in for?' There were plenty of clean cut, well spoken, well mannered and educated men that made you quizzical, so much so that it was the staff that sometimes appeared uncouth and roguish. But now and again you would get an eye opener.

Career criminals are pretty much all similar animals, on the whole they have their own brand of honesty and integrity, which naturally varies from person to person, but everyone is aware of the unwritten rules. You don't snitch, you don't steal from your own, women and children are not fair game, and you pay 'double bubble' on anything you borrow in jail, in other words one hundred per cent interest in kind. So if you run short of tobacco, jail's everyday currency, or chocolate, and you have to borrow an ounce of smoke or a bar of confectionery, then you would have to repay two ounces or two bars respectively come canteen day. If you consistently flouted any of these codes of conduct then inevitably there would be a price to pay, which would most likely be of a violent nature, but at least you knew the beast you were dealing with. I always found watching the frenetic activity of payment day most entertaining, especially as I was never involved in it. It was fun to see who was ducking who, and I enjoyed noting the reactions of lenders and their hired collectors to difficult debtors. They could be as astute as bank managers, or as ignorant and ruthless as loan sharks, dependent upon the nature, attitude, loan history, and negotiation skills of their clients. For my part I never lent anyone anything I could not afford to write off to experience and was treated with an elder respect for doing so. But there was another type of prisoner that made me feel distinctly uneasy.

The best way that I can relate the kind of person I am talking about is with the story of Steve. He was white, early thirties, approximately five feet eight inches tall, and one hundred and thirty pounds dripping wet. I met him when he came to work on my section in industries and it was clear that not only was he extremely bright, but also that he liked to talk a lot. At the time we were building wiring looms for motor vehicles and had to assemble them vertically on specially constructed metal frames. The job was of a technical nature, we were supplied with computerised blueprints of each loom which had to be built to its own specification, with wires cut to exact measurements, run through intricately mapped routes, and fitted and attached with distinctively defined components, all of this to a high standard. The looms were then tested by computer, faults rectified, and then processed through to the company that supplied Rye Hill with the contract. By no stretch of the imagination would I consider myself gifted in this type of vocation, but after my experience at school I adopted a 'How hard can it be attitude?' and applied myself with due diligence. I learned every facet of the process that the jail was responsible for so that I could supervise efficiently and very quickly became a key on-site decision maker. It was a fairly interesting way to pass the time.

With his boffin-like disposition, it was no surprise to see Steve take to his post as a loom builder with ease. It was when he started to lecture on chemistry, physics, and other Open University programmes, that he used to watch at 4am, and ask me why I hadn't watched them myself that the penny started to drop. Everyone else used to avoid conversation with him as once he started he was relentless. Unfortunately for me, not only am I the type of person that the lunatic always sits next to on an empty bus, but as supervisor I had no choice but to inter-act with everyone. While verbally pinned down by Steve one afternoon I asked him what crime he was in for, my reasoning behind this was that most people do not like to talk about their offences, and unless you know someone well, or they offer to tell you, then it is one of jails unwritten laws of etiquette that you do not broach the subject. I figured that this move might cut our conversation short so that I could make my escape and get on with some work. Some hope!

Steve had been an arsonist since he was in his early teens. His parents had upset him so he lit a fire and burnt their house down. And here was me, Mr Naïve, thinking that he was a fraudster or involved in some other white collar crime. His career as a fire-starter then progressed to the property of next door neighbours, factories, offices, and the abodes of anyone else that dared to rankle him. I had wondered why some of the officers had backed off when he had heated words with them. He told me later it was because they were aware that he knew where they lived. I resigned myself there and then to be as polite as possible to him no matter how exasperating he became. He was clearly the type of guy that couldn't be intimidated by threats of violence, or even violence itself. The truth is, Steve's mind didn't function like everyone else's, he had gears all of his own and if I ever see him in my neighbourhood I'm calling the police.

Another very seemingly innocent character, Paul, came to live on the same unit as I did, unlike Steve he was a large portly fellow, again early thirties, white, very well mannered, and shared my interest in National Geographic magazine. I used to collect it from the library or wait for it to be delivered by any of the other lads on the unit who had accessed it before me. Paul received his own copy personally by subscription and when informed of my interest in the title offered to regularly pass it on along with some back issues that I had missed. He made for very pleasant conversation especially as we had the magazine in common and I enjoyed talking to him. He had told me in passing that he was only serving a five year sentence and I figured, once again, in light of this information that he was guilty of a white collar crime, such a shame I thought as he was probably a responsible family man.

What was explained to me later, in fairness this was by Paul himself, was that he was not serving a fixed five year term, but a minimum life tariff of five years, he was a lifer. In other words he would not be considered for release until he had served at least five years in jail, and then some.

I was keen to hear the details of his case as I just could not picture the circumstances in which this quiet, educated, and gentle guy had committed such a severely punishable crime, so once again I took it upon myself to ask him what happened. With head bowed he told me how unfair his predicament was and that the courts should let him go post-haste as his five years were almost up and he was no closer to release than the day he was sentenced. He explained how the two lads that lived next door to him and his mother used to continually play loud music and ignore his pleas to be more considerate, finally he could take no more and went around to remonstrate with them. It's lost on me whether Paul said they verbally abused him or slapped him around a little. The rest he says was a blur and that the authorities should show more sympathy towards his case. He professed amnesia at the resulting carnage, but when he came to his senses, both of his neighbours lay dead in their hallway, the result of multiple stab wounds inflicted with a fishing knife, which Paul told me he did not remember he had on his person as he often went fishing. Paul was a double-murderer.

The roughest and toughest guys that I knew never intimidated me, or tried to, but these guys were a different breed, you would just never see them coming. There was no bravado, no rippling physique or gestures, no shouting and swearing, just a steely resolve to do whatever they felt warranted for the slightest altercation, with no thought of consequence. It was amusing to note how much space they were given by the alpha-male tough guys, which is why tough-guy reputations mean very little to me. It's a fact that people are as bad as you let them be, we all get away with whatever we can, with whoever allows us to get away with it. This applies all the way through our lives, until integrity kicks in and our consciences mature into barriers of self-discipline. Unfortunately this does not happen to everyone, and there are those who will take advantage of any given situation until their dying day. I loathe the behaviour of such people, groups, or governments. Bullies can get my respect easily enough, all they have to do is try to bully everyone, but they do not, they are not that stupid, and while reticent to admit it are usually the first to know their limitations. In Rye Hill this was true of both inmates and warders.

One particular officer, who was one of the very few below management level that stayed at the facility from inception right until the day he got sacked almost four years later, was typical of the type of insecure prick that preys on the less fortunate. He was arrogant and rude to most inmates, to be fair he never openly disrespected me, but you always got the feeling that he thought of prisoners as the scum of the earth and that the punishment of exclusion from family and society was never enough. It's the old school of thought that was at one time endemic in the prison system and one can easily understand some of the older officers who still have that attitude, it was ingrained in them after a life behind those walls, but this guy was late twenties at most and was not trained in a government institution where such an attitude could have rubbed off on him. He was a bastard all on his own initiative.

You can usually tell a lot about people by the little things that they do and I remember having just finished shaving one morning when I heard the familiar rattling of keys for breakfast and early gym unlock. The keys rammed so loudly into the metal door of my cell that I thought there was some sort of problem, especially when the door was flung open and crashed into the wall. I figured there must be a fire or some such emergency so I stepped out onto the landing to see who had opened my door so dangerously and what the problem was. But no, there was no problem, it was just this young knucklehead trying to show the cons who was boss and that they had better get out of bed because he had demanded it. Almost every prisoner who was up and ready to start the day stepped outside of their pads in pop up fashion to observe him, all shaking their heads in agreement, what a dickhead. He was not a regular unit officer and had bagged himself the inmate and goods admissions post, it was to become clear later why he had done this.

I only ever saw him open the doors like that one more time, it was years later during a lunchtime opening, when the nature of the jail had changed somewhat and there were new prisoners in the establishment that couldn't care less about being made subject to disciplinary procedures, they were all experienced cons who towed the line, but only just. Pedro, a young guy from Handsworth, the type that genuinely hadn't been dealt the best cards that life had to offer was one of them, and I took to him quite readily mainly due to the fact that he displayed an interest in reading books and always asked politely if he could borrow some of my research material, every time bringing whichever tome he had borrowed back within the time-scale he promised and in respectful fashion. When his door was flung open by the wannabe Hitler I was standing in the dinner queue almost exactly outside it and was glad to witness the ensuing scene.

Pedro flew out of his cell demanding to know who dared to open his door so wildly, he was furious at the disrespect, stating the many sensible reasons, in between the curse words, as to why this should not be done, the inmate could be ill, could be sitting on the toilet, could have been standing by the door and got injured, could have been practicing religious observances, and a host of other intelligent comments that were at odds with his demeanour as he approached the officer in question in menacing fashion. What made it worse for the warder is that Pedro had everyone else's nodding approval as he confronted him. Even the other officers stood back as if this comeuppance was deserved. At first I thought that we were going to have to drag Pedro off him, but after he had verbally let rip he simply turned back to his pad to get his plate and cutlery and emerged to the welcome respect of the men in the dinner queue who pushed him approvingly to the front of the line. The remaining doors were opened so quietly that it was embarrassing. Someone had been put very firmly in their place, for the day anyway.

To receive anything from the outside world into the prison, unless the item came via a corrupt officer, it had to pass through the security network of admissions, whether it was money, jewellery, clothing, a compact disc player, books, or any other item on the allowable list. Each unit would be allocated a time slot during the day or evening when they could collect their goodies under the supervision of a unit officer and whichever warder was working the admissions counter. Whenever it was the numbskull in question there were always problems. I have seen him disallow cons from receiving items that they were clearly entitled to, ruin brand new compact disc players by claiming that he had to search them for security reasons, and regularly claim that lists of items that had been delivered by post were incomplete and did not fully contain what the sender had claimed was included. I still did not suspect a thing, I wondered why he felt he had to be such a 'jobsworth' when other officers used a more common sense approach when fulfilling the role, and like everyone else figured he was just a 'hater', someone who was either bullied at school and was now exacting his revenge, or who had such a miserable life on the outside that he was even envious of the lifestyles of society's confined rejects. Still, the old adage was to later prove true, what goes around comes around!

On the other end of the scale there were officers like Alison Adams, the wife of British Olympic Judo Gold Medallist Neil Adams. I first met her when I was on remand at the Green and we struck up conversation. Miss Adams (prisoners refer to female officers as 'Miss' in government run institutions) was tall, attractive, and very pleasant, clearly intelligent and well educated she was being fast-tracked through the system to governor status. As you would expect this entailed her having to learn every facet of the job, from unlocking cell doors to let inmates out of their cells, to the comprehension and implementation of the most fundamental rules of the prison system, and there were many of them. What was most impressive about her was the fact that although physically an attractive woman, she earned the respect of the inmates without being nasty, raising her voice, or using her sexuality in any overt or lewd fashion. She displayed even-handed behaviour with inmates and her fellow staff, a trait that was evident to everyone that she came across. There were no vulgar or disparaging comments made in her vicinity by the cons, which was often not the case with less respected female staff, and it was noticeable that she was held in such high regard that no one wanted to disappoint. That was the crux of the attitude towards her, and why? Because she treated prisoners with respect and honesty, it also didn't hurt matters that she was very efficient at her job. The guys used to queue around her whenever they got the chance, primarily to air grievances and raise issues that they knew she would attend to.

Amazingly, I had never met Neil Adams, her husband, which is only odd because most of the higher ranking martial artists, no matter what discipline they practice, invariably cross paths at some function or the other, nevertheless martial arts was the subject that formed the basis of our initial conversations which were always interesting and made Miss Adams stand out in my mind as someone destined to last the course in her profession.

There were other equally impressive officers that I came across throughout my time inside, men and women that gave everyone a fair crack of the whip and interacted with us as if we were human. To my mind this was an important part of the regime, because it would be so easy to exit those walls as a bitter person, I cannot tell you the amount of times that it crossed my mind to make a career out of crime just so that I could get my own back on the system, the main thing that stopped me from pursuing that line of thought was my children and my mother, I could not bear to think of the pain that it would cause them if I were to be locked away again. I can only imagine how much greater the temptation would have been had I been a single man with no such restraints, but one thing struck me from my conversations with the guys that had served more than one sentence and were still intent on leading a life of crime. They were always convinced that they were never going to get caught again even though they had already been proved wrong once, or even more. It really is a mugs game.

To my mind, the pain of not being able to mentor, hug, encourage, and console my children was already horrendous, and to think of it happening again was an unbearable notion. It seemed as if I watched them mature and grow a little older on almost every visit, Nick seemed more contemplative, Chris, a deep thinking child anyway, seemed to get even deeper, and Kelis, my little girl, just got taller and taller, all of this causing me to worry about whether I could bridge the gap that would inevitably widen between us. You can only maintain relationships to a very limited extent in ten minute telephone conversations and bi-monthly two hour visits and my obvious concern was whether I would come out of jail a stranger to my children. Still, like them, I had to harden myself to the situation and plough on with the one thing that could ease my burden, the completion of my book.

It had become clear from my discovery of the origins of the Noah story that to pass any commentary on the authenticity of religion I would have to read and compare a great many texts in detail, this included the Bible, the Koran, the Egyptian texts, the cuneiform writings of ancient Sumer, and the Hindu manuscripts. I not only had to read them, it was also necessary to at least attempt to decipher their coding, a feat which could only be achieved by comparison and analysis of the meaning of many passages in their original language, especially as mistranslation was rife. The reason for these 'errors', to my reckoning, became too obvious to be refuted.

The Old Testament, the first section of the Bible, contains the story of Hebrew history, from their creation and propagation, through to the existence of the entire population of the world. What is odd is that the land of their origin, according to the Genesis account, was not Israel, but the land between the rivers Tigris and Euphrates, a land which the Bible gives many titles, such as Shinar, Babel, Chaldea, Babylon, and Mesopotamia. It is the land where the demi-god, Adam, was created and where the Flood hero Noah returned to after the deluge. This point was not one to be neglected during the course of my cross-referencing. It seemed to me to be a Freudian slip of quite some magnitude. Today we know this country as Iraq, and it is a mystery why the chosen people of the Old Testament accounts did not refer to it as the 'land of their fathers', as by their own account this is where they began life.

It was pretty much normal for the ancient creation stories of many cultures to suppose that they were the first people on the planet and that their God favoured them above all others.

This notwithstanding, the notion in itself is eyebrow-raising as no logical reason can be given as to why a supreme being would be racially biased, and promote cultural, political and sexual superiorities, especially if he had created the universe and all its contents. Fortunately, many such accounts are flawed, simply because they are so blatantly patriotic, originally penned to build and sustain social order and control within defined borders. Nevertheless, although open to the abuse of power-mongering, they served their purpose well and were as good a tool as any in the enhancement of national development. Once outside of these confines however it was a different matter, they would be confronted with other creation stories and tales of other gods, which would challenge the veracity of their detail. In essence these were not religious differences, they were polit-ical. The battles of the gods were a disguise for the supremacist struggles of national leaders and their psychologies.

In this regard the Egyptian and Sumerian worship systems were arguably the first to be developed on a national scale, and the depth of the meaning of their stories, now appreciated as being far more than the ranting and literal beliefs of pagan savages, are recognised as legacies of some worth to modern man if they can only be deciphered correctly. The monuments constructed by these empires already testify to their mathemat-ical and astronomical advancement, so much so that even today we have no real idea of how they came to facilitate such achievements. Their religious stories seem little different and to some extent are clearly based upon the scientific knowledge of their time.

I had already noted how the land of Egypt was divided into two portions, the North and the South, and how the Sun was acknowledged as the creator of the solar system. Ancient man had already documented the solar government of the cycle of life and nature as farming had long begun, and mathematics had developed enough for them to measure the precession of the stars and thus configure the astrological houses and their movement. Everything was cyclical, thus it followed that this must also include the life of man, who would perish and be reborn again just like the sun each year as displayed by the seasons. It would 'die' in the winter, be reborn in the spring, grow to full power in the summer, and begin the waning of 'old age' in the autumn, in never ending fashion.

I also had a good idea why it was assumed that the 'gods' had taken up residence in the centre of the earth as well as the heavens. Man had seen the 'gods' descend in balls of fire, as they roared through the sky, parted the waters, and made the land tremble as they penetrated the planets surface, a physical phenomenon followed by the assumption that such powerful beings could not stay dead, but were rejuvenated by their apparently similar and senior entity, the Sun on its westward descent as it seemed to disappear into the earth each night, taking its creative light with it. The biblical Old Testament also contains its own version of gods within the earth, a point that modern religion does not advertise, or to be blunter, one which it goes to some lengths to disguise.

In the story of the death of one of Yahweh's chosen 'judges', Samuel, a holy man whose birth was brought about by God himself, we are told quite plainly how he went on to become a deity resident within the underworld, a story I will expand upon later.

It is not the only reference to gods existing within the earth in the biblical pages, but it is the most blatant, the others thinly disguise lower realm activity in the form of 'dreams' and other metaphoric imagery. In one account the hero Jacob meets a 'Lord' when he arrives at *'a certain place and stayed there all night because the sun had set'*, this 'certain place' was of course the underworld, a fact confirmed by other details in the story and Jacob's revelation, *'How awesome is this place! This is none other than the house of God, and this is the gate of heaven!'* The underworld was exactly that, the means by which access to heaven was granted, which is why in the Jesus story the Hebrew messiah had to spend 'three days' there before his resurrection, the number 'three' emphasising the symbolic amount of time it took to travel from one supernatural realm to another.

After constantly researching and re-checking the evidence that lay before me and scrutinising different topics to make sure that I was not deceiving myself, it became apparent that the Hebrew authors of the Old Testament had quite wilfully rewritten the philosophies of the earlier super-cultures within their own framework. Whether this was done as an act of literary theft, or in homage to the worship systems of Egypt and Sumer is unclear. But I was certain that I was not mistaken.

They divided their Promised Land, Israel, into two portions, the north and the south, the same as the country that they had just left, Egypt. The main Egyptian city in the biblical records was called *On*, which means 'sun', the Hebrews nicknamed their holy city, Jerusalem, *Zion*, meaning 'little sun'. They wrote the ritual of circumcision into their religious canon, one that the Egyptians had already been practising for millennia, a fact not mentioned in the Bible. They took to practicing prayer, chanting, and fasting, rites also originated within the Egyptian religion. Most cleverly they then denounced the Egyptians and Sumerians as superstitious pagans and sun-god worshippers when the Bible in its entirety is devoted to sun-god worship. The adopted title of these nomadic wanderers is one of many testaments to that fact.

They chose to adopt the name, *Israel*, a word which is defined in its translation from Hebrew to English as 'God contends'. This definition is challengeable from the fact that the word is made up of the names of three of the major neighbouring and earlier gods who are featured under disguise in the biblical works, and the term can be more aptly described as 'gods in contention.'

The first of these foreign deities is the Egyptian goddess, Isis, she was the mother of light, the illuminatrix and as the mother of the Egyptian messiah, Horus, became the role model for the later Virgin Mary. Indeed one of Mary's titles is also 'mother of light'. Isis was so popular that her words *'I am the first, the last, and all that is to come'* were later ascribed to the Hebrew Supreme Being, Yahweh, in the final biblical book titled Revelation.

The second is also of Egyptian origin, the chief sun god *Ra*, who actually makes a cameo appearance in the book of Genesis at the scene of a well. The third is the Canaanite god, *El*, who dwelt and conversed with his people from his habitat in the mountains*. It was the behaviour of this god that is reprised in the book of Exodus where God continually talks to Moses from a 'mountain' retreat after the Israelite exodus from Egypt. It is also from the influence of this deity that the Hebrews adopted the word 'el' to mean 'god'.

Thus the title Israel can be broken down clearly to *Isis-Ra-El*, which renders all too conveniently the meaning 'Light of the Sun God'. This is not an isolated red-herring and the misleading translations were continued by the Church in a worthy attempt to silence those who could see that the emperor wore no clothes.

The word 'holy', very artfully dictionary defined as meaning 'universal', literally means 'sun' and is derived from the Greek word 'Helios'. Its etymological history runs *Helios-Hely-Halo-Holy*, and indeed the 'halo' was the sun symbol used by early Christianity, and other religions, to glorify its saints. Thus the term 'holy books' actually means 'sun books', a definition that can be confirmed by detailed reading of their contents. The pot was to call the kettle black and the whole world, courtesy of the Roman Empire, was to fall for its propaganda. Israel had stolen the key tenets of its teachers and then denigrated these elder cultures with a neatly-spun history. These parodies were the tip of a very large iceberg and there were many points to be researched and still yet many questions to be answered in order to confirm my conclusions.

I also faced another problem. This was my first venture into a scheme of such magnitude. I had previously written articles for martial arts magazines and even had my own monthly column in one of them, but the skill level required for such publications was not exactly of the highest order, this project was another matter entirely. I would have my work, if I could

---

*In ancient culture theology the word 'mountain' was often a euphemism for 'heaven'. The holy books are no exception.

succeed in getting it published, compared with that of some of the most experienced authors in the world, so even if my research was flawless it would mean nothing if it was presented in garbled or uninteresting fashion. As they say, for a joke to be funny, it is not the joke itself, it is the way that it is told. I knew that I had my work cut out when I began to re-read some of the material that I had put together earlier, it was unclear, boring and drawn out. Writing has to be punchy, to the point, informative, and enthralling to have any chance of success. I had written over seven hundred way-too-long pages when I decided that I needed to start from scratch and relegate anything I had penned previously to the ranks of helpful notes. Giving up however never once crossed my mind.

8

One of the things I was warned about by the other cons while inside was my habit of being too frank during open discussion and debates in front of prison officers, especially in rehabilitation sessions which were often recorded on video. The first time that a more experienced con took me aside to whisper such advice was during induction sessions at Rye Hill. The danger, apparently, was that it was not wise to be seen as too smart as the assumption could be made that you had the ability to fool the system into thinking that you were a rehabilitated criminal, when in fact you understood what was required in terms of attitude and behaviour and simply played the game, while biding your time to re-launch a lucrative career in crime. Reports of that ilk would of course seriously harm your chances of gaining early release on parole. I gave it considerable thought and felt it best to err on the side of caution, biting my lip instead of passing comment on many topics. This attitude changed as I became more comfortable with my surroundings and the prison system, mainly because I love nothing better than a good debate.

A topic which seems constantly under discussion in male prisons is what behaviour is acceptable from spouses and girlfriends while their man is locked up. Sometimes I felt so much in the minority in my opinions that I began to question my own ethical stance on the subject.

Many men, and indeed women, feel that once they enter into a committed relationship that they are in ownership of another human being, it's something that I could never get my head around. Unsurprisingly, the problem is predominantly a male one. If someone is with you it's through choice which should be the whole essence of the partnership. Couples meet and are mutually attracted by looks, mannerisms, and traits that they find impressive, and yet many men try to deny the individuality of their new partner in such a dominant fashion that heartache, unhappiness and resentment must surely ensue. Is it any wonder that the relaxed atmosphere and fun of courtship soon dissipates, to be replaced by a relationship based upon psychological power struggles, insecurity, and mistrust? Naturally then, when Mr Dominant gets locked up, his opposite number rediscovers her independence, sense of fun, and what it was like to be a free spirit, and wants to keep it. I'm not espousing something I've read in a book here as in a lot of ways I'm a guilty party, but fail to see how if anyone analyses the situation objectively it is possible to arrive at any other conclusion.

It used to be great fun watching from the balcony as guys waited until the last possible moment before the telephones were switched off to ring their wives and girlfriends at night, many of them checking that she was staying indoors and leading as mundane an existence as they were. I've never seen anything more pathetic or indeed selfish. If she was going out, how on earth could a phone call at eight o'clock at night prevent that? Sure, he might succeed in heightening her guilt for a while, but how long would that last, and what would happen when the resentment of him not being there for her kicked in? I could just imagine some of the girls that I saw on visits, dolled up to the nines and clearly good time girls, psyching themselves up for their acting roles when the insecure numbskulls called. They must have been dressed to the hilt, while putting on the yawns and listless voices that the guys inside wanted to hear as if they were ready for milk, cookies, and a soap opera or two before dragging themselves off to bed. I don't think so! And I certainly hoped not. The bulk of them were not responsible for their man being inside so why should they be imprisoned too? I raised these points during many conversations only to be met with the most mind-numbing of arguments, and indeed ferocity, about what would and wouldn't happen if she was found to have been out enjoying herself, or even worse decide that the relationship was over.

To my mind it all boiled down to a matter of choice, most of us were serving years and not months, so to demand that someone wait unreasonable lengths of time to continue a relationship was an insanely self-centred notion. Even if the con had been the most loving of husbands and fathers, if he was to be away for many years then surely the decision to wait for him or move on in life was entirely the woman's.

The only thing that I asked for in my own case was honesty. If Nia was seeing someone else then that would be perfectly amicable so long as she wasn't hiding the relationship and be seeking to continue ours when I got out as if she had waited patiently for me. I knew she was too strong and classy for that kind of nonsense anyway, and I did feel for the guys who were being led astray in that fashion. I cannot recount the amount of times that someone came to my pad to 'let out' emotionally about how badly their woman had treated them, how disappointed they were, and ask what I would do if I was in their position. I always listened patiently while usually leaning towards the female point of view when offering comment, even when I received my own 'Dear John'.

Some women have what I have found to be the most attractive of qualities, they just never realise when men fancy them, everyone sees it coming but them, and that obliviousness is the most endearing sort of humility. Men and women that imagine that they are God's gift to the opposite sex, or even their own, no matter how physically attractive they indeed might be, are a pain in the ass.

One of the parents at the school that assisted Nia on school runs while I was on remand was Sean, a pleasant guy, who doted on his children and possessed admirable family values.

During my time on bail, he sometimes visited the house with his common-law wife, and Nia became something of a confidante for him, as he suspected that all was not well within his household, and that his own relationship was beginning to fray.

He had a close circle of friends, and during my time at Rye Hill, one of them, asked Nia if she would assist him with a new business venture that he was setting up. Nia's secretarial skills are quite adept and she readily agreed so long as she was going to be remunerated. She explained the situation to me on the telephone and I suggested that she give it some serious consideration if she felt that the business had a sensible chance of success. It all seemed fine until the guy in question asked her if she would also like to go out on a date. I'd seen that coming from the very first time she mentioned the whole scenario, and I figured Nia must have too. She hadn't, and she felt so let down by the situation that she chose not to participate in the venture. What surprised her more was that Sean, whose own relationship had by now totally disintegrated said to her that if she and his friend did become an item that he would have to curtail their friendship. Nia was proving to be a popular lady, which is only fair as it was by now common knowledge that she and the now incarcerated hot-shot world kickboxing champion were into the later stages of divorce proceedings.

I telephoned her one morning before going to my job in industries as it was my habit to speak to the children before they went to school. She told me that there was something that she wanted to tell me as she did not want me to hear it from anyone else. Oh-Oh I thought. She told me that she had begun dating, I enquired as to with whom, as if I didn't know, and as much as I was happy to hear it in one sense I didn't want to hear it either. What was all that advice that I had doled out to other cons again? She and Sean were now an item and she told me with such an honest and exuberant voice, *'I'm having fun Howard'* that it resonated throughout my memories of our marriage. Such a simple statement spoke volumes about how much I'd neglected her throughout so many years, and now she had someone who she believed would make no such mistake. I felt like a weight had been lifted, as our situation was at last clear cut, but it was also one of those moments, again, when it hit home just how much I had lost through my own stupidity.

My acceptance of the situation however did not mean that it was plain sailing for Nia and Sean, there was someone who was not overly impressed with this new development, Kelis. She was now nine years old, going on seventeen, and displayed her disapproval by slamming doors and adopting disapproving facial expressions whenever Sean visited the house. This became such a problem that Nia, in her exasperation, mentioned it to me and so I decided to have a word with 'young lady' as I often call her. I spoke to her on the phone and on a visit and explained that I approved of her mother dating, and especially a guy that seemed quite decent, all the time stressing that his presence would never make me any less her father. She took this on board, gradually, and came to accept matters just as her brothers had already done. What was to become obvious was the protective nature of my children towards my mental welfare, I just never looked at things that way, to me it was one way traffic, the old man does the protecting, physically and emotionally, period. Alas, not so.

I remember one system of training that I set myself consisted of seeing if I could complete a six mile run on the gym treadmill within the 50 minutes or so that we were in the gym each day. I've always been a fairly decent middle distance runner and more often than not achieved this new goal by setting the machine speed at between 7-10 miles per hour after a two to three minute warm-up. Inevitably, as fit as I felt, I lost a lot of weight within a few weeks. I was forced to stop this routine when Nia brought the children to visit and I phoned the next morning to make sure that they had arrived home safely. She told me that they were inconsolable at the sight of me being so thin. I stopped the running and reverted to a weight training routine that very day.

Still, as far as our break-up was concerned and as much as I thought that I had an emotional handle on the situation, it became clear later that it was not an immediate acceptance, and only as time passed by and I began to look forward to the prospect of being a single man upon my exit from prison, did I realise that any psychological changes I experienced were indeed gradual. Like Nia, I did not spend too much of my youth having fun, we started a family early, which, to be fair, has its rewards, as no one can believe that we are actually the parents of Nick and Chris, who are as much my pals as my sons. They can even give me a run for my money in the boxing ring (they wish!). But I imagine that Nia and I now both felt the same, there was much lost time on the fun side of life that needed to be made up.

If it seems that Nia's decision to end our marriage was solely based upon emotional neglect, I have drawn an unfair picture as there is more to the story. But even if I say so myself I do have some merit points, for instance, I believe it is to my credit that I have never believed in violence towards women, or anyone less able to defend themself than I, as I said, I detest bullies. Only once during our twenty-two years of marriage did I ever put my hand on that girl and I remember it like yesterday.

It happened during the early years of our co-habitation, and in truth was quite comical. Nia used to display quite a temper whenever we argued, which is only because I used to fuel it by goading her with sarcastic comment when she did not agree with my point of view. Who was usually right in whatever we were arguing about I could not tell you, but if she did not accede to my opinions I would become a psychological pig until she eventually lashed out at me and I would have to ward off her blows. Being a fighter I always thought that this was extremely funny and any punches, kicks, or attempted head-buts when I trapped her arms, served to heighten both her fury and my amusement. She could even spit at me and I didn't mind, only one thing was out of bounds, do not slap me in the face, and she knew it.

When Edge and I used to regularly street fight at the Silver Blades Ice Rink we made a habit of not exerting ourselves with guys that we knew were no match for us, no matter how game they were. We couldn't let them hit us so we used to slap them across the face as we strode towards the tougher members of their group, the alpha-males. The lesser members of rival gangs were not even given a second glance after we had dismissed them with a back-hand slap. We used to cheat sometimes though, as it would appear that we had merely slapped someone and yet they would stagger around or collapse, the truth is that if they looked like being a serious disruption we would use a martial arts technique to the temple to despatch them, either 'haito', a rapid blow with the open palm facing upward and the strike landing with the knuckle of the folded thumb, or an open-handed back-fist with the top two knuckles of our open fist making contact. This was done as we walked past them with serious intent, which would also serve the purpose of intimidating our main targets as they watched their friends reel around from apparently light blows. In face to face confrontations some of the guys used to 'slap' with the heel of the palm into the chin, which was effectively a palm-heel strike, a very solid and dangerous blow, followed by the verbal punch-line to their wobbling foe, 'that was my slap, here's my punch!'

We were so immature that we did not realise the serious implication of all of this, it was glorified violence, the opposite of the true essence of martial arts, a point that I'm glad I grasped sooner than most. Nevertheless, now you can under-stand my psychological approach to being slapped, no one can dismiss me with a wave of the hand, not even Mike Tyson. Whoever I confront should have to pay close attention, and I like to think that no matter how good they are at combat, they will have to take me seriously. It's a childish hang-up I admit, but as they say, it's my bad.

So what did Nia do during one of our more heated arguments? Without even showing that she was mad enough to get physical she slapped me straight across the face, hard! Clever girl! I laughed at the indignity of it as I stared at her and sure enough I should never have laughed! She slapped me again! She knew it would get both my attention and my ire. She was right. I was impressed at how fast she was but in my most daunting baritone I warned her not to do it again and kept my hands akimbo in true machismo style with no intention of stopping her, as if she would never dare to contemplate such a silly move when I was in serious mood. I should have known that would provoke more than scare her and sure enough there she went again, wham! Slap number three. I retaliated. I slapped her with the palm of my hand onto the side of her cheek, I pulled back instead of following through, as no matter how mad I was, I'm not insane, still, her eyes rolled into the top of her head and she fell straight back. Fortunately we were upstairs and she landed on the bed, out for the count, or so I thought, as to this day I'm not sure whether she was faking it just to scare me, because I was pretty sure that I had only hit her hard enough to sting her. My reaction was instant. Panic! I tried to bring her round by cradling her head and patting her face, kissing her cheeks and forehead, telling her that I was sorry and didn't mean it. I did everything but take the sensible action required for someone that was concussed. My amateurish attentions worked anyway and she came around to have the most attentive and apology bearing husband in the history of the world. There was one time however, that my apologies were not enough, and our marriage never really got over it.

I always sought to be a consummate professional when teaching martial arts, I treated man, woman, and child with the same amount of respect and attention, I'd seen too many relationships and classes fall apart because the instructor had an eye for the ladies or had his head turned by some pretty girl. Realising this point made my classes more successful than most, people know when they are getting value for money and my input was always one hundred percent, not only because it made for enjoyable classes for all concerned, but it was also good for the bottom line.

One of my advantages was that I was not a natural at martial arts technique, I excelled at the strategy and thought behind it, but had to work hard at the execution of the more complex manoeuvres, and as a result spent hours practicing what Edge and other guys used to pick up in minutes. So whenever teaching someone that had difficulty in learning I could always empathise and found it easy to show patience and impart advice with a genuine concern to speed up progress. This created a lot of goodwill and I attracted a lot of students, both novice and experienced martial artists to my classes. The word also spread that I did not fool around with the many pretty girls that attended, sure I used to share the odd joke, but in exactly the same manner as I did with the guys, I was proud to be seen in a professional light, much like a doctor. This must have been evident even during the early stages of my teaching career and was not something that I had to focus on but was a natural instinct.

However, I was still taken aback when first approached by a parent after a class and asked if I could have a word with his son about doing his school homework on time. My initial thought was 'What on earth has that got to do with me?', but I spoke to the lad concerned anyway and was surprised that my advice had a positive effect. This type of request became quite common, no matter what part of the country I was teaching in. One evening I could be in Wolverhampton, the next in Bristol, Telford, London, Stoke, or Nottingham, there were classes being operated all over the country, and I taught regularly at most of them. It was hectic but I enjoyed it, along with the respect that I garnered as being Britain's first world kickboxing champion. To this day I am proud of the fact that I am the only British fighter to have held an undisputed world title both as an amateur and as a professional, a feat that may never be repeated due to the proliferation of governing bodies that now exist within the sport. I am equally proud that I form part of an historical team as Edge also went on to become a bona-fide world champion and not many brothers achieve this feat either. Teaching from such a respected base was most enjoyable.

There were several cities that had an overwhelming response to the newspaper adverts that were placed by the organisation that I belonged to, so from a business point of view a responsible and experienced instructor always had to be installed to run classes in those areas, someone that would not only do a professional job and retain custom but would also build on it. Nottingham was particularly busy so it fell to me to run it on a permanent basis, it was only fifty miles from Birmingham so I readily agreed. There were over one hundred and fifty regularly attending students over the two nights that I taught at the city's Victoria Leisure Centre and the place was abuzz with kickboxing fever.

Because it was so busy I had to take a secretary along with me to collect the class training fees, a logistical decision so that I could start and end the classes promptly without losing time performing administration. No matter which guy I took did not mind the journey either, the time flew as they carried out their role, and they spent much of it talking to the attractive girls who turned up early to register and then had to wait around for their class to start. This was because Nottingham had an amazing anomaly for a modern city, the females outnumbered the males in some estimates by as much as five to one. If you were a 'player', or indeed just a regular guy looking for a female partner, Nottingham was a candy shop.

I had an abundance of ladies on my classes and although I did not fraternise with the students myself I used to encourage them to mix with each other. You always know if you've got a good class if people who are injured and cannot train still turn up to watch and mingle afterwards, at my classes that was the norm, and I was aware that many of my students used to visit the leisure centre bar after classes to socialise so I used to direct a lot of new members in that direction while declining every invitation to attend myself. I used to merely jump in my car and head home after chatting for a short while with the students of my advanced class which was always the final one of the evening. It was a habit that I found easy to keep up no matter how many stunning looking girls from my sessions were in the bar as I could hardly wait to get home, relax, spend time with Nia and check that Nick, who was only a toddler at the time was ok. He was at that fun age of two to three years old and would wake up sometimes as I stood over his bed when I got back late at night as if checking to see that Dad had got home safely, before spinning back into his covers and nodding off.

I had left the bank and was teaching full-time by now, and because of the constant travelling, or if I had car trouble, I would sometimes travel to certain venues by train and spend the night in a local bed and breakfast before heading home in the morning. I was still competing at international level and was often worn out by my day-time work-out and early morning runs, the drive to and from classes was an added burden and it was sensible to escape it when I felt unduly tired.

On one of the many successful enrolments that we had for new students there were over fifty applicants who wanted to register so I had to shuffle some classes to fit them all in. My classes ran on a Thursday and Friday evening and we had a Sunday overspill that was taught by a good friend of mine, an excellent martial artist named Ivan Riley. I directed who I could to Ivan's sessions to ease the size of my own as many students wanted to double up on their training and attend on both Thursday and Friday classes. I created a new 7pm class on both evenings and moved existing students into the later 8pm slot. What made me smile was the amount of my more senior grades, notably the male brown and black-belts, who turned up early to attend the 7pm beginner's class and help me teach it. I was not naïve enough to think that this was done out of any sense of altruism or empathy for my plight as an overrun instructor, they were checking out the ladies, which from both a business and amusement point of view pleased me no end. They were not the only ones, my secretary had his eye on one too, a particularly attractive and demure young lady that had joined with her friend.

I remained as aloof as usual about the situation until a month or so later when my secretary, who drove us both to the venue in his car as this not only lowered travel costs but also allowed me to get some rest, suggested that we take up an invite from Linda, the friend of the girl in question, to have a drink with them in the bar after the final class. He had worked things well, having become quite friendly with both of them while collecting class fees from week to week. It was breaking a taboo for me to do such a thing, compounded by the fact that I didn't want to give my senior students the impression that I was invading their territory. I eventually succumbed to the arm-pulling and told my colleague, who was also a long-time friend, that he had better hurry up and find out whether he had any real chance of a date or not.

When I entered the upstairs bar, it was packed with my students, and every head seemed to turn in unison as I made my way through. What in the world was I doing there? I was uneasy to say the least, but as a dutiful guy, I felt that I had to provide the required back up. I won't deny that the evening was quite pleasant, the girls were a lot of fun and I also took the chance to mingle and chat with whoever I could, but I was never going to make a habit of it, no matter how improved his chances seemed to have become.

The following week, he asked me if I was in a hurry to go home because Linda had invited us back to her house for a drink, which sounded appealing because we had got on so well the previous week. This was also much less of an encroachment into my business and I thought he had done quite well to advance matters to a safe distance so quickly and at the same time speed up his progress. It crossed my mind that all of my secretaries must have had some interesting times outside the training hall while I was teaching, no wonder they were so keen to accompany me to my classes. Once again, the evening went well, so well that it was agreed that we would do the same thing after the following night's class and this time take in a video too. Once again, great night, but I felt duty bound to get home and urged him to ask Elle, the object of his desire, out on a date and hurry up about it!

At the end of the day no advance was made and our after class liaisons with Elle and Linda developed into a fun platonic relationship. My secretary was the top administrator in the organisation and so was inevitably called to other busy enrolments and I was left to fend for myself in terms of travel and paperwork, but this was no problem as with my banking background it was something that I was equipped to handle with minimum disruption. I often did not relish the trip back home after such nights and regularly stayed over in a Nottingham hotel while still sometimes taking up the invite for a drink with the girls who would transport me to Linda's house. I would always get a cab back to my hotel after a couple of hours of chit-chat and a glass of wine or two.

Elle worked for a well respected firm of solicitors in Nottingham city centre and asked me if I would like a lift to the train or coach station after my stay-overs as it made no difference to her journey and would save me a lengthy walk. It was from this scenario that our relationship developed into a romance that was doomed from the start. It was always going to be an uphill struggle as neither of us had planned our liaison and we were both married.

I don't know how long it took Nia to figure out that I was having an affair and looking back I imagine that the signs must have been there from an early stage. I had gone from stopping over in Nottingham sometimes to all the time. When I started to meet Elle after she had finished work for an hour or so before my classes began it meant having to leave Birmingham earlier than I normally used to, and on Saturdays I would come home later and later after exiting my hotel. I cringe when I think of the pain that I must have caused Nia during this period.

Elle and I became closer and closer and planned to set up home together, we had a property organised for us to move into and arranged a date for us to leave our spouses. She waited patiently that day for me to arrive. I didn't. When it came to the crunch I folded. I got as far as telling Nia that I was leaving and packed my bags, but I just couldn't take that final step. The key factor of course, and I'm not just using this as an excuse, was Nick. I idolised him and when all was said and done I felt that this amount of upheaval would have seriously affected the mental security of my little boy. I stuck to my sense of duty and let my head over-rule my heart, not that I still didn't care deeply for Nia, but I wanted to be with Elle too.

She and I were together for just under two years and would have made a great team, she was one of those women, like Nia, who was loyal, smart, a hard worker, and one hundred per cent behind her man. She helped me with promotional work, set up pre-fight television interviews, and was full of sound advice. With all of the investment that she had put into me as a person it was only natural that when I didn't fulfil my part of our bargain she felt desperately let down. She was not only hurt, she was livid, and curtailed our relationship in a face to face meeting. I had caused her just as much pain as I had caused Nia and I have always felt that in some ways it was one of the worst periods of my life.

I was truly devastated, holding out the hope that somehow the situation was solvable. I remember wishing that Nia would meet someone that was truly worthy of her as I genuinely felt that I was not. It was to take another twenty years for that to happen. Such wishes of course are a form of cowardice, hoping for others to make decisions that are entirely your own responsibility. For months on end it was all too obvious that I pined for Elle and I was aware of how distant I was when in Nia's company. All of this of course only adding to the hurt that I had already caused her. There was also of course the nagging doubt, the thought that if I left Nia for Elle, would it be Nia that I would then miss inconsolably in what would have been a major mistake? To be in love with two women at once, what a predicament! Millions of people, both men and women, go through this experience and always have, it is part and parcel of a condition that if we let it, is all too often beyond our control, the human heart.

For me the situation was extremely difficult to comprehend as I was so inexperienced with women. It is easy to say that I foolishly allowed myself to fall in love with someone other than my wife, and the same can be said of Elle, she was far from the female temptress. It was her friend Linda that had led the way in the friendships that blossomed, and Elle, like me, was an innocent bystander. A fact that made our liaison seem all the more fated. Still, it was over now, and I became consigned to the fact that I had lost her because of circumstance and weakness.

It was some years later that curiosity got the better of me and I tried to track Elle down just to see how her life had turned out. I was genuinely hoping that things had worked out well for her and was not seeking in any way to rekindle a romance, we were so close that it seemed the natural thing to do and so much time had passed that I hoped that in the least we could have had a good-natured conversation. As usual I was a poor judge of the temperament of the opposite sex. Elle was far from impressed and wouldn't take my call. She had moved on. People tend to do that.

In between this time, Nia and I eventually patched up the wounds that had been caused and tried to put the situation behind us, we had two more children, Chris and Kelis, and looking at my offspring I was glad that my sense of duty won out, but obviously things in my marriage were never to be quite the same again, I had broken that so sacred element of trust. When I made that phone call from HMP Rye Hill, almost twenty years later, and Nia told me that she was seeing Sean she said to me, *'You know why, don't you Howard?'*, I replied *'Yes, I know why Nia.'* Women and elephants.

My motto on situations like my own is simple enough, 'What's good for the goose is good for the gander!' I just could not believe how many men disagreed with that philosophy. The argument that guys can play away but women must stay dutiful is chauvinistic tripe, and doesn't even merit discussion, but what I found disturbing was the mind-set on this matter of a lot of men. They overstepped the mark though when they brought God into the equation to back up their nonsense. I was quick to point out that their God, had a wife too who was also considerably wiser than him, and so well respected that their 'divorce' was handled with the utmost reverence, before her existence had been hidden from the masses. As expected by then I was given the usual looks of disdain, fury, fascination, or puzzlement, all of them begging the same question, 'What on earth is he going to come out with now?'

The holy books and the church are openly misogynistic, which is why women are not allowed to take to the pulpit. Even the religiously minded guys that seem to agree that women are equal to men ratify it by condescendingly stating that this is as a partner in marriage, and that in all other respects the laws of God must be observed. I stated that this was because the laws of God were invented by men, which is why the creative force was given a male gender and the creative mother-goddess, Eve, was demoted to the role of a disobedient and foolish female.

The Bible canon clearly features God as one of the worst and most unsuccessful fathers in the history of parenting, a female touch being sorely needed to temper his judgement. One of his own sons became his arch-nemesis, Satan the Devil, his human children continually disobeyed him, and his constant resolution to this problem was to kill them or promise to. What kind of an example is that? I am just a fallible mortal, but I cannot foresee the situation where I would take the life of one of my children because they disobeyed me. But there is a simple reason that the female input in his activities is missing, it was deleted.

When the Hebrews re-wrote the ancient tales to bolster their struggle for national independence and security, they had a serious problem to overcome, the power of the priestess, for their role model society, Egypt, was a maternal one. This dumbing-down can be seen quite clearly especially in the Old Testament. The role of wisdom, one of the 'brides' of the chief God, Yahweh, was female, and continued to be so in the New Testament sequel. The reason for this was because no man, or god, could be seen to be a success without the counsel of the female intuition, which was sought from either his mother or his wife. This did not change until the advent of Judaism, Christianity and Islam, which taught the opposite, that the woman was prone to foolish thought and should bow to the wisdom of her husband. With these new philosophies the power of the priestess was driven underground, a persecution which continued throughout the centuries. The Witchfinder Trials of sixteenth, seventeenth, and eighteenth century Europe, which were essentially a purge on midwives, such is the male insecurity of modern religion, saw thousands of innocent women mutilated, tortured, and murdered in the name of Yahweh and the perpetuation of this dogma. (Midwives eased the burden and pain of childbirth which was not only viewed as contrary to biblical tuition but was also seen to lessen the female fear of sex which would lead to them being 'equal' to men).

The Hebrew kings knew what they were doing when they sought to eliminate the power of the goddess within their society, for with the female influence in the household diminished, and the fragile male ego given a royal boost, the implementation of their new philosophies became a much easier task. The men could not see that not only were they being manipulated, but they were also losing an asset that had been prized for many thousands of years. Nature has displayed quite openly that the physical slave in the male/female relationship, is the man. He was given a predominance of the muscle producing hormone Testosterone for this purpose, the woman, the voice of reason, planning, feeling and intuition, was to help guide and support him in his roles as provider, defender, and father. That blend was the essence of equality of the sexes.

In the religious tales of all of the early worship systems this is well reflected. The male gods were haughty and impetuous in their behaviour, while the goddesses were denoted as thoughtful and compassionate, an accurate reflection of male and female relationships. It is to his own loss that any man would consider himself naturally smarter than his female counterpart.

In the biblical Old Testament the power of female wisdom is lauded as a consort of Yahweh instead of as a goddess, she was then known as *Chokmah*, in the New Testament she is referred to as *Sophia*. In both documents her references are reduced to the metaphorical, in other words these ladies became abstract forces and not creatures of human personality, unlike the Hebrew supreme God, whose foolishness, tantrum-throwing, insecurity, and rashness are an open-book. He was proud to claim that he was an '*angry* and *jealous* god', the two worst emotions of the human psyche, and if analysed objectively his actions in many passages reveal psychotic and genocidal behaviour. Nevertheless, the political spin of the governments from that period onward have concreted the female role into one of second-class-citizen subservience, thus ensuring that most households would ultimately be reliant upon the wisdom of the state.

It is of no real surprise then, that it has been kept hidden that the supreme God of the Bible and Koran had a much more overt bride, a goddess named Asherah. Someone so revered at the time that her demotion was handled with much thoughtfulness and respect. In spite of the need for her removal from such a vaunted position, there is not a single disparaging criticism of Asherah or her priests in the Hebrew accounts.

On this point it should be noted that the Old Testament can be divided into two segments, mythical time, and real time. The mythical time relates to the compilation of ancient folklore, some of it Hebrew, and much of it borrowed from Egyptian and Babylonian religious tenets and tales, the Great Flood being an example that I have already mentioned.

The real time portion relates to when this material was put into written form, a period of a hundred years or so spanning the captivity of the Israelites in Babylon and their subsequent release. They were then presided over by real life kings such as Josiah and Hezekiah, who allowed the problems that they encountered in convincing their subjects to accept the new one-God, Yahweh, to be incorporated into the nation's written works. This was tabled in slanted fashion, and they continued to borrow heavily from the deeds of other more accomplished nations to bolster their literature. The Hebrew people were steeped for centuries in the more ancient worship systems of their successful neighbours and resisted change to a new arrangement over and over again, which is why the biblical propaganda is so anti-Egypt and anti-Babylon. A trend perpetuated and reflected in the religious upbringing of modern black youth, who instead of calling the police 'pigs' like their white counterparts, call them the 'Babylon' a word that has become synonymous, due to biblical influence, with evil.

During this revamp the Hebrew kings also thought it wise to eliminate all traces of the reverence for foreign gods held by their people and systematically destroyed temples, idols, and any other examples of foreign religious influence that they came across. This also extended to their own written works, and in the Old Testament accounts the female deity Asherah was reduced to a grove of trees instead of a well-respected goddess. It is only through archaeological excavation that the truth has emerged, proving that things cannot stay buried forever.

If the situation is analysed logically this revelation should be of no real surprise as ancient documentation demonstrates quite clearly that no early culture would have made sense of a God operating without a Goddess. It was contrary to all the laws of nature, which is ultimately what ancient worship systems were based upon.

During such arguments I managed to sway many guys as I tried to stick to a common sense approach rather than bombarding them with the academic information that I was by now quite well equipped with. What struck me was how little people knew factually about what they were talking about and the amount of cons that were 'going to get their vicar or imam to come and challenge me' was growing. This actually happened once or twice, and I found that the teachers were barely more knowledgeably equipped than their devotees. This became so embarrassing on occasion that I often held back in respectful manner when I had them cornered, although from the looks on some faces I'm quite sure that once again, if it were not common knowledge that I was a fighter I would have been given a thump or two.

Some observers to these discussions were fascinated by my knowledge and the factual detail that I would relate to either back up my arguments or stop silly talk in its tracks, and many cons, and officers of both sexes approached me in my cell while I worked and said, *'Howard, hurry up and finish that book!'* It was very encouraging.

For my part, in terms of my relationship with the opposite sex, I again stress that if I had listened to Nia more often, having also noted the same pattern in many other relationships, then my passage through life would have been much easier and more successful. However, having come from a family that underwent the rigours of colonisation and the associated indoctrination of religious dogma, my thought patterns were cast in a mould that proved difficult to break. Underestimating the value of the female input is not a mistake that I will make again.

9

As soon as my sentence was passed I had conference in a Crown Court holding cell with my barrister who proposed launching an immediate appeal against the imposed term which he felt was extraordinarily long. He feigned surprise, distress, and outrage, probably thinking that would make me feel better, but I never bought any of it for a second. It will take some convincing for me to believe that he did not know in advance what my fate was to be, the legal system consists of wheels within wheels, and judges and barristers are all close proximity players within its pantomime, all sitting at the same table and eating from the same pot. Still, I held no grudges, he had done the best that he could, although I would have much preferred blatant honesty. I find insults to my intelligence by people that I think have a fair assessment of my character both condescending and disappointing. However, I did on the strength of his apparent sincerity, and my solicitor's comments that my penalty was 'savage', believe that I would get some reduction in the length of time to be served.

The court appeal process is slow, but harbours the faint possibility of clemency after sentencing, and it is odd how prospective court dates seem to speed the days along. They serve as great bench markers of time, and by the time my appeal was heard I was just a few months away from having served one year behind bars, which did not include the two month period that I had spent on remand before obtaining bail. I had a suspicion that if successful I was not going to get a generous result, and if the appeal court judges had discounted even one year from my sentence it would have been something to celebrate.

I was given the option of attending the court hearing in London but decided against it, I considered the various pros and cons of being present and whether this would make any difference, and finally decided that I would wait to be informed by Rye Hill rather than go through the rigmarole of the prison limousine service. There was also the chance that the 'meat-wagon' would not return from London on the same day, effectively leaving me stranded and shacked up in HMP Belmarsh or some other similar hell-hole for weeks on end.

When notification of the appeal outcome arrived it was delivered to my cell by a unit officer and I closed my door before opening it. It was one of those documents that I had to read, and then re-read to get the message to sink in. The content though was clear enough. The judges agreed that my sentence was substantial but its harshness was negated by the discount I had received in reward for my guilty plea. They indicated that as the maximum sentence possible was fourteen years that I should consider myself fortunate that I was only given ten. They felt that I operated within the upper limits of the criminal scale and although the penalty was severe it was not excessive. Their decision was final, no reduction. I sat and pictured the appeal court judges laughing at my apparent impudence. The only thing that grated me was that I now had to inform Nia, who was hoping that she could at last have given the children some good news.

When I phoned and told her the outcome she said that it was what she was prepared for and anything else would have been surprising. She had not mentioned anything about my pending appeal to Kelis, but shared information she felt relevant with our sons. I felt once again, that I had let them all down, but I was getting used to this feeling now and it serves no purpose to psychologically punish yourself forever. The positive thing about having finality in the matter was that I could now plan my life accordingly, it was another weight lifted.

On the plus side the children were making great progress on the education front. Kelis was immersed in violin lessons and taking part in school concerts, and Chris in spite of the stain that my situation had placed on the family name was made deputy head boy at school. I was bursting with pride when I received the pictures of him in his school uniform with the gold bands stitched onto his blazer sleeves. We were allowed our own picture frames in our cells and that particular photo took pride of place. Imagine that, my children were setting me examples in life.

Of course there were the obvious down sides too. Chris had shown an aptitude for lawn tennis when he was about eight years old and was being sponsored by the Cliff Richard Tennis Foundation. The tennis world is an extremely competitive one and his mother and I had to take him to tennis matches every week, and this just so that he could maintain his ranking. For a child to succeed in this sport is not just about skill and dedication, but also about climbing the British rankings which could only be done if they won the required matches in their talent level. Arranging these contests was difficult enough, but it seemed logistically impossible to attend them all, nevertheless Nia and I shared the burden of transporting Chris to all the matches that were arranged through his tennis clubs.

We enrolled him in three tennis centres in order to maximise his chances of success and even arranged for him to get coaching lessons in New York with an ex-training partner of tennis champion John McEnroe, Rex Miller, a tennis pro who also happened to be one of my brother Edge's kickboxing students, eventually attaining instructor grade himself. Rex told me that Chris certainly had the skill level and was at the right age to make the grade which was enough for us as parents to put ourselves out even more than we had already to support him. My incarceration changed everything.

The main tennis centre that Chris trained at is in an upmarket suburb of Birmingham called Edgbaston, an area world renowned for its cricket and tennis facilities boasting sites that host professional events at top level. In spite of my arrest and imprisonment Nia continued to take Chris training and was pulled aside one day by representatives of the Edgbaston Tennis Centre Board. They told her that Chris's position at the club had been considered in light of my conviction and that a special meeting had been held to discuss the matter, they could not afford to be seen allowing people steeped in crime to use their courts, but in the light of Chris's exemplary manner and conduct it had been decided to allow him to continue his progress with them. Nia told me that in spite of their magnanimity she had never felt so embarrassed and once again let rip, as usual I had no choice but to remain silent. Eventually the strain of having to transport Chris to all of his matches on her own became overly burdensome and mother and son made a conscious decision that a future in the sport was no longer viable.

Kelis was going through a similar experience at school and although it was a serious matter, I suspect it had its comic elements. She would break down from time to time during class and the teachers, who were very sympathetic did their best to console her and one or two even recounted their own experiences of a loved one that was presently in, or had been, sent to prison. Although I'm sure their attention helped, Kelis would still have panic attacks, burst into tears unexpectedly, and seem detached in the classroom. The sympathetic reaction of her teachers was always the same, and more often than not they would contact Nia to come and collect our daughter and take her home. I don't know whether she played on it or not but at one point young lady would get time off from school on a weekly basis. When Nia told me about the problem I was extremely concerned, but she suggested that I do not mention it as it might make matters worse. I am assured by Nia that all of these breakdowns were genuine, still, although it may be wishful thinking on my part, I hope that my daughter milked the situation for all it was worth. It serves me well to think such a thing. It eases my guilt.

My eldest, Nick, had resigned himself to finding employment so that he could help out financially and so any of his further studies had to be modelled on whatever job he managed to get. He had been dating steadily for the past few years, and Sarah, his girlfriend, had become part of the family, regularly staying over at our house when she was in Birmingham. I had even met her parents who were very pleasant and decent people. I have no idea how much my later situation affected their opinion of me, but Sarah seemed to take it in her stride.

As expected, Kelis idolised her eldest brother's girlfriend and they had a great relationship. Sarah used to make her feel womanly and even let her wear some of her clothes, usually the sort of skimpy adult tops that didn't look out of place on a seven year old girl. Whenever Sarah was at the house, Kelis wanted to know where she was and traipsed behind her, everyone else became secondary in importance. I enjoyed seeing her have a new female role model, the look of excitement on her face, and her obliviousness to my existence, was so amusing that it made me feel excited for her too. So it came as quite a surprise when at Rye Hill Nick told me that he and Sarah were going through a trial separation, and when they eventually finished their relationship it was a tearful time. Sarah visited the house, Nia gave her a necklace as a goodbye present, Kelis burst into tears, Sarah burst into tears, and Gemma, Chris' girlfriend, was doing her best to hold them back too. The day after that scene, Nick sent his mother a text message to tell her how much he appreciated her support. I know she was touched by it and the whole episode proved how galvanising a sad event can be for a family. Little did I know that there was a world event looming that was to enforce that message on a much larger scale.

As a main supervisor at work I was sometimes allowed to take my gym session just before lunch if we were not too busy and on one particular September day I was about to do just that. I had been let back onto my unit so that I could change into my training clothes and did not even make it to my cell when I realised that something major was amiss. At first I thought that it was a joke when told that someone had flown a plane into one of the Twin Tower buildings in New York but as I walked along it was the topic of conversation among every group of huddled inmates. I ran to my pad to switch on the television and sure enough, every station featured images and reports of this bizarre crime. My first thoughts were the obvious, where were Mom, Junior, and Edge throughout all of this? Mom could easily have been caught up in the tragedy as she would often go shopping in Manhattan, and even worse Junior was working for the Municipal Credit Union in the city, which was housed in a building directly opposite the towers. Edge was in a transition of jobs, but lived in lower Manhattan with his wife and daughter, goodness knows where a free spirit like him could have been. My heart was in my mouth as I raced down to the phones to see if I could get through and check that they were ok.

The lines were jammed and as I wasn't the only inmate that had relatives in New York there was inevitably a queue for the payphones. We all stood by them quizzing each other to see who had achieved any success in making contact. No one had. I tried unsuccessfully to get through and on the odd occasion felt hopeful when mom's phone started to ring but became more and more despondent when her voicemail kicked in. I called Nia to see if she had heard anything. Not a word. Coming to prison was bad enough, but the thought of losing a loved one while I was so powerless was too much to bear. There was a phone in industries so at least I could still attend work and try to make contact throughout the afternoon. Those calls proved equally fruitless and my evening efforts were the same.

I had a sleepless night of course and as soon as I was unlocked in the morning raced down to the phones to see if Nia had heard anything. She had. Mom had called to say that no one in the family was hurt and that she had also being trying to get through but with the telephone traffic it had taken her a while.

The story of Junior's experience in this event took a few days to filter through. When the first plane impacted the tower it was with such force that it threw some of the staff in the

Municipal Credit Union to the floor and panic swept the building. As a manager Junior said that he did his best to try and keep his colleagues calm, as the surreal sight of a plane embedded in the building across the street had them terrified. He and the other senior staff kept cool enough to help implement the safety drill procedures and shepherd everyone out in orderly fashion. But it was a tentative calm and only lasted until they managed to get out onto the street. After that it was mayhem. Not only had the second aircraft now impacted the other tower throwing those still exiting against the wall of the Credit Union building, but people in the towers were now leaping out of high level windows to their deaths. The whole scene was a nightmare, a collection of carnage, rubble, and dead bodies. Many started running, or at least trying to. Those that kept their senses made effort to help others while worrying what new catastrophe might befall them as they tried to get to safety. Was it some kind of bizarre accident? Was America under attack? Was it Armageddon? He told me that all of these thoughts raced through his mind as he tried to keep his legs, which as they do in the horror movies, felt like jelly and kept buckling underneath him. I was just grateful that my brother was alive.

Edge's situation was completely the opposite. He was celebrating his baby girl's second birthday at an apartment on 10th Street and was called out to the rooftop to witness the first plane embedded in the North Tower. He and a group of friends then stood aghast as a second aircraft careered into the other one a mere 15 minutes later. They could scarcely believe their eyes. Their shock however was yet to manifest itself in more physical fashion.

About three weeks after the tragedy, Edge was overcome by nausea and headaches which left him bed-ridden for almost a week. In his mind there is little doubt that this was caused by the toxic dust clouds that formed and lingered above the area for weeks after the crash. The topic is one of some controversy even now.

In a bid to get the lower Manhattan financial and stock markets functioning as quickly as possible, New Yorkers were urged to go back to work as soon as they could by federal and state officials. This, even though these officials knew that the collapsed twin towers contained hundreds of thousands of tons of asbestos, much of which would have been released into the air in the form of microscopic fibres. When inhaled, asbestos is deadly, but unfortunately, counting the cost takes decades. In spite of federal and state officials insisting that the asbestos levels in the area were tested, and although increased, found to be safe, independent tests have shown otherwise. Many respected analysts estimate that up to ten per cent of people living in the lower Manhattan area will be afflicted with lung-related cancers within the next twenty years. Clearly, we will not be able to fully assess the damage inflicted by 9/11 for some time. Edge moved his family to California within 3 months.

As the detail and intention of the New York atrocity came to light the feeling in the jail was an odd one. The Asian prisoners in both the Green and Rye Hill were predominantly Muslim, and there were comparatively much fewer Hindu's or Sikhs. The underlying reasons for this cannot simply be put down to religious belief, and although I have thought about it I have never researched or debated the cultural and socio-economic factors which must also be responsible. Without a doubt though, the attitude of Muslim inmates was definitely more defiant in regards of conforming to western culture. I would not go as far as to say that their response to the 9/11 attack was one of glee, but it was clear that they were almost unanimous in their feeling that it served the Americans right and their respect for Osama Bin Laden was both alarming and overwhelming. On this point I was well aware that I was talking to societies rebels, and that the rank and file law-abiding followers of Islam might well offer a different perspective.

Politics is a game of intrigue, guile, and public manipulation and I suggested to quite a few Muslims that to take the apparent enmity between Bush and Bin Laden at face value might be falling for the ultimate confidence trick. I'm no more a conspiracy theorist than anyone else, although I admit to finding them both entertaining and thought provoking, as they always leave you with that 'you never know!' feeling. I remember the shock and disbelief that Princess Diana's death caused and even phoned Edge to gauge what the feeling was in America, he said that he imagined the James Bond 'mission completed' theme music being played as soon as the fatal crash took place.

The fact that they did not immediately trace the white Fiat Uno car that allegedly impacted the Princess of Wales' Mercedes is one of the many mysteries of this intriguing episode. The current official line is that the French police did indeed question, but then discounted as being involved, the owner of the vehicle, a French taxi driver. The reason? Because the paint on his 'newly' re-sprayed car did not match that of the one that collided with Princess Diana's. This even though he gave conflicting accounts of when he had the car re-painted, and not just to regular police officers, but to the investigators into the death of the most famous woman in the world!

It is difficult to believe that the French police could be so inept, or as has been suggested, interferingly resentful at the massive resources being poured into what they saw as a simple car accident. Yet in spite of the latter late revelation the smart money seems to believe that the Fiat in question actually belonged to a 'Diana-fanatical' journalist, James Andanson, who not only had a habit of pursuing her relentlessly but was also an MI6 informer who owned just such a vehicle. Andanson had no alibi for his whereabouts that night, and was found dead three years later in a burnt-out car in mysterious circumstances. Whatever the truth of the matter, it is no wonder that so many people, both public and officials alike, suspect foul play.

On the subject of the world's most infamous modern terror attack I devoured factually-based articles, books, and documentaries by respected and sensible commentators such as Gore Vidal, John Pilger, and Noam Chomsky and was not at all surprised by the public backlash against the Bush and Blair administrations. And yet, public outrage and public hypocrisy, it seemed to me, were closely allied. Many people feel that the incursions on Afghanistan, and later in Iraq, were illegal, a fact represented by numerous media polls and debates. Yet every morning I would switch on the breakfast news to note the traffic gridlock in most major cities. George and Tony must have been scratching their heads. Did the public want oil for their cars, one of the seemingly obvious ulterior motives for their Middle Eastern forays, or not? They could not have it both ways.

This hypocrisy extended across all religious and racial boundaries, as it included everyone that was critical of Western aggressive policy whether they were Jewish, Christian, or Muslim. In a sense it could be argued that they were actively asking for the war effort so long as they drove a petrol or diesel fuelled car.

On the conspiracy theory front the history of the Bush and Bin Laden relationship is even more absorbing. The families of these two men have been friends for decades and it seemed to me, that Bin Laden's actions and his claims to be hiding in Afghanistan suited an American agenda that was an open secret. If, with all of his wealth and contacts, Osama Bin Laden was a friend of the Afghan people, why hide in their country when he knew America yearned for an excuse to invade it and had such a proposal on their foreign policy table for several years prior?

My candid approach did not go down too well. Again, good thing I'm known for throwing a punch or two. To suggest that the hero of many Muslim inmates was a quisling was tantamount to blasphemy and I chose my words carefully when debating the issue. I'm glad I took that approach, and it seemed to have a positive effect as more than one of the Muslim lads that I spoke to told me privately that the same thoughts had already crossed their minds.

My suspicion of this situation has grown over the years as quite frequently when George Bush's approval rating needs a boost, Osama pops out of hiding to issue an anti-west declaration of war to prop up his old friend. It seems to happen too many times, and always at the 'right' time to be coincidence. It is a proven statistic that belligerent world leaders make their subjects feel safer in times of war and the propaganda of the war on terror is doing George Bush Jnrs presidency the world of good. I have a big mouth though, and I couldn't help also telling them that the present situation was history repeating itself and the Koran, their revered Holy Book, like the Bible, was not original in content, but was a collaborative work overseen by the Roman Empire. They must have thought that I was insane.

The Islamic belief system teaches that the Koran was literally handed to the prophet Muhammad while he was hidden in seclusion by the angel Gabriel and was originally written on the skin and bones of an animal. It also teaches that unlike the biblical texts the Koran has never been subject to alteration as it made its way through time. This declaration was founded on the basis that as it was such a revered tome no one would ever dare to tamper with its divinity. In reply to this I asked the most obvious of questions, 'Who then took it upon themselves to put it into chapter and verse format, especially as the Arabs did not possess this type of numerical system fourteen hundred years ago?' It certainly wasn't the angel Gabriel. In other words, who took it upon themselves to decide that the original format as handed down by their supreme God, Allah, was not good enough? Because whoever it was, had tampered with their God's work and changed its tone permanently. I tend to pose questions like this one to stop people in their tracks, especially when their ignorance exasperates me and this was one of many.

What was even worse, was that the grammatical form of the Arabic language had changed considerably with the passage of time as evidenced by the later inclusion of the 'dot' or 'nuqta', which when placed over different letters of the alphabet changed the intended meaning of the word. The original text possessed no such grammatical paraphernalia. This of course was without stressing that there is no language on earth that can retain its original meaning and nuances in translation, and the con that Arabic was confined to one language would not work on me as I knew that there were scores of Arabic dialects and the most common modern day translation of the Koran was conducted in Farsi. And all this without the fact that far from being a unique or original language, approximately half of the Arabic vocabulary consists of words borrowed from other Semitic tongues.

A comparison of Arabic words to Hebrew ones bears this claim out, for instance the ancient Hebrew word for Peace , 'Shalom', became the Arabic 'Salaam', 'Ab' meaning 'Father', became 'Abu', 'Haggai' the Aramaic word for pilgrimage became 'Hajj', 'Walad', the word for 'Boy' became 'Walid', 'Yom' the word for Day became 'Yam', and some words such as 'Dam' and 'Wahy', the words for 'Blood', and 'Inspiration' respectively, even remained in their original format. In turn, the Hebrew language was heavily influenced by the Egyptian tongue, and with this transition of language, it was only natural that there would also be a similar trail of ideas that had been passed down the same line. The Koran bears witness to this in hidden fashion.

It is the most recent of the Holy Books, penned over a debate-able period of time some fourteen hundred years ago, Muslims claim that it is the final work of the Supreme God of Judaism, Christianity, and Islam, correcting the errors and alterations of its predecessors, and in many ways, they have a valid claim.

As we have already seen it is not difficult to prove that both the Old and the New Testament borrowed the main themes of the Egyptian and Sumerian works and then tried to deny that fact with slight alterations to detail. The Koran goes one better, it corrects some of the altered details by re-presenting them in their original form.

In the biblical creation story, the first man, Adam, was created from the 'dust of the ground', whereas in early Mesopotamian versions man was created from clay. The Koran reverts to this ideology and states that Adam was indeed constructed from clay. Even more importantly it reveals that one of the secrets of God was that the earth and heaven were 'one piece' until separated by him. This was one of the core elements of both the Egyptian and Mesopotamian belief systems, the separation of these two realms yielded the Hermetic saying, *'From the below comes the above, and from the above comes the below, the work of the miracle of the one.'* This of course, notwithstanding the fact that the Koran also includes the story of Noah and the Ark, a proven biblical theft from earlier pagan sources.

The plagiarism does not end there however, and becomes even more widespread with allusions to Greek myth, such as that of the cruel king, Tantalus, who was damned in hell, with hanging fruit and flowing water being teasingly close but yet permanently out of his reach. There are also the claims that Allah provided the twelve month calendar, an undisputable Egyptian invention, as well as the very important and subtle use of the 'East' and the 'West' as the main points of geographical reference. Just to recap, the value of the latter is not the obvious one, that is, as denoting the difference between western and eastern cultures as is so happily promulgated in religious and political propaganda, but exists, as I was quick to point out, because in ancient culture the East represented Heaven and the West represented the Earth and Hell. Thus in tandem these two points encompassed all creation, a point the Koran makes in much clearer fashion than its counterparts.

The inclusion of the original unity of heaven and earth is the most ironic insertion of all, and as I mentioned earlier it was born out of the ancient belief that the heavens had exploded and fallen to earth, this assumption because of the phenomena of the meteorite. This is noteworthy because the most revered object in the Islamic religion is a stone that fell from the heavens which is known as the 'Black Stone' or in Arabic, 'Hajrat Aswad'. Prior to the advent of Islam this same stone was equally sacred to the followers of the Greek goddess Diana for the very same reason, it came from the gods. Today all Muslims that make a pilgrimage to the Ka'aba at Mecca, march around it seven times as part of a holy ritual that is imperative to followers of their religion.

When writing Rulers & Lies' I made several references of comparison between the presence of various versions of the

God Yahweh and the Egyptian deity Osiris within the pages of the Old Testament, and it was to my surprise that I was to find a similar vein in the Koran, as Allah is claimed to be the 'Lord of Sirius'. I reasoned that of all the stars of the heavens why single that particular one out for special reverence? With its wealth of other early culture influences the only conclusion that I could make was that the Koran, like its predecessors, was also heavily influenced by a select group of people. But more intriguing than all of this was why would they go to the effort of constructing such an opus and yet submerge hidden messages so easily spotted by anyone familiar with the earlier works? And just as teasingly, who would have done this? A sojourn into the politics of the time would give me my answer.

The Roman Empire, like all others of its ilk, nurtured its own enemies, and it was as much the creative masterstroke of Constantine, namely the birth of the Roman Church, as it was military might, that should take credit for helping it to survive as long as it did. The western section of the empire was surrounded by relentless barbarian hordes such as the Vandals and the Goths who were determined to destroy it and in the year 410 A.D. Rome fell to the Visigoths. The colonies of Spain, Africa, and Gaul, were already lost, with the latter being captured by the Franks to later become known as France, all of these losses precipitating the fall of the capital itself.

With Rome vanquished, the eastern portion of the empire became the new stronghold, and Constantinople (modern day Istanbul), formerly known as Byzantium, became its new centre. By the sixth century, with this replacement for Rome as a power base, the newly named Byzantine Empire, was showing some of its old form and a revival to re-gather its fortunes was spearheaded by a superb general named Belisarius. He overcame the Vandals to retake North Africa and temporarily recaptured Rome from the Goths. This success was the catalyst to a series of wars between the Byzantine forces and the regrouped Goths, which all but decimated Italy. To make matters worse for the Romans they were also undergoing serious internal instability with much political infighting and treachery as politicians fought for power. But this was not all, an old enemy, Persia, the former ruler of the Holy Lands, had regained its strength and was on the march.

The Persians re-conquered Jerusalem and Damascus in 613 A.D. and then Egypt the following year before gathering themselves for their assault on the heart of the Byzantine Empire.

At this time Arabia was a key strategic region in the battle between the Persians and the Byzantines, and the bulk of its domain consisted of a mixture of villages and towns, which harboured a majority of pagan multi-god worshippers as well as Jewish and Christian elements who belonged to the religious minority that worshipped the one-God, Yahweh. This was a major problem for the Byzantines and much like today amounted to a war of ideas, a religious struggle that reflected the bigger picture of world politics. A battle for hearts and minds was imperative, and was not unlike the earlier task of the Hebrew rulers to establish the Torah as a Holy Book and unite the religious beliefs of their subjects, the Roman Empire similarly had an uphill task that required great contemplation, planning, and assistance.

It was coincidental to this that the Prophet Muhammad's rise to dominance and his propagation of the newest version of Judaism, Islam was born. Islam holds that the Koran revelation first occurred to Muhammad in 610 A.D. and that he initially restricted his guidance to friends and family before announcing his divine tidings to the masses. The timing of his public disclosures dovetailed perfectly with the confrontation between the rival world factions. How opportune.

What is even more coincidental is that this new revelation drew on elements from all three of Arabia's resident religions. It kept the Hebrew Yahweh as the supreme one-God but changed his name to the same as that of the chief god of the Arab pagan pantheon, Allah. The pagan venue of the Ka'aba became the pilgrimage for the Islamic religion, a fact admitted in the Koran, and the ancient rituals of fasting and chanting were maintained. There was one major sticking point though, the question that asked, what was the true essence of the character that had become the pivotal figure in the religion of the Roman Empire, Jesus the Christ?

The new work revealed by Muhammad stressed the monotheistic uniqueness of the one-God, and insisted that to have him share any of his reverence with a mortal or any other god was blasphemous (It seems that Muhammad was excluded from this policy). Thus Jesus presented a two-fold problem. It was readily alleged for centuries that Yahweh had experienced marital unity with Asherah, and in his guise as the pagan Allah had previously also been allied with Arab female deities, which, as Salman Rushdie discovered, is a fact emphasised at one's peril, even in a novel. The Koran outlawed the reiteration of such tales and the concept of female power was allied to devil worship. Jesus being labelled God's son lent credence to a female divine input and such a philosophy was also forbidden, as was the concept of the three-gods-in-one, the Holy Trinity, thus in the eyes of Islam the Christian messiah although rendered as special, was relegated to the guise of a mortal prophet.

The other difficulty lay in the fact that Jesus was regarded as a god in his own right, which was also a problem for believers of the Jewish faith who, like the newly formed Muslims, also had difficulty with him being labelled God's son. They eventually came to accept him as a real person, as someone who like Abraham and Moses before him had been born of divine providence and was sent to help educate God's chosen people, but nothing more.

The dumbing-down of Jesus from a son of God to a special mortal was necessary to the advent of Islam, the human focus of whom, Muhammad, was, and still is, revered as much by Muslims as the Christ is by Christians. The authors of the Koran wanted the people of the 'one-God' united in war against the Persian forces. For Jesus to be relegated to the same status as Muhammad was the perfect compromise, and one that in the Arab lands proved acceptable to all parties

This arrangement succeeded in uniting the Jews and Christians of the desert regions as well as gaining many pagan converts. As a result, the tide of opinion in this key location turned against the Persians.

After studying this topic in detail it is extremely difficult to accept that the grouping and manipulation of these religious factions was merely fortuitous and not orchestrated in its entirety by interested political parties. For the Roman forces it was all too ideal. They had as an ally a new prophet, Muhammad, a man who turned out to be one of the finest military commanders of all time as well as an astute religious leader and politician, who would smooth over any discrepancies in divine history for the final time. He had a new book, and a new doctrine, one that brought back in a time of war the angry Old Testament God, Yahweh, whose belligerent image Christianity, in its all-embracing global strategy had sought to alleviate. The supreme God of the Torah was thus reintroduced with a new name, but the same cause, to convert or exterminate those that did not believe in him. This reverse transformation can be seen in the attitude of many modern day followers of Islam who would have little hesitation in resorting to violence, although not necessarily of an extreme nature, in the defence of their God. In their minds they are simply following the divine example and believe that such aggression is justifiable.

An example of this is the intimidation and aggressive displays of outrage exuded by Muslims even when resident in non-Muslim countries at any disrespect shown towards their faith. When a Danish newspaper, depicted the Prophet Muhammad as a cartoon terrorist it became clear that many followers of 'the way of peace' would, if allowed, have taken matters too far. In other European countries such as Holland they already have. The sentiment of 'kill those who offend Islam' is far too strongly supported for anyone to suggest that the religion is operated as a pacifist one.

You won't find many conscientious objectors in the Islamic faith. Apart from its deep-rooted use of indoctrination one of the factors that fuels such mind-numbing ire is a lack of external education in Muslim states. The politically correct brigade will no doubt detest such a statement, but for progress to be made the reality of any given situation must first be acknowledged before it can be countered or improved.

It is a fact that predominantly Muslim countries do not encourage the reading of open-minded material and that a small European country like Greece imports and digests more reading material for the education of its residents than all of the Islamic states combined. This is an alarming, shameful, and dire statistic. It is the same state of mind that afflicted Christianity just a few hundred years ago and saw its intolerance inflict physical cruelty, suppress minds, and deny psychological freedoms, all on an international scale and supposedly in the name of God. God is love, so long as you do things his way.

To counter this it must also be stressed that to suggest that the majority of Muslims are potential terrorists and suicide bombers is also a gross misrepresentation of both them, and their religion. The word Islam, does indeed translate as 'Way of Peace' and I have no doubt that at heart there are many Muslims, men, women, and children who sincerely believe and adhere to this tenet. The use of news images from the daily violence perpetrated in the Middle East can emphasise a one-sided nature to the Islamic majority and essentially confuses religion with politics. Retaliation for hurt caused to loved ones is a separate topic, and it is here that religion is slanted to discriminate rival parties, religious belief per se has little to do with it. Still, its ability to divide, unite, or incite, has always been taken advantage of, a fact aptly demonstrated throughout history.

The Koran, in its dual function as a political tome nods its head to the convenience of the ancient Roman alliance and its thirtieth chapter is aptly entitled, Romans. However, as is the way of things, the understanding that the Byzantines and the Arabs enjoyed was not to last, as the war inflicted these allies with contrasting fortunes. The new Roman Empire became even more stretched and battle weary, while the Arabs, had become a force to be reckoned with, they were now united in politics and religion, and seasoned, experienced, and organised in battle. The former world rulers were no match for them and all knew it. The students had become the masters, giving birth to the spread of the latest political-cum-religious tool of conquerors, Islam, and the latest incarnation of the Hebrew God, Allah, throughout the Middle East, Africa, Asia Minor, and Eastern Europe. A situation which in many of these areas has remained virtually unchanged to this day, and forms part and parcel of current world politics.

It would be wise to consider that many comparisons from this historical model can be made to the modern relationship between the new Roman Empire, America, and current Islamic states such as Iran. America, in its self-appointed role as the policeman of the world has overstretched itself on the global front and its appetite for military engagement will almost certainly wane. At this particular moment, Iran, North Korea, and several other opponents of its belligerent foreign policy have stated openly that the intrusive giant is running out of oxygen.

What is most disturbing about so-called modern day religious terrorism such as 9/11 and subsequent atrocities, most of which are largely perpetrated in the Muslim world, is the inability, or indeed unwillingness, of Islamic religious leaders to denounce suicide missions as contrary to the teachings of their faith. Yet the sayings of the Prophet Muhammad known as the Hadith, expressly forbid such behaviour, stating that anyone who takes their own life, no matter the reason, will be forever condemned to continuously repeat the act of their death in hell as punishment. I did not come across a single Muslim that knew of this, and whenever I informed them of it they were always visibly shocked, not just at the fact that I was privy to such information, but because it was so alien to them. There is no doubt in my mind that deep down they have been taught to commend the act of suicide in its use to destroy the perceived enemies of Islam as one of glory, with many Imams either directly, or indirectly, promoting eternal bliss in paradise as a reward for such insanity.

In his well argued work, *'The God Delusion'*, the academic Richard Dawkins makes the very lucid point that moderate Islam has a lot to answer for in this regard. One must surely concur, because by staying silent on the occulted details of their faith, for whatever reason, they are implicit in providing a breeding ground for extremism. Suicide bombers would not be so eager to sacrifice their lives if they knew that their faith taught eternal damnation instead of heavenly bliss was the reward for such actions.

There is another trend in their faith that proves equally ironic, and it is that despite Islamic claims of one-God, and one-religion, they are just as diverse in their interpretation of their Holy Book as Jews and Christians are of the Torah and the New Testament. The schisms within Islam are numerous and deeply factious, consisting of blood feuds that have lasted for centuries. The united façade that is often presented to the western world is just that, an illusion. Muslims kill more followers of Islam than non-believers in their faith on a daily basis, which begs the question, which of them gets to go to paradise?

With this in mind it becomes even more transparent that the extreme thought and activity that is supported by religion, no matter which denomination conducts it, is nothing more than political spin. It is the control of the many by the minds of the few, with the influential taking advantage of the ignorance, vulnerability, desperation, and need of the masses to escape turmoil and despair, while sating their growing egos and improving their own lot in the process. Wheels turn but nothing changes.

10

Tim Caines is a good friend of mine. He possesses the qualities that I like in a person, he is polite, self-effacing, intelligent, and as is the common consensus of opinion of anyone that has ever met him, a gentleman. He is one of those old-fashioned fair and square British types. I've known him since we were teenagers as he also used to frequent the Silver Blades ice-rink, and although not indulging in the fisticuffs that was so popular amongst my friends and I, he was well-liked and well-respected. His sense of fair-play and maturity would not allow him to become involved in such nonsense and he thought we were all quite wild, I found this quite admirable as he was several years younger than many of us. We became closer when he started practicing Karate and began training at Birmingham's most famous Karate Centre which was located in the City Centre. It was known as the Temple, and was founded by a superb Japanese Karateka named Toru Takamizawa.

The Temple Karate Dojo was known for producing international standard competitors and Tim, a natural athlete revelled in its competitiveness and high sporting standards. He and his regular training partner, Clarence Mckew, used to travel to the kung fu and karate clubs that their friends trained at to pick up tips from the different styles, a typically open-minded and sensible tactic, as when it came to inter-style competitions they would have a good idea of their opponents pet techniques.

Everyone knew where Edge and I practised as our reputation in England as kickboxers was growing and Tim and Clarence would regularly journey over to the Hachi-Shin Kai to join us in some kick-boxing training. They figured that the extra attention that we paid to conditioning and endurance would serve them well in the less physically demanding world of sport karate. Very wise, but even though our sessions were conducted with good grace and a sense of fun we did our best to give them some licks.

The affinity that Tim and I developed was assisted by the fact that he had begun work in the insurance world, (I was in banking), and over the years he gathered a wealth of experience and contacts in the money lending market, especially in the field of home purchase loans, which as ever was extremely lucrative. Tim used to make an executive style living from arranging loans for clients in addition to the commission based fees for selling-on the necessary insurance schemes.

It was in the early nineties, while running a keep-fit business from my offices in Birmingham, that I was approached by officers from the Criminal Investigation Department (C.I.D.), affectionately known by the British as 'Coppers in Disguise', because they wear civilian clothing while on duty, to ascertain what I knew about Tim's activities. They quizzed me about his character, and wanted to know how often I fraternised with him. I was later to discover that these questions related to a murder enquiry.

There had been a large scale fraud investigation in the city when it was discovered that criminals had infiltrated the loans market during the mid to late nineteen-eighties when building societies and banks were lending money like confetti and Britain was letting the good times roll, 'Greed was good' was the Hollywood expression used to sum up that brief bohemian era, and it was entirely accurate.

Elaborate chains of corrupt house purchasing networks, which included building surveyors, estate agents, solicitors, bank managers and lending agents, collaborated to line their pockets. They would develop a rapport with property sellers, present front men as buyers, ramp up the value of buildings, then authorise loans well in excess of their true worth and pocket the difference. The buyers would then disappear after making two or three monthly repayments making the scam seem like a default instead of what it truly was. The lender would then repossess the property and naively list it as a statistic before reselling it via auction or on the open market to the first sensible bidder. These schemes went on for three or four years before imploding and resulting in jail sentences for those who had not fled to Spain or some similar foreign destination, or had not been astute enough to cover their tracks. Greed tends to get the better of most people when they are making easy money.

Many of the older bank managers were tempted to knowingly lend money in this manner as the sentences for this type of fraud were not excessive, and they would often be treated leniently by Judges who not only empathised with them but were also members of the same fraternal societies. The way it was often perceived was that it was a worthwhile risk. They often felt that they were being treated shabbily by their employers, this due to the fact that the old style bank managers were being phased out, to be replaced by smart-alec young bucks and computerised credit-scoring systems. So for the sake of eighteen months in an open prison, they could give their pensions a healthy buffer and always maintain that they had no idea that such a ruse was being perpetuated under their very noses. Such cases are nearly always impossible to prove conclusively.

These frauds increased in complexity as funding moved into more commercial areas such as industrial property, foreign lending, arbitrage, and the inevitable, money-laundering. For the educated white-collar criminal the potential gains were huge, and the risk of being caught was minimal as frauds can be completed before anyone is even aware that a crime has taken place. The police do not have the resources to investigate the majority of complicated white-collar crimes simply because standard manpower is not enough, they need well educated police officers to even attempt to fathom the felony let alone prosecute it, and the drain on their financial resources made the Crown Prosecution Service wary of sanctioning too many detailed investigations.

The police were not the only ones given pause for thought by these ruses, as complicated structures also worried the less educated criminals whose funds had become embroiled in such schemes due to the promise of life-changing returns. These guys would pretend that they understood what was going on, when in truth many of them were lost at the first hurdle, and when unexpected delays arose in even the most basic of procedures such as an international money transfer, they would lose it and start physically threatening all and sundry who wore a suit. It was the only method they knew of trying to control such a situation. To the solicitors and other professionals that were working with them they were showing their true colours as the knuckle-dragging Neanderthals that they were suspected of being. At best they were secretly regarded as a joke, rabble whose thuggish antics would be laughed at over a private drink, and at worst, they were covertly despised by their other-world colleagues. Educated people brave enough to get involved in crime do not scare easily and are usually great actors anyway. It does not take a genius to see that such a mix is boiling water, and if something were to go truly awry with these clandestine projects, it was inevitable that they would not remain secret much longer.

A solicitor named Colin Hickman, paid the ultimate price in what appears to be exactly such a situation, he lost his life, after brutally being stabbed to death in his own house. His common-law wife, Vera Philip-Griffiths, saw the murderer flee the scene, a tall, male, fair-haired Caucasian who has to this day never been apprehended. As I write, Tim Caines is serving the eleventh year of a life sentence for this crime. Tim Caines is black.

Tim, in his capacity as a lending and insurance consultant was involved in the surrounding fraud issue, to what extent, I do not know, and he readily admits that he was at Colin Hickman's house only some thirty minutes or so before the murder took place, and was party to a meeting between the solicitor and his alleged assailant, having been forced there at gunpoint by the unknown assassin, and that the meeting, the essence of which was a financial dispute, did indeed become heated. He even remonstrated with the aggressive third party, attempting to physically intervene at one point, before being asked to leave by both men. Unfortunately for him, and Colin Hickman, he did just that.

When the police arrested Tim, they insisted that he knew who the killer was, they knew it was not him, but the murder was high profile, and killing solicitors is not like taking the life of a factory worker. They are connected to the legal system, as well as being respected pillars of their community. Someone had to pay, and if Tim was not going to fess up, then it was him. Tim has always stated that the first time he saw the mysterious third man was on that very day and although he could describe him, he knew nothing else about him, not even his name.

British legal legislation in such issues is covered by a law known as Joint Enterprise, which is often used in murder cases where there is confusion as to who actually performed the deed that caused death. This is normally reserved for group killings where more than one person is present at the commitment of a murder, and even though only one of the group may have performed the fatal act, if this detail cannot be proved or extracted by confession, then all present are sentenced for the crime. They are all deemed equally guilty by association, whether bystander or not. In Tim's case, his gold bracelet was found at the scene of the crime, inferring that he was physically involved in the fatal struggle. The police alleged that he had physically held Hickman while the assailant repeatedly stabbed him, a large leap in terms of assumptive analysis, but one that stuck. The fact that Vera Philip-Griffiths had a clear view of the attacker while he was still in her house and saw him leave, yet did not see Tim, and that Tim admitted to attempting to restrain the alleged murderer before leaving the house, explaining the presence of his bracelet which was lost during the altercation, held no water. A jury of his peers found him guilty by a majority verdict of nine to one.

The suppression and mislaying of vital evidence have formed a large part of the many appeals, television, and radio interviews that have covered this case for the last ten years, and Tim continues to protest his innocence vehemently.

It is my personal opinion that the more time passes, the more his chances of a successful appeal will fade. There are two simple reasons for this, money is one. If Tim were to be absolved of this crime, the legal payout that he would be awarded would certainly exceed half a million pounds, and the embarrassment that it would cause to an already beleaguered police force would be another blow to their esteem that they do not need. To my recollection, never before has a black man been locked up for a crime that was acknowledged as being perpetrated by a white person in the history of British crime. There have been many high profile cases of miscarriages of justice, but never one of this nature. I believe that it would be international news if Tim were to be acquitted at this very late stage which is the second reason for my assessment. He will be released from his sentence when it has run its full course and not a moment sooner.

To my shame, I only visited him once after he had been sentenced, he was still resident at HMP Winson Green and had not begun his filtration through the penal system. I was caught up in the running of my business and personal health issues as I underwent a serious illness at that time, but that is no excuse, I should have supported him more. And yet not once has Tim even as much as uttered a word to me about my shortcoming. Not an innuendo, not a whisper. He's as stoic as I am which is why many people think we're similar. No doubt he'll have a dig at me when he reads this though. I'm just thankful that he has a great family network and many reliable friends, both men, and women, who have stuck with him throughout the years.

When it sank in that I was going to be convicted myself it crossed my mind that our paths might cross, one guy at Rye Hill, a young Rastafarian nick-named Fire, also a lifer, said to me that I reminded him of an inmate he knew from another jail, I knew who he was talking about before he even mentioned the name. I was at work in industries some months later when told that someone had arrived from another jail and wanted to know which unit I was on, once again, the description given and my gut instinct told me straight away it was Tim Caines.

Tim was placed on a different unit to me so we could only really meet in passing or at the gym. When his transfer to my wing was approved, we reminisced for hours on end. He had been in almost eight years by then and it is a testament to his character that many inmates thought that he was serving a short fixed-term sentence. He was, as always, immaculately presented, very clean, tidy, well-pressed, and constantly smiling. Not many lifers are like that, they usually seem to have the weight of the world on their shoulders and drain your energy as soon as they start talking. Tim also had something else going for him, and that 'something else' included lots of female admirers, both staff and visitors. I used rib him all the time about it and called him 'Mandingo' or 'King ding-a-ling'.

He had three ex-girlfriends who were all still in regular contact with him whether they had a new partner in tow or not. Remarkably, none of them had yet started a family and I got the impression that this was because they hoped to start one with him upon his release. If that was the case then they had good judgement, I've seen him in the company of children and I think he would make a great father. I know that having his own offspring is one of his foremost ambitions, with his warm personality and having missed so much of life it is only natural.

I also wondered what his reaction to my own new found aspiration, to publish a book on one of life's most controversial issues, was going to be, and gave him my updated preface of *Rulers & Lies* for his opinion. Tim is not easily impressed and I found his positive reaction, especially for a black person, most encouraging.

Well into my sentence I was asked by a white prison officer who was an aficionado of Roman history what my opinion was of the holy books as it was common knowledge that I was writing about the subject. I answered by stating it would be very difficult to objectively research their background and come out a believer at the end of it. He smiled and nodded acquiescently. Generally speaking, this was not the reaction that I would get from the many black or Asian people who asked me a similar question.

There were a group of Rastafarians that worked together in industries, I had become friendly with them as they were all pretty cool guys and two of them, Silk and Archie, used to work out in the gym as much as I did. Each morning in industries before work commenced they would read passages from the Bible in prayer while at their workbench, which although unusual, is not that surprising in prison, as many people tend to become more religious when incarcerated. I was to research why this was at a later date.

On one of their sessions they asked me to join in instead of bypassing them as I normally did. The mischievous side of me readily consented and I stood there while their self-appointed leader, Nigel, piously read a passage from the Old Testament. Closing my eyes and saying amen was out of the question as even though I was being patronising, I try not to be a hypocrite. When Nigel finished, I stated that it was an interesting passage from the Book of Psalms, (this without having sight of their Bibles), and that it was describing a journey through the underworld in replication of the Egyptian Book of the Dead. I enjoyed the look of bewilderment on their faces. Affronted, Nigel asked me what was so special about the Egyptians. I replied that I could not believe that someone was asking me such a question as there are programmes on television every week about the achievements of that culture that are still unfathomable today. I was about to walk away when Nigel threw a red rag to a bull, he told me that as I was such a smart-ass he was going to bring in his Bible of a 'thousand deaths' to our afternoon work session and show me the power of God. Trying to psychologically intimidate me is pointless, I told him to bring two.

The only other person in the group to comment was Bigger, who asked me if I believed in Jesus. I told him that I did not and got the usual Hollywood reaction. He raised his hands, exclaimed loudly that I must be a Satanist and followed me to my workbench in disbelief that another black man could fall so low. Considering where we were all resident I found that observation quite amusing and have never been able to make neither head nor tail of the argument that if you do not believe in God then you must be a Satanist.

The devil is part and parcel of the biblical canon and is God's nemesis, so if you believe in the existence of one of them, then it follows that you concede to the existence of the other. Conversely, if you do not ascribe to a belief of the holy books then neither character features in your psychology. To my mind any other rationale is nonsensical. Like heat and cold, dark and light, or soft and hard, they represent opposite ends of the same spectrum, and philosophically speaking, if you are a believer, neither can exist without the other. This was another of the corrections that the Koran emphasised over the New Testament. In the Christian doctrine it is prophesied that after Judgement Day, God would eventually destroy the Devil, whereas the Koran states that he would not. On this issue, the Koran makes more sense, if God were to destroy the concept of evil then the world would implode. It would be like having permanent light, or no such thing as hard or soft, that there would also be no scale of measurement in terms of human behaviour is a totally incomprehensible doctrine.

The determination of 'good' and 'evil' are both points of view in many areas, and man's capacity to commit what we would all generally consider to be evil acts stem from a warped expression of our need to survive. The need to protect and provide for our loved ones is clearly as much dependent on our 'dark' side as our good and is vital to our existence. The desire to survive is a natural human instinct, and one noticeably displayed by the God of the Old Testament, in fact the stories of that text make it clear that his own survival was entirely based upon the need for mankind, or more pointedly, the Hebrew nation, to believe in his existence.

With this need in mind it should not be too surprising that it was God who introduced the concept of violence and murder in the Genesis story and perpetuated it throughout. He needlessly performs the first act of slaughter in the biblical canon when providing Adam and Eve with the skins of animals to clothe themselves, and this at a time when the innocently-minded duo were happy to sew fig leaves together for bodily covering. How do we define 'good' and 'bad' in that scenario?

Couldn't explain any of this to Bigger and Nigel though. But what did stand out was that throughout all of the chatter, Silk and Archie never raised their voices or used any animated expressions, not even once. I got the impression, almost immediately, that they were more on 'receive' mode than transmit. Not knowing what they were thinking I once again felt it wise to choose my words carefully and not be too dismissive of what I considered to be infantile argument. Both of these guys were serious players in the weights room.

That afternoon, Nigel, or 'the Sheikh' as he appointed himself, brought his deadly text to industries and we spent most of the afternoon in debate instead of working. He knew his Bible thoroughly but his lack of any detailed external knowledge and pompousness made him an easy target and I enjoyed myself. The next day, while on the way to work, Silk accosted me and told me that the reason that he was so quiet during the previous day's discussions is because some of the points that I had mentioned concerning the Old Testament's plagiarism of Egyptian documents he already knew to be true and he just wanted to hear what else I had to say. It seems that it was my turn to be taken aback.

Silk had many articles and books in his cell that he had gathered over the years and was committed to analysing them all. Many were new to me and featured writings on philosophy and historical social structures that pertained to religion and the organisation of ancient and modern cultures. I was more than a little impressed. Even more so because Silk was one of the most feared inmates in the facility, I'd already seen what happened to a couple of inmates that had crossed him in one way or another. It always gave me a little giggle. This though, was a completely different side to him, I doubted he was going to let too many other inmates see it.

One of the topics that we spent much time discussing was the esoteric nature of the Old Testament. It was already clear to us that the tales were not literal and needed to be decoded to obtain their core message. I already knew that like the Egyptian texts, the Hebrew ones were also dedicated to sun-gods and that two of the most popular and well-known characters, Samson and the 'wise' king, Solomon, were exactly that. Samson was of particular interest because he, like Jesus, to the Rastas anyway, was also a Rastafarian.

The Jamaican sect of the Rastafari was heavily influenced by the ideologies of the social reformer Marcus Garvey, a man whose influence and drive indirectly led to the formation of the Nation of Islam, and was an inspiration to notable black reformers such as Malcolm X and the African hero, Kwame Nkrumah. Malcolm X's father was an avid Garveyite, and it was this in part that led to his murder by unknown redneck assailants in America's Deep South. Garvey, a Jamaican, was a pioneer for self-advancement amongst coloured people and from his base in New York sought to link a world-wide movement between the blacks of America, Africa, and the West Indies, a visionary and monumental task. His enemies came from both within the black community as well as the establishment and his ambitious projects were to take many steps forward before being brought to heel by treachery, bloody-mindedness, and envy.

Garvey died amid relative obscurity in 1940 while resident in London, which completed the dissolution of his followers and stymied the notion that black people could independently achieve self-advancement if they presented a united front. My father was a keen admirer of Marcus Garvey and believed in the philosophy that a man's destiny was largely in his own hands. The thought of ever having to rely on anyone else for his survival, whether it be the state, friends, or even his own children during old age, was an anathema to him.

Many of the Jamaican followers of Garvey's movement, took to a more religious expression to replace their deceased hero, they viewed Garvey as a prophet, and came up with their own branch of Judaism, one based upon the Old Testament followers of Yahweh that were called the Nazarites. This biblical group consisted of children and adults who were 'dedicated' to God's service and as such were forbidden to cut their hair or partake of the 'fruit of the vine', and the biblical strongman was one of them.

His name, Samson, literally means 'like the sun', and his story tells of his demise when he falls for the feminine wiles of the treacherous Delilah, whose name has its roots in a word meaning 'night', one of several allusions to her underworld nature, another is that she hailed from the 'Valley of Sorek'. The word 'valley' is more key underworld symbolism and is commonly used as a metaphor to inform the reader that events were not necessarily taking place upon the earth but quite possibly down below as in the oft quoted 'valley of the shadow of death'. The word 'Sorek' means 'choice red vine', which without going into too much detail should have been a resounding warning to our hero that this woman spelt trouble for any Nazarite.

The symbolism and coding of this story is laden with hidden meaning to such an extent that even a surface knowledge of ancient philosophy makes it clear that the tale is not a literal one. Samson is the sun itself and strongest while he has long hair, and weakest during the night, while resident in the underworld, that is, under the influences of Delilah, who subsequently shaved his locks thus rendering him powerless.

His story perfectly sums up the ancient depiction of the sun as a young man during the summer with long, flowing, golden locks, (a metaphor for the sun's rays), who ages and loses his glow and his hair during the autumn and winter, to begin rebirth during the spring amid renewed vigour. The astronomical nature of the tale is further emphasised as Delilah is readily identified with the house of Virgo through which the sun passes on its yearly autumnal phase. When viewed from this perspective the story, far from losing its appeal, not unlike most of the other Old Testament legends, takes on a much more interesting aspect, particularly because it is one of the easier ones to decode. What I enjoyed about discussions with people as open-minded as Silk, was that they would see points that I had missed, one's that filled gaps or accelerated my own understanding of certain topics, their ready interest made me feel even more certain that my project was worthwhile.

The story of the 'wise' King Solomon has the same tell-tale signs of sun-god presence in the name of the featured character. The word Solomon displaying both Egyptian and Greek influences, both of which are prevalent throughout all of the holy books. His name is actually Sol-Amun, a combination of individual terms for the sun, and is a reference to the body during the last phase of its daily activity as it appears to descend into the earth on the western horizon. In each of its three phases, its rise, peak, and descent, the sun was a recognised deity and formed the original three-gods-in-one concept of the trinity. In ancient lore the descent phase, the Amun, signalled the sun's entry into the lower depths, the underworld, where it enlightened the gods and beings that dwelt within that realm. It is a theme that is rife throughout the Old and New Testament and features heavily in the story of Jesus. The 'Amun' is also paid much covert reverence as the 'Amen' in the teaching of several New Testament writers.

Solomon's appellation of the 'wisest king' was not, as is implied by the Old Testament a unique one, but one that was bestowed on many ancient kings whose names were linked to the sun. This was simply because in its 'all-seeing' nature, the sun was thought to be the wisest of all. It was the ultimate accolade.

There is still much debate over the real existence of many biblical characters, and Solomon is one such figure. In my mind whether he existed or not is indeed arguable, but whether he achieved the towering claims as laid out in the Old Testament is not. The scale of his kingdom, his achievements, and other events that took place during his reign are clearly mythical, and like the story of Samson, were two-fold in intention. On the one hand they were designed to embellish the history of an impoverished people who sought to establish a new and credible nation that could rival its neighbours, and on the other they were meant to impart esoteric information to those thought worthy enough to receive it.

An example of this is the visit that Solomon was said to have been paid by the 'Queen of the South', an epithet used for dark-goddesses, i.e. female deities of the underworld, of which the Egyptian goddess Isis was the first and foremost. This is confirmed for us in the New Testament in the words of Jesus who stated that the 'Queen of the South' would rise up from the dead to pass judgement on the day of reckoning. That particular passage is one of many in the Bible that could well have been lifted directly from the Egyptian Book of the Dead and the basis of its theology cannot be disputed. As a sun-god, Solomon could indeed have held court with an underworld deity, but as a mortal king the notion is nonsensical.

As far as Solomon's alleged wisdom is concerned it is clear from his story that he was far from flawless in his decision making and was constantly at odds with his God because of his love of foreign women and his frequent adoption of their systems of worship. His spending habits were equally wanton and from the design specifications laid out in the Bible the construction of his legendary temple would have cost in excess of ten billion pounds by today's monetary standards. The fact that not a solitary stone of such a magnificent edifice has been found to date, or any clue as to its location, when many much older and valued monuments are easily pinpointed does raise some suspicion. This is compounded by the neglect of any of the neighbouring cultures of that time to mention him at all in their records, even though he was purported to have been a king accorded world-wide fame, wealth, respect and grace.

If we analyse his compilation of gold then matters may become clearer. His income of that material from various sources was '666 talents' per annum, which is clearly an esoteric figure, and presses home a point that once again relates to our old friend the meteorite.

The biblical mention of precious metals and gems begins in the Genesis account and the acquirement of physical wealth is clearly important within the lives of the main Hebrew characters and priests. So much so that one could easily argue that the Hebrew God was encouraging his chosen people to be as materialistic as possible, as this seems to be the main yardstick by which their success was judged and their faith rewarded. But this is not entirely the case.

The ancient gods had originally entered the earth in dramatic fashion as beings of immense physical brilliance, lighting up the sky and filling the air with sound as they made their approach. For anyone, king, hero, or priest, to become a god, they had to achieve this same physical presence before they could be considered worthy of re-entering the heavens.

It is from this philosophy that the institution of jewellery as royal regalia and the royal fanfare of trumpeting were born, they mimicked divine status, and with all royals claiming to have had divine birth, these adornments were vital. Thus upon death these divinely decorated humans could descend into the earth before making their ascension, in effect retracing the route and appearance of their alleged mythical entry in exact fashion.

The Old Testament makes this clear in its second book, Exodus, where the detailed construction of garments required for the priesthood are outlined with some precision and the emphasis on glistening adornment is an important one. If we note the activities of many biblical characters, whether as groups or individuals, they had to empower themselves before they could 'travel', and quite simply, the more 'brilliant' they appeared, the more progress they could make in trying to get back to heaven.

The first five books of the Old Testament, known collectively as the Pentateuch, are entirely about man's meteoric fall from heaven's grace and his attempts to regain his former status. This he could not do without re-energising, no 'brilliance' equated to 'no movement' and any detailed reading of the ancient Hebrew stories bears this point out. In the story of the Exodus the Hebrew's could not exit Egypt, which represented the depths of the underworld, before plundering their Egyptian neighbours and stealing their gold, it was not greed, it was a basic requirement for ascent and is a recurring theme in almost every subsequent story. Whether it was achieved by trickery, theft, murder, or good grace did not matter, exit from the lower realm was the primary objective, and jewellery and the other material possessions needed to 'rise up' from the below were vital to this.

In the texts of the earlier cultures an escape from the underworld was only possible if a life was given in exchange for the one that was departing on a 'like for like' basis, i.e. a god for a god, or a human for a human. The Hebrew mythology changed this rule in the story of Abraham and the intended sacrifice of his son Isaac, where the Hebrew God decided that a human life could be exchanged with that of a ram or sheep, and cements the 'blood of the lamb' as a key theme in the biblical canon (this point is a little more complex than I can outline here as the 'Ram' was an animal also equated with a 'god', in particular the Egyptian deity Osiris). It is for this reason that the possession of livestock was as much a necessary requirement for the travelling Hebrews as precious metals.

When viewed from this standpoint, then Solomon was indeed the wisest king, for he gathered more gold, livestock, and other material possessions than anyone else and thus, metaphorically speaking, shone as brightly as the sun itself.

On the subject of the Amen, you may have already worked out for yourself that its use to end Christian prayer is an esoteric link to its true nature. The descent of the sun-god Amun into the underworld each night is why the translation of the word is 'so be it'. Thus every time a Christian finishes their prayer they are unwittingly paying reverence to the third deity of the original trinity. They should not worry, for their belief system and holy book are laden with such hidden homage.

As this analysis points out, verbally explaining what my research had uncovered so far was not always easy, as when I was asked what appeared to be the simplest of questions, the answer sometimes needed a background explanation before it could be substantiated. As a result I often ended up not answering certain questions at all especially if I felt that my time was being wasted. Having said that, very few people actually challenged me in debate, for once I had mentioned a few etymological or other factual details they normally ran for cover. The imam at Rye Hill actually told me when I threw a question to him about his religion, that he was not a scholar, inferring of course that I was. I think he meant it as an insult, as the most revered human character in Islam, Muhammad, apparently could not read. I challenged that claim too by stating that he could indeed read, but when he relates in the Koran that 'I am not a reader' he was talking about the classical Syretic Arabic that he was being confronted with. He could read the language of his tribe, Quraish, just fine, and he was actually appointed as business manager for his first wife, Khadijah, before falling in love with her. Still I took the imam's comment as a compliment, and an admission that he could not entertain a serious conversation with me even about the religion that he was allegedly expert in. I had already come across the same wariness with many priests and preachers and was alarmed at how unaware they were of relevant information that was not readily supplied within their belief systems.

Tim and many other guys were impressed by episodes such as that one, and they had a habit of marching people to my cell, or fetching me out of it to present my opinion on some topic or the other. To be honest I learned as much as I expounded in many conversations because there were some very intelligent guys on the education unit, who were well-read, experienced, and great fun to debate with, especially on a Sunday morning after we had all read the tabloids.

It is one of the things about prison that I miss, the time and opportunity to discuss and debate almost everything that was topical with a varied range of inquisitive minds, and more importantly, by noting the reactions of those involved it helped me to decide who I would want to keep in touch with upon my release and those people that I thought might not only be a threat to my liberty but also to my trust.

Silk and I continued our cross-referencing and kept each other up to speed whenever either of us discovered any literary material of any interest. Quite often we were at odds in our conclusions, and debated our points of view furiously. I loved it. 'Yes men' do nothing for progress. Our discussions took place in industries as much as anywhere else as he and I both worked on the loom building team. Eventually, and through no overt influence on my part he and Archie stopped bothering with their prayer meetings, and when I asked Archie why, he told me that 'they just tell too many lies', 'they' of course being organised religion. He then left me with a quote that summed up exactly how I felt about my project when he said, '*Howard, keep doing what you're doing because there's one thing about the truth, people might reject it, but they'll never be able to refute it.*' I thought it was a great saying and I've used those words so many times since then that I've lost count.

11

One topic I find truly fascinating is racism. The notion that any ethnic group should consider themselves superior to another because of their skin tone or culture is the most comical of delusions. I know that in reality it is a serious and always ugly subject, but I've got to be honest, when I listen to the rants of some far right extremists I laugh so much it makes my belly hurt.

I remember an article written by the Daily Mirror columnist Tony Parsons on the subject which asked the question, 'Which white man could look at Muhammad Ali in his prime and hand on heart say that he was superior to him?' Unanimously voted the greatest athlete of the 20th century, the young Ali had the good looks, physique, and athleticism of an Olympian god and for a man that had little formal education was acknowledged by many academics as having one of the sharpest minds they had ever encountered. In fact, the author and journalist, George Plimpton, lobbied for one of his quips to be officially credited as being the shortest poem on record. It never happened.

The poem currently credited with this distinction is one that I love because to my mind it sums up my current focus perfectly. It is called *Lines on the Antiquity of Microbes* and is generally thought to have been penned by the American poet Strickland Gillilan. It reads:

Adam
Had 'em.

Personally, I've a suspicion this clever little ode is about a lot
more than tiny organisms, or *Fleas*, which is its alternative title,
as it aptly describes the effect of organised religion on the minds
of believers. Still, I digress. While visiting Oxford University
during the height of the American Civil Rights issue Ali was
asked to recite one of his famous off-the-cuff rhymes by the
attending group of excited students. He thought for a moment,
raised his arms, and said:

Me...We.

Tony Parsons could hardly have picked a better example to
make his point and it seems George Plimpton had a strong case
too.

I take the same stance on the racial issue with black people
who espouse this supremacy nonsense. Wladimir Klitschko, the
world heavyweight boxing champion, whose elder brother,
Vitali, gave Lennox Lewis such a fright in his final world heavyweight title defence is just shy of six feet seven inches tall and
has a physique that would give Bruce Lee a run for his money.
Not to mention the fact that he's movie star handsome, fluent
in five languages, and has a doctorate in sports science. I do not
know of any black man that could try to convince me he is
superior to this Ukrainian superman without me rolling around
in laughter. (In 2002 the Klitschko brothers were selected to
work specifically for the UNESCO [the United Nations
Educational, Scientific and Cultural Organization] which
supports more than 180 projects in 87 countries).

If you are a winner of the genetic lottery, as Messrs Ali,
Klitschko, and many others of both sexes and every ethnic
group have been, it does not make you superior to other
humans, you're just lucky. Superior is all about behaviour,
which means that sometimes we are all at the top, and equally,

all slide down and around in the barrel when the mood takes us. I remember being shown around his lovely house many years ago by a well-heeled middle-class Englishman, Stan Ball, who said to me as I took in his success, '*Howard, in spite of all this I realise I'm no better than anyone else,... but no one is better than me either.*' I think that goes for us all.

Sadly, in spite of the fact that most honest people are aware of its stupidity, ethnic division and animosity, mostly due to ignorance, religion, and the migration of peoples, is on the up worldwide.

Being aware of this madness is one of the reasons I've always thought sport is so important. It is a massive barrier breaker. One of the joys that I really got out of my martial arts career was in watching trainers in the corners of their protégés as they went out to fight. On many occasions I've watched black fighters with white coaches facing white fighters with black coaches as they've slugged it out in the ring, and the only thing their trainers wanted was for their charge to win, and boy do they get emotional. I've always found a real beauty in that, it is racism totally abandoned. So when the medical bodies talk about wanting to ban contact sports I wonder if they have truly analysed the many social, psychological, and fraternal plusses that such competition brings. I doubt it.

Unsurprisingly I have found that the one form of bigotry that as a black male I have come to express a minority opinion upon is homosexuality. There is no beating around the bush, the black community as a whole is extremely homophobic. So much so that homosexuals are considered to be less socially acceptable than rapists, murderers, and in some cases, paedophiles. This antagonism, once again, is borne from the edicts of the holy books, and emboldens the adage that 'there is no arrogance like religious arrogance'. To tell consenting adults that they are 'evil' for expressing love, just because of an ancient and warped philosophy, if one can indeed classify it as such as there is little reasoning, substantiation, or any form of objective debate on the matter, is dictatorship in its most basic form.

The religious bondage that this bigoted belief yields is both sad and deplorable. Metaphorically speaking it often gives birth to children that will do anything to get free, this is quite simply because the offspring of repression is rebellion. It is like encasing them in cloth from head to toe and being surprised that they struggle because they need to breathe. The more tightly they are bound the more they will resist, damaging the cloth, and perhaps themselves in the process. (I use the analogy of the 'cloth' intentionally!) Those that settle for a life in their confinement will suffer in silence or with minimum protest, maybe even becoming convinced that their prison is a comfortable haven and shouting to others in the same predicament to stay put as at least the bag is safe and warm. The truth however, is that their enclosure limits growth, respiration, and vision. It is this experience that is abnormal, not one human loving another, and it is a repression that inflicts bruising and wounds that require both time and therapy to heal.

In fact, the psychological damage is such that many who have seemingly escaped this cerebral prison re-seek its confinement at a later date as their consciences struggle with the concept of real freedom. In other words they turn their back on what really makes them happy to return to the life and falsehood of pleasing others. I know of several homosexuals in religious subservience who struggle to fulfil a life based upon indoctrination, denying themselves companionship and love as a consequence. They are martyrs to their own happiness and I feel for them. They would do well to remember that life is neither a rehearsal nor a popularity contest.

The attack on 'men who lie with men' in the New Testament may well be a comment about the openly gay conduct of many men of that time, but in particular was a warning to the emerging Christian priesthood, who in undermining the female power encouraged men to remain single in their pursuit of godliness. Their paranoia was self-inflicted as living amongst and travelling in almost exclusively male groups to spread this new dogma nurtured the very temptation that the Bible strives so ardently to condemn. Anyone doubting this would be wise to note that the Greek scriptures do not issue a single word of disapproval about lesbian relationships. The hypocrisy and mean-mindedness of the situation needs no underlining.

That black society abhors homosexuality so vehemently is one of the world's greatest ironies, for the debt that it owes to feeling people is immense, and no truly objective person would doubt that the gay community is one of the most feeling of all. At the forefront of both the abolition of slavery and the American civil rights movement of the 1960's were many gay people who lent both their voices and physical liberty to the cause of human rights. In light of this, especially as a black person, I would feel embarrassed to persecute them as a minority group, their sexual orientation is their business and my attitude is simple, live and let live.

It was pleasing to note that the gay guys on the main population units at Rye Hill were treated the same as everyone else, and discussed their love lives quite openly, I certainly did not hear of any bullying or harassment. There were incidents of one or two gay clinches in the showers, and indeed in cells, between inmates who had decided to start a relationship, which were met with the same amount of scandal and gossip as when some lads were caught out with female officers. Modern adult jails have moved with the times and respect for another inmates space, whatever their sexual preference, is part of prison protocol.

I have had several friends and acquaintances over the years, both black and white, whom I have suspected of being gay or at least having homosexual tendencies but this has never been confirmed so maybe I am wrong, but I hate to think that by confiding in me they thought they would have lost either my respect or my friendship. In fact the opposite would have been true, such confidential revelations would have flattered me and I would have been honoured to think that they held me in such high regard as to confide their secret.

While right-wing religion continues to condemn gay behaviour as inhuman, it cannot be neglected that the slavery of the African nation was imposed and maintained by a Christian majority who vigorously fought for a 'God-given right' to own and bequeath another person. The hypocrisy of religion and politics is indeed boundless. Their interpretation of a biblical curse placed on of one of Noah's children was their justification for this inhumanity, so is it any wonder that the proof that Noah's existence can be easily demonstrated as fictional was kept hidden from the masses? This is compounded by the fact that the Bible record is littered with the concept of human slavery, condoning it in both the Old and New Testament. These documents make it clear that the Hebrew God and the Christian messiah are supporters of this abominable principle, which if one has any background knowledge of the texts, is not a surprising stance. (Not to be outdone, the Koran dictates that women will continue in servitude in the afterlife).

In this regard, interpretations of the holy books as the words and edicts of a supreme God have much to answer for. But such an argument is purely semantic for this God has never been proven to impose his will, it is only pious, indoctrinated, and corrupt men that have done it for him.

As far as my life is concerned I have never really encountered much blatant colour prejudice. I remember walking through Birmingham city centre once when I was about thirteen years old and a policeman called me a black bastard for no reason whatsoever. I couldn't believe my ears, but I just ignored him and carried on walking, but from all later experiences I have to say that was an abnormal occurrence. My arrest for the charge on which I was convicted highlighted behaviour at the other end of the spectrum, the police could not have been any more polite and accommodating. Ok, I was a sporting hero in my home town, but even so, I think that there has been some growth in attitudes over the years, and combating racism is all about that, education and growth, whether it be personal, institutional, or social.

I also find it quite fascinating that I know black, white, and Asian people who remind me of each other, sometimes this is in physical appearance and mannerisms, sometimes character, and sometimes habits. People are people, period, and with the world getting smaller, so to speak, we had all better get used to it.

Now and again I've been privy to groups of black guys talking about the white man this and the white man that, the kind of generalised talk that one can easily get sucked in to, and I would honestly state that I agree with them in terms of the behaviour of certain people, and indeed, the establishment. But I have white friends that are like brothers to me and at the same time some black guys that I cannot stand the sight of, so to my mind it is all about the heart and intent, a case that I always state when debating the issue. In such situations ninety-nine per cent of guys present would agree with that logic, not everyone though, because you always get the odd jerk, but it was heartening to observe that I was not the only one to make the points that I did.

While on this subject it is interesting to note a major irony that is rarely mentioned by opponents of racism in western countries, and it is that colour prejudice is also endemic within the sub-strata of many black societies.

In countries like Cuba, Brazil, India, Pakistan, Mexico, and until the civil rights era, America and the West Indies, lighter complexioned 'people of colour' would always get the best jobs. For a darker-skinned person to excel he or she would have to do so in the traditionally accepted fields of sport and entertainment, in line with accepted stereotypes. To try and do so in a business, literary, or scientific field would be frowned upon and actively discouraged, and sadly, sometimes violently, and yet these cultures are quick to point the finger at European countries and accuse then of various inhumanities. They have a point but they had better acknowledge and clean up their own act too.

I was at Rye Hill for some time before an undercurrent of racism came to my attention, I had heard rumours that certain officers were ex-members of the British National Party, a far-right minority political group, but did not pay it much attention as I knew the officers concerned and to say that they were at the lower end of the social spectrum is to flatter them. The issue that brought it to light was something much closer to home, gun crime in the area that I was born and raised in, Handsworth.

I was discussing the issue of parole with one of the younger black inmates on Carling unit and asked him how he thought he would fare when his parole answer, which was due shortly, came back. He quickly replied, *'No chance!'* He was so firm in his retort that I asked him how he could be so certain when the granting of release at the halfway point of your sentence seemed a lottery, and just like sentencing for the crime itself there was no apparent parity in its application. People guilty of the same offence under similar circumstances can receive wildly different punishments dependent it seems upon where they are sentenced and the attitude of the sentencing judge. The lad in question answered me succinctly, *'Too many gun charges blood!'*

When we first met I asked him his name to which he replied *'13'*, I asked him what his real name was and he replied it was Yohanne, I told him I was going to call him by that name instead of his street one as I thought it was already pretty distinctive, and as far as I knew I was the only person on the unit that ever addressed him that way. We got on well, very well, and he had a respect for me that belied his street credibility. Raised in a Christian household he was fascinated by the amount of time and effort that I was putting into my project and like many others often came to my cell to discuss the merits of religion and learn more about the history of what so many take to be literal truths. I think what intrigued him more than all, like it did many guys, was my manner, especially after they had seen me get involved in some serious sparring sessions in the gym. I told him that I had learned that it was best to be as rounded as possible and not to neglect the brain in muscle building workouts. I noted that he always listened intently before making comment, which when they were voiced showed a keen brain, and watching him interact with other inmates, there was no doubt that Yohanne was leadership material.

He was athletic too. He turned up to one of my boxing classes and picked up the basic stance, footwork, and guard effortlessly. I told him that he was a natural and should consider taking up the noble art as a serious hobby. He smiled but never came back to the classes preferring to lift weights during his gym session instead. I guess he figured that boxing wouldn't be too much use to him on the outside. He was right.

When his parole answer came through as positive he made a point of telling me that I was correct in my assessment after all, and it is a mark of how pleasant a lad he was that the whole unit was not only happy for him, but also concerned. His street reputation, and just as pointedly, that of his enemies, was common knowledge, and make no mistake, in a given situation, this was one very dangerous kid.

Yohanne was as enterprising as he was bright, and admirably decided that he was going to become an events promoter upon his release and turn his back on crime. The guys that specialised in graphic design in the prisons computer unit were going to handle all the ticket, poster, and leaflet artwork for his gigs, and he put together a professional ensemble of celebrities from the singing and comedy world for an entertainment event that was to held at a respected venue in Birmingham known as the Tower Ballroom. It is actually the last arena that I ever competed at as a professional kickboxer when I knocked out Italian Champion, Michael Baldasarre in the fourth round of my final world title defence.

Yohanne's 'Christmas Comedy Explosion' was a big talking point within the prison and it seemed certain that he was going to be off to a profitable start in his new career as the owner of the fatefully named 'Dynamite Entertainment' as tickets were selling well and many inmates had relatives that were attending. It was not to be. He was shot six times, twice in the head, while he sat unarmed in his Mercedes car on the West Bromwich High Street exactly three weeks before the planned event. Like me, Yohanne was also born and bred in Handsworth, dying the proverbial stone's throw away from where Bob Hazel had honed his soccer skills. He was 24 years old.

His killers, members of a rival gang known as The Johnson Crew, pulled up alongside him in a black BMW and exacted what they considered to be revenge for the slaying of one of their own just a few years previously.

In March 2000, a member of the Johnson gang, Christopher Clarke, was brutally stabbed to death and Yohanne was charged with his murder. The charges were dropped due to a lack of evidence.

As we know, it is an accepted principle of philosophy that violence is self-perpetuating and the retaliation for '13's' death was one of the most tragic events in the history of the Handsworth community. Yohanne belonged to an outfit known as The Burger Bar Crew, a name stemming from the café bar that the group used to frequent in the days of their formation. Both the Burgers and the Johnsons have grown in numbers, stature, and ruthlessness over the years, and the cause of their rivalry, now enshrouded in the mists of urban legend, seems almost irrelevant to the enmity currently displayed by the newest players. As the situation being outlined now aptly demonstrates, they have their own new and ongoing beefs.

Nathan Martin, a.k.a. '23', Yohanne's older brother as well as a Burger Bar member, was never going to let the matter of his sibling's death rest in the hands of the police, he felt the same fury that the relatives of Christopher Clarke did when he was murdered, and so the cycle continued. '23's' weapon of choice to square matters? A sub-machine gun.

The Mac 10 isn't really a machine gun, it's more of a machine pistol. Designed by the American weapons manufacturer Gordon B Ingram in the 1970's it soon set its mark as the most reliable weapon of its type in the world and embodied a technological spirit that has gathered pace throughout the world of science, smaller is better.

The attractiveness of the machine, its compactness and high rate of fire at one thousand rounds per minute, is also its downfall, as it is extremely difficult to control. As a result it only saw limited demand from the military, with only specialised and highly trained units taking it on board. Yet somehow this and other extreme weapons have repeatedly found their way into the urban areas of Great Britain.

Rumour has it that the shedding of weapons by the IRA and other para-military groups during the late-nineties and turn of the millennium in the run-up to decommissioning, led to an influx of guns to be bought and sold for profit both alongside and within the illegal drugs market. With the cheapness and ready availability of such weapons throughout the country the commercial implication is that the numbers on offer must have been vast.

The deaths of two innocent girls having a night of fun, were to drive this assumption home. For Charlene Ellis and Letisha Shakespeare, both Handsworth girls, their celebration of the 2003 New Year was to be their last. They were mown down in a hail of bullets sprayed by a Mac 10 as they stood outside a party hosted at the Uniseven Salon in Aston, Birmingham. Two of their friends, Sophie Ellis and Cheryl Shaw were also wounded, but survived the onslaught.

The ironies in this story bear out the amateurishness, immaturity, and ruthlessness of gang-culture, and provide a back-drop worthy of the most talented storytellers.

Nathan Martin, Michael Gregory, Rodrigo Simms, and Marcus Ellis, were all found guilty of the crime. They were charged and tried for murder under the legal grounds of 'transferred malice'. The reason for the use of this legal application? They clearly did not intend to kill Charlene and Letisha, but instead a member of the Johnson Crew, one Jermaine Carty, who was also present at the same party. They missed him completely. Under standard legal practice they could have been charged with the less severe offence of manslaughter, i.e. accidental murder. But their intent was clear, they meant to kill, and kill they did, and in the eyes of British justice the issue of who the victims were, was beside the point.

That they took a Mac 10, a weapon that they had no experience of using, to a crowded venue to eliminate a single foe, when even the best trained soldiers in the world would never have attempted such a feat. That they thought that they acted in a professional manner in the planning of this atrocity. That they thought that they would never be punished for such a crime, even if they were successful in their original intentions. That they thought that they were morally justified in their intent, show the truth. That this was all sheer lunacy, and of dramatically tragic proportions. '13' had been assassinated as he sought to turn his back on this life, in an ill-judged act of vengeance his brother had now also sacrificed his own future, and those of his closest friends, as they will almost certainly spend much, and possibly all, of the remainder of their lives behind bars. And to add to this catalogue of misery, in a final twist of fate, one of the gunmen, Marcus Ellis, had also taken part in the murder of his own flesh and blood. Charlene Ellis was his half-sister. Letisha's surname notwithstanding, his Christian name, and that of young Sims are truly portentous, for the word Shakespearean could not apply to a saga more fittingly

I mourn Yohanne Martin's death, because I knew him. Had I known Christopher Clarke, I would probably feel the same way, for it is my experience that when outside of the macho gang culture, many of these young men are fun, polite, and respectful. However, when they catch sight of each other, it is like a meeting of pit bull terriers, and their ire is raised to such a pitch of uncontrolled fury and emotion that it makes them unrecognisable. The contrast between their normal behaviour and the one exhibited when amongst their peers is immense. This is aptly illustrated by the reaction of one of Yohanne's elderly white neighbours who was both stunned and saddened by his death. Why? He used to help her bring her shopping in.

Great Britain is gripped and understandably wary of this new Hollywood-style violence being perpetrated within the heart of its major cities, and unless extremely punitive measures are employed on a wide and sustained basis, it will see a lot more.

The reaction at Rye Hill to the death of the girls was primarily one of shock and it surprised me to hear that there were celebrations taking place on Farley unit. Apparently a small group of white convicts ran through the wing shouting 'Hurray, Hurray, the nigger bitches are dead', and other slogans to that effect. I was quite surprised for several reasons. The first is that there were quite a few black inmates on every unit and I wondered what the reaction of those resident on Farley was to this nonsense. It seems that for some reason it was quite muted. The second is that girls are normally exempt from such antagonism, especially to villains, who do not normally see women and children as fair game. So in the minds of many inmates, both black and white, this behaviour was below the belt. The third was that one of the guys that took part in the carousing was a guy called Buzz, someone who I had previously thought to be a pretty amiable guy.

Buzz was a big lad, about six feet two and two hundred and twenty pounds, he was shaven-headed, the old mark of the racist, but one that does not necessarily carry the same meaning today as it is also a fashion statement. I met him in the gym when he used to attend the open boxing sessions and we sparred once or twice. He used to box himself, not to a high standard but he was too big and too good for many of the inmates that were having their first foray into the sport. Buzz was in that no-man's land where he was also not quite good enough to have real rumble with the experienced lads and when I sparred with him I bore this in mind. He commented when we first put the gloves on that he did not want to get embarrassed by being knocked out by someone half his size. With my sense of fair-play that was never going to happen unless he started to take liberties and throw cheap shots while I was taking it easy with him. He was not that brave or that stupid, and although I made it clear in our sessions that I was the boss, I purposely avoided embarrassing him at the same time. After the reports of his racist behaviour I wished that I had not been so civil.

It is not the first time in my life that I have totally misjudged someone's character, and I am sure that it will not be the last, but I am also well aware that I cannot take it as a premise to judge matters of racism either. What am I to do, assume that everyone of Buzz's description is a racist and treat them aggressively? It would not only be out of character, but would also be a major step backward in my evolution as a person. I don't remember seeing Buzz again after the incident, and I surely did not speak to him, but if I had seen him, no matter who he was with I simply would have said 'Buzz, I heard about the episode on your unit the other day and I have to say I'm surprised, I thought you were bigger than that?' It would have been fun watching him squirm and it's what I like about the fact that I am well trained in both the practice of violence and its psychology. I get to speak my mind.

On the subject of racism I used to enjoy telling various vicars and priests, while in front of an audience, that Jesus was a racist. It's one of those one-liners I like that gets a reaction out of everyone, whether they are believers or not.

One first has to be familiar with the concept that all ancient messiahs were sent to the earth to rescue a particular race of people, and it is only later in the gospel writings, a blatant tampering, that his mission changes to accommodate people of all nations. Jesus' initial task was to make the Hebrew people believe in both him and the revised teachings of their God, Yahweh, in order for them to achieve salvation. No other race counted.

This is highlighted in a gospel story where a non-Hebrew woman, she is either a Canaanite, or Greek of Syro-Phoenician origin, depending upon which of the gospel accounts you prefer, asks him to perform an exorcism on her daughter, he abruptly tells her that he was only sent to the *'lost sheep of the House of Israel'*, as in keeping with the nature of an ancient saviour. She persists and begins to worship him and yet he retorts even more strongly with the abhorrent and blatantly racist statement, *'It is not good to take the children's bread and throw it to the little dogs.'* Confirming that her standing in his eyes was even less than human. She is admirably relentless in her pursuit of his favour so he concedes and grants her wish.

It should be noted that even today a line in an orthodox Jewish morning prayer states, *'Blessed be God King of the universe that Thou has not made me a woman.'* This narrow-minded nonsense is amplified by a verse in another popular Jewish prayer, *'Praised be God that he has not created me a gentile. Praised be God that he has not created me a woman.*

Praised be God that he has not created me an ignoramus.' I fail
to see how the latter of these statements can logically be used
in conjunction with the other two which are bigotry exempli-
fied, but the point is that the prevailing view of orthodox
Judaism is both racist and sexist, and in this light why should
we be surprised that the 'king of the Jews' displayed both
tendencies.

Obviously, as the need for the Hebrew stories to be taken
on by the wider Roman world became a necessity this attitude
had to change, and by the book of Acts, the narrative following
the gospel stories, Jesus is portrayed as a fully-fledged humani-
tarian.

Yet taken in context the inclusion of this tale should not in
itself be unexpected, for it is essentially a Hebrew one, meant
originally to bolster the self-worth of the Hebrew people. Only
the fact that it was allowed to remain within the gospel texts at
a later date should be considered a surprise.

Propagators of the holy books make the claim that the
Hebrew supreme God is a being of pure love, and the term
'unconditional love' is often used to describe his benevolence
and that of his son, the messiah. Yet the fact is that nothing
could be further from the truth.

The gods of these tomes never express unconditional love.
Conditions are the main keys to the success of organised
religion and the kindness of their deities must therefore come at
a price. The first and foremost being that you have to believe in
them, otherwise they promise to make you suffer, and in some
horrific way, before condemning you to death. This flawed
feature does not reflect absolute power but instead absolute
insecurity, and is one that is in direct contrast to their claims of
omnipotence. The truly all-powerful, and all-loving, would not
be so churlish as to care whether you believed in them or not.
These rules of engagement pile up to such an extent that they
can only be described as psychological blackmail, enforcing an
imaginary grip on the believing mind, that billions struggle to
break free from for fear of supposed eternal damnation, peer
pressure, and sadly, physical violence.

The reasons that they were imposed vary due to various cultural and political factors, but ultimately it was to maintain social control of the masses. The Old Testament was compiled to create a new nation for the Hebrews, the New Testament to bring cohesion to a fragmenting Roman Empire, and the Koran to convince and motivate the Arab peoples to assist the Romans in their war against the resurgent Persian forces. All succeeded in their design, to such an extent that similar ancient material is considered myth while they are regarded as fact.

I have pointed out my realisation that all ancient writings can only be seriously reviewed if considered against the background of their period of construction, and so, knowledge of the relative history, politics, mind-set, and traditions of the time are essential in trying to make any sense of them. This part of my opus was going well but there were other areas to consider.

I therefore also decided to analyse the forecasts of the doomsday-mongers, who claim that the end of the world will be at hand when the prophecies of the Bible and Koran are played out, and found that in a sense, they are right.

These prophecies talk of numerous earthquakes, pestilences, persecution, famine, international war, and family feuds in the run up to a divinely wrought Armageddon. The fact is that these signs of doom have actually occurred time and time again since their prediction and yet we are all still here, so we need to ask the question, do we need to use other common denominators to pinpoint both their fruition and their true meaning?

Let us remember that they were written for people who expected to see these forecasts completed within their own life-times, or certainly that of their children. So could it be that the end of the world has already taken place? The term used to pinpoint what it is that will end is the Greek word 'Aeon', which does not mean 'world' but refers to an 'age'. The term 'age' is one that relates to a specific, but un-exact period of time governed by the movement of the astrological houses and their effect upon the planet earth. How the ancients came to compute these time-scales and their effects on the planet is not only mysterious but mind-boggling, like many of their achievements.

As most people know there are twelve astrological houses based upon the astronomy of the planets, and in common perception they rotate in a yearly cycle. They also host another calendar, a precessional one that is not determined by the earth's yearly conjunction with the sun and the moon, but by the more intricate changes in its elliptical orbit as it revolves on its axis. These take thousands of years to complete, in fact almost 23,000.

These periods, like their more common annual divisions, are also divided into 12 sections, being of roughly 2,200 years each, which are known by the same names as the yearly ones. Thus we are now firmly moving into the 'age' of Aquarius, the 'water-bearer', having just left, or possibly still at the tail end of the age of Pisces, the 'fish'. This may seem like mythical nonsense but these 'ages' may actually have a scientific value.

The Age of Aquarius may well be known as the 'water-bearer' because it refers to the presence of more water on the planet, caused by naturally higher weather temperatures and the increased melting of ice-caps that the additional heat would bring. Because these 'precessional cycles', as they are known, are predictable, many scientists argue that global-warming is a natural occurrence and that man has not caused it, but added to it, hence the extra danger. A definite conclusion may or may not be reached in that debate, but what is certain is that to some degree the earth was heating up anyway. With the temperature and climate changes caused by precession also come various shifts in geological activity as the earth adjusts to its new position and the changes in heat and cold on different parts of its body. Hence the unexpected and extreme changes in weather and natural disasters. Is it this that the holy books were outlining?

Let us consider that the impending doom of a divine Armageddon is stressed as being unknowable, and guaranteed to strike when least expected. The gospels state that it is known by no-one save the supreme God himself, the architect of the universe, and in the Christian canon not even Jesus knew it. Which rather complicates the early Church's version of the three-gods-in-one doctrine if Jesus and his father are essentially the same being. (As I have already pointed out we only need to be aware of the original trinity of the Egyptian belief system to comprehend the true nature of this dogma).

This mystery of the 'end-of-days' is interesting because from an astrological perspective the transition of the Ages is in fact incalculable. No one can predict the exact day, or even year in which a change is complete, the shift is too gradual and complex. It is like colours fading into each other and to date has proven too difficult for astronomers to pinpoint.

I noted that the astronomical and astrological interests of the biblical writers was intense and their constant use of numerology in the texts seems quite likely to have been for this reason. The only question about the biblical Armageddon is whether it was meant in application to the change from Leo to Pisces, that is during the beginning of the new millennium AD, or for those of us alive today from Pisces to Aquarius, or maybe even both.

One thing is for sure, it has nothing to do with some catastrophic end-of-the-world scenario specifically aimed at the 'ungodly'. If the very large dormant volcanoes on this planet decide to erupt, or a huge meteor shower strikes the planet as they have in the distant past, then we're all going to be wiped out, believers or not. Until such time we will no doubt continue to be our own worst enemy.

Just to clarify my perspective on this matter, I felt it was also necessary to consider the identity of one of the Bible's chief doomsday-mongers, the messiah, and why he was so vital to the New Testament texts. The question of his existence is a highly emotive subject and certainly one that cannot be discussed lightly, and it is for that reason that I spent much time and energy, trying constantly to be as objective as possible, before reaching what I found to be an inescapable conclusion.

12

My stance on religion is not an inverted evangelicalism, in fact, after these books are published I don't mind if I never, ever, discuss the subject again. The whole purpose of writing *Rulers & Lies* was to spread some factual background information in a '*did you guys know about this?*' fashion. My research was topical for its time and just as much so for my predicament. Religion is a big issue in prison, mainly due to the fact that so many people of so many different beliefs are living in such close proximity to each other. That is why so many guys who were fed up with being bombarded with appeals for conversion used me to deflect such attention. I was an anomaly, but a popular one.

There is certainly nothing wrong with anyone depending upon a religious belief to get them through this journey called life, my only beef comes when it is rammed down your throat as a necessity by people who are indoctrinated, pious, ill-informed, or even worse, have their own hidden agenda. My feelings are augmented when this leads to violence, cruelty, and ill-feeling, or as is usual enters the realm of politics. And so I felt it necessary, especially as I had the time, to point out the flaws I had spotted in the major worship systems just to take a little shine off their piety, to make them think twice before acting so self-righteously in that superior 'we're-so-humble-but-right' approach that impresses so many people. The biggest contradiction of all is that this behaviour is magnified, excuse the term, to high heaven, when law-breakers are incarcerated, with Christians and Muslims by far the worst culprits.

So you can forgive my mirth when one of the vicars at Rye Hill was escorted off the premises when it was discovered that he was giving fellatio sexual favours to inmates on the vulnerable prisoners unit. The term 'vulnerable prisoners' is the one used to describe inmates that have to be segregated from the mainstream offenders due to the nature of their crimes. They are not all sexual offenders, and some are there because they owe money to serious men on the main wings and have to hide out, or are ex-law officers such as policemen and judges. However, on the whole these units are reserved for child-killers, rapists, and paedophiles, and are so dreary that many of these offenders often begin their sentences hidden amongst the mainstream population while telling other inmates that they have been locked up for drug dealing or some other more socially acceptable offence. Inevitably the lie is eventually found out and they are escorted post-haste for safety reasons to either the VP block or to another facility to begin their facade again.

Prison officers are taught that these inmates are not criminals, but patients, and should be treated as such. They are thus extended privileges and courtesies that are denied to the bulk of offenders. As liberal as I am, I cannot bring myself to agree with the kid-gloves treatment that they are given, especially as the nature of some of their crimes is truly despicable. My attitude towards rapists and paedophiles makes me wonder if it is me that is inhuman, for the punishment I would mete out in cases proven beyond any doubt would be truly horrendous. Very few would be shown leniency on the grounds of diminished responsibility. And there lies the rub, how do we decide if someone is truly guilty, not beyond reasonable doubt, but beyond any doubt?

Assumptions, which are in many instances the only way to decide such matters, are a precarious business. As a result I have seen and heard of men issued with summary prison justice when they were truly innocent, and so I could never be party to any form of vigilante retribution.

It is hard to separate urban legend from the truth, but one of the most popular prison tales is of a convicted rapist who refused to be housed in his facilities segregation unit. He did not invent some other reason for his presence in the jail, and told all concerned that his charge was rape adding that he was innocent and would not be confined with the VP's. He was warned by several inmates to leave their wing, but remained resolute in his protests. He was given a 'Mars Bar' for his stoicism, the cockney rhyming slang term for a facial scar, inflicted with a makeshift razor that ran the entire length of his cheekbone, marking him out as what he allegedly was, a sexual deviant. He was moved from that unit for his own safety but still adamantly refused to be put onto a segregation block.

I wonder how those that inflicted his punishment reacted upon his release when his alleged victim confessed that he was in fact an innocent man? With some serious soul-searching I hope. Knowing the mentality of many inmates I have little reason to doubt the veracity of this particular story, for if it is not true, then there will certainly be ones similar to it that are.

Without a doubt, being accused of something that you have not done is a horrible feeling, and sometimes the more you protest, the more guilty you appear to be. To be punished and scorned on the basis of such an accusation only adds to the trauma, and in the case of the latter story, the innuendo is life-long, mud sticks as they say, and no amount of compensation can truly heal the family, psychological, and social damage that is suffered. The compassion that is felt by many for such a wronged individual is only matched by the amount of hypocrites ready to claim that they believed he or she was innocent all along. Nevertheless, we have all at some time been in a similar predicament, and so our empathy is both natural and profound.

The essence of the latter tale is one of the ingredients that makes the story of the Christian messiah the most compelling ever told, the tale of a god, coming to earth as a man, to be rejected, despised, tortured, and killed for a crime that he did not commit. In light of the human psyche it could not have been woven more magnificently, but perhaps a little more smoothly.

The relationship between the Old and the New Testament is not without contradiction, and indeed there are many prophecies and accounts that are at odds with each other, even though Christianity does its level best to explain these differences, it cannot. A square peg does not into a round hole go. One of the most glaring, important, and perhaps the most revealing of these irregularities is the name of the expected messiah of the Hebrew people. In the older text his name was foretold to be Emmanuel, a detail acknowledged in the gospels, and yet without any further ado he was given the name Jesus for a motive that is not explained, just merely accepted. The reason for this silence is because the answer is a magic trick, cleverly deceptive in its simplicity, and we must delve into the history of that time to see why it was necessary.

The turbulence within the Roman Empire that led to the rise of Islam in the seventh century AD had begun much earlier, and the beginning of the third century saw more than twenty emperors come and go within a fifty year period in their bid to quell various uprisings and maintain internal stability.

Eventually the soldier-emperor Aurelian succeeded in reorganising the Roman military forces and managed to stabilise the eastern region, but this did not complete his task and there was still much work left to be done if empirical fragmentation was to be stemmed. As much through wisdom and negotiation as through physical might Aurelian also secured the west of the empire and brought a stability back to Rome that was to last for almost two centuries.

He was not the first to recognise that a unity of minds was the key to equilibrium and as a sun-god worshipper who venerated the then main Roman deity 'sol', he pursued the philosophy of 'one god, one empire' by propagating his god to all and sundry. Quite astutely he refrained from persecuting non-believers for maintaining their former religious beliefs and instead tried to woo them through tact and diplomacy, arguing with some success, that they could adopt his one-god without betraying their own. This policy was continued in part by the emperor Diocletian, and further maintained by the ruler that entrenched Christianity upon the world, Constantine.

Unlike Aurelian, Diocletian was not so liberal with those that did not follow the one-god principle, and he mercilessly persecuted those that did not believe in his creed, singling out the Christians in particular. A point which they have played on ever since, while conveniently neglecting to mention their own historical intolerance and the gruesome retribution they exacted for this period of suffering.

Diocletian, like his predecessor, was also a military emperor, a trend which existed simply because it put the Roman people, who were constantly under the self-inflicted threat of invasion, at psychological ease. Better to have a guard dog as their leader than a diplomat. With the election of Constantine they were not disappointed.

At the time of his succession, the empire was home to many cults spawned by the nations that it had conquered. Judea, the home of the Jewish people, was among them. Many of the Jews had by now become Hellenized, a term that meant that they had in some measure succumbed to Greek influences, and a number of them had even become Christians.

The Greek effect on the ancient world began with the conquests of Alexander the Great in 333 B.C. and even after that empire's fall to the Romans it continued. The new rulers adopted Greek gods and practices just as much as everyone else. To be Greek in attitude and philosophy was to be considered educated and civilized, a trend that was popularly aspired to.

Many cities within the Roman Empire were cosmopolitan in nature and outlook and its capital city was home to a hotch-potch of travelling and resettling peoples. Amongst these were the Jews of the Diaspora, the mass dispersion that followed the Roman destruction of the Temple of Jerusalem in 70 AD. They traded and lived in Rome itself for centuries and took readily to the fact that a Jewish born god, Jesus, was being worshipped by foreigners. This new god preached the laws of their forefathers and observed the rites of their national religion, his bloodline enhancing their feeling of superiority as God's chosen people. Their affinity to him was quite explicable, but what explained the loyalty of the Greeks and the other nations that also took to this growing cult called Christianity?

The Greek religion was based heavily upon the canon of the Egyptian deities such as Asaru, Aset, and Haru, who had been renamed as Osiris, Isis, and Horus respectively, and formed the Father, the Mother, and the only begotten son. In the Egyptian system Horus became Osiris upon his death and rebirth, thus he was the image of both 'Father-and-Son'.

The Greeks also retained a religious independence of sorts with their reverence of Zeus, a sky-god who, as was the norm, adopted the traits of deities from other lands, and as ruler of the sky was seen by both the Greeks and the Romans as the supreme god. To ask the followers of Zeus to rally behind a Hebrew god named Emmanuel would have been an impossible mission. But to ask them to support a god who was all things to all people, might appeal to their intellect, especially if it could be shown that he and their own ancient deity were one and the same.

It was out of this need for cultural cohesion within the empire that a merger of gods again took place, when the Old Testament Yahweh and the Greek supreme deity were united into a super-God, a messiah named 'Yah-Zeus', who would be both Father and son at the same time. A saviour called Emmanuel would never have achieved the required effect, one called Je-sus would. The expansion of this name into the title 'Jesus the Christ' or more correctly 'Yah-Zeus the Krishna', only serves to confirm the true origin of this political construct. *(This titular merger appears to have taken place once before in Hebrew history with the invention of the Old Testament sun-god Joshua, [a Hebrew variant on the name Jesus], who actually made the sun stop in its orbit around the earth. Like many before and indeed after them, the early Hebrews were unaware that the sun remains at a fixed point within the galaxy).*

Let us not be fooled by the apparent simplicity of this religio-political spin, for the Christian messiah was well constructed and continued to embody much of the esoteric thought of the ancients. He and his mother were most reminiscent of the Egyptian Madonna and child, Isis and Horus, and early church depictions featured the holy duo with the iconography of their older proto-types, which included the sign of the sun, the halo, in deference to their true origin. The goddess Isis was worshipped as both a virgin and a mother, although the Egyptians did not claim that she was both at the same time as in their minds such an assertion would have been nonsensical. The Christian dogma went one step further in this area as well as others in denunciation of its true origins, and the prudery of Mary as a Virgin Mother, and Jesus' own dismissal of her importance in the gospel accounts, paved the way for the misogynistic attitude of the Roman church and its protestant offspring.

Horus, the original son-of-god saviour, was the sun on the horizon, and it is this image that yielded the story of Jesus 'walking on water' just as the solar body appears to do every day. The Christian messiah was not so much the 'Son of Man' as he is shown to so often refer to himself in the gospels, but the '*Sun* of Man', and his Father, the Hebrew supreme God Yahweh, was already long revered as the Aten, or 'Most High', the sun at its mid-day peak.

The vastness of the Roman Empire meant that the leaders of its subject nations had to be assisted in the application of this indoctrination as well as the appeasement of their peoples, a feat that was performed using a variety of methods. Physical force was used with discretion as a first and last resort for two main reasons. It caused the necessary trauma to show its victims that their own gods were powerless and had deserted them, and also left the psychological vacuum for indoctrination to take place. The old tricks are the best and the slavery of the African continent was achieved in similar fashion.

Nevertheless, as religion was so important to life in ancient cultures any drastic shifts in philosophy were either avoided, or in the very least carefully considered. This was a principle that the Romans recognised and catered to very well, and quite favourably for them they were assisted by the fact that a common thread ran through most belief systems, and the saviour figure was a bastion in most of them.

With the initial creation of Jesus, attempted claims to authenticity and originality were something of a problem. The ancient Egyptian worship system was so impressive that it yielded many imitations which largely maintained the concept of a messiah son-of-god whose exploits were altered to suit adoptive cultures. His history began with Horus, who was to take many names in his journey through time as a redemptive figure in the later guises of Adonis, Attis, Tammuz, Dionysus, Buddha, Mithra and others.

All of these shared similar experiences as later attributed to Jesus in the gospel stories, such as the feeding of the multitude with five loaves of bread, the turning of water into wine, walking on water, being a target of assassination at birth, dying sacrificially for their people only to be resurrected after three days and taken to heaven, and so the list goes on.

Fledgling Christianity had a particular problem with the followers of Mithra who were notably affronted by the similarities that this new god shared with their own and accused the new group of plagiarism citing that their cult was much older and had existed for six hundred years beforehand. The Christians refuted this by saying that the Devil had foreseen the coming of the true messiah and had gone back in time to invent Mithra in order to usurp the Christ. This infantile argument aside, sheer force of numbers aided by political influence meant that the old was inevitably going to give way to the new.

My discovery of all of this was intriguing enough, but became truly absorbing with my analysis of the appellation referred to as 'the Christ'. Horus was known as the 'KRST', which if we install vowels as used in the names of Osiris and Isis, becomes the 'Krist'. Like his parents, he was a 'dark god', and if we latch onto his trail in his eastward travels we see this meaning is maintained

The Hindu messiah, Krishna, also shares many of the traits of Horus. The story of his birth sees him come under threat due to an ancient prophecy, just as both Horus and Jesus did, the light of the sun was likewise blotted out at the moment of his death, which is an esoteric incident of quite some magnitude, he too had his feet pierced before dying (albeit only one) and was taken up to heaven in glory upon his resurrection after being dead for 'three days'.

As usual, what interested me most in all of this was the etymological connection. The common theory of the origin of the term Christ is allegedly that it was based upon the Greek word 'Kristos', commonly translated as 'anointed one' or 'messiah', which is supposedly a Greek translation of the Hebrew word *mashiach*.

To put it diplomatically, especially after all of the research I had done, I knew that this was unlikely. The similarities to the other earlier messiah figures could not possibly have been coincidence, and it was when I came across the meaning of the word Krishna in its original form, KRSNA, that I knew I was right.

Depictions of Osiris and Isis generally showed them to be black in colour, this was a feature that highlighted their underworld status, and I was mildly surprised to discover that Krishna was also featured, like other Hindu gods, as being either 'blue' or 'black'. It is clear from the variations in his birth legend that he was born in the 'underworld' as the metaphors in his story for such a location are clear enough and the revelation of the meaning of his title cemented my findings, and it was inspiring to note that Hindu iconography had remained true to the concept.

The word Krishna is the Sanskrit term for 'black' or 'dark' and completed the link in the trail of messiahs from Horus to Jesus, showing clearly that the academic explanation for the origin of the term was yet another red herring for the masses who have been taught to believe that the biblical texts are both original and unique.

The principle of the 'dark god' did not end here however and the Catholic Church has long been embarrassed by its expression in another of its most revered divine figures, the Virgin Mary.

The cult of the 'Black Madonna' is linked with the two most significant females of the gospel accounts, Mary, the mother of Jesus, and his main female companion, Mary Magdalene. Black figurines of the Virgin Mary are by far the most popular and often feature her with the infant messiah à la the 'dark' ancient representations of Isis and the baby Horus. This much is undeniable hence the unease on the matter of the Catholic Church. The reason, no one (apparently) can explain why these paintings and statues of the holy mother and child are black-skinned.

Afro-centrists state this is because Isis and Horus are African characters and the later black Madonna and child imitations were merely being true to their source. In part this may well be the case, but begs the question, why would even the figures with European features, of which there are many, also be black in colour? If the explanation were so simple then when the physiological nature of the images were changed the colouring would also have been altered.

Some theologians argued that the Black Madonna's were not always black, but became discoloured over time due to the soot residue of the candles that were lit alongside them. This was countered with the common sense argument that, if this excuse were true, then the rest of the image should also have turned black and not just the face and hands of these icons.

The situation is such a delicate one among the priesthood that in his book *The Cult of the Black Virgin*, the writer Ean Begg reported events that took place at the American Association for the Advancement of Science in 1952 where papers were being presented on the subject of Black Virgins. He stated that 'there was no mistaking the hostility... every priest and nun in the audience walked out.'

To my mind the reason that these figures were presented as black was quite obvious and also very important in terms of the nature of their message. They were not people, but far more important than that, they were principles, archetypes that articulated deeper meaning than could be garnered by a literal reading of their stories. Their blackness expressed quite clearly that they were all 'dark gods', in other words, they were reborn amidst darkness in the belly of the earth after a fiery descent from heaven. Whether we talk about Osiris, Isis, Horus, Krishna, Buddha, Jesus, the Queen of Sheba, or the two Mary's, the message was the same. They represented the primordial human concept of the gods, one that the Church was not keen to reveal to the masses, but also one that it was equally keen not to discard.

Even today, the cult of the Black Madonna is particularly strong in France and she is represented in some French Gothic Cathedrals as *Notre Dame de Souterrain*, meaning, 'Our Lady of the Underworld' where she is complimented by another female figure, Mary Magdalene, arriving, presumably to France, in a boat. It is noteworthy that the most popular form of underworld travel in the ancient accounts was also a boat.

That the veneration of this cult is still hugely popular with religious devotees, even though apparently frowned upon by the Church, is an enigma, as it seems quite certain that pilgrims to statues of the Black Virgin and Child have no real grasp of their hidden meaning. This public ignorance was never more apparent than in the furore that surrounded the death of Diana, the Princess of Wales.

Diana was commemorated in many ways, some traditional, and some unconventional, but none was more controversial than when a black granite statue of her was unveiled at a funeral services exhibition in England's second city, my home town, Birmingham. The statue was branded 'demonic' and 'wholly inappropriate', and was even, to my surprise, denounced by her own relatives, the Spencer family. This situation was even more interesting as before this particular depiction, the princess had also been controversially featured as the Virgin Mary in a statue unveiled in the city of Liverpool. I could not refrain from commenting on the whole scenario in *Rulers & Lies* and wrote:

...for the late princess to have been commemorated as both the Virgin Mary, and then have her likeness carved in black granite, is not only interesting, but plainly esoteric. The fact is, it was deeply reverential.

There is no doubt that I am not the only person to have spotted that this commemoration was a huge mark of respect to the late princess, and just as certain is the fact that those that knew the real reasons for such depictions were never going to come out openly in their defence.

As usual I rubbed some people up the wrong way when dragged into discussion of such matters, and one line of defence that was often tried against me was the pigeon-hole, an effort to allocate me to a certain religious group. This was a sensible mode of defence, as subconsciously my would-be critics were admitting that every religion or cult had its weaknesses, none are authentic, and all are flawed in terms of both historical development and philosophy. The Imam at Rye Hill even alleged that I was probably someone that believed Jesus was a black man with an afro. I don't know whether this was an attempt at mirth or some ill-contrived effort to demean me in front of others, but I was on my way to something that I take very seriously, the gym, and had no time to be clever. I retorted that I could not care what colour he was, he was a Roman invention so they could make him pink with blue spots for all I cared, and I raced out of the unit door. The Imam was not my nemesis though, and I enjoyed our banter, as much as I did with one other inmate who tried every psychological ploy possible to show me the error of my ways.

Chris Obi was a devoted Christian, he did not ally himself to a particular denomination and preached the good news of the Christ to all and sundry, whether inmate or officer. I believe he was serving a sentence of similar duration to my own, but could never ascertain what his crime was or how long he had left to serve. He would constantly tell me that everything was in 'the hands of the Lord.'

The first time we met he invited me to a bible discussion that he had organised one evening in the unit meeting room which inmates were allowed to use upon request, and I told him that not only was I a non-believer, but boy had he got the wrong guy. This only spurred him on even though I stressed that my presence would only be a disruption. His opinion was that the Holy Spirit would transform me, a similar perception is held in Islam, where it is alleged that if you read the Koran from start to finish then you will become a believer. I have read it from start to finish more than once and have scrutinised its pages in cross-reference on numerous occasions, a fact which has embarrassed many Muslims who have entered debate with me by asking if I had read their holy book, as most critics have not. Upon discovering that my knowledge of it was greater than theirs they always switched to speaking in Arabic, or some other Eastern tongue, the gist of their confusion however was always blatantly clear.

Chris seemed similarly perplexed by my staunch disbelief, and totally taken aback by my arguments that the Bible did not bring civilisation to the world as most Christians seem to think, and was a copy-cat tome that paid hidden reverence to the cultures that it had stolen from. I know that I disturbed his calm, as after that first night he took every opportunity to convert me to the 'light', and took to the tactic of ignoring every factual statement that I made about the origin of his belief system. When I quizzed him for a retort he told me to believe in the Lord, which I found highly amusing, but I liked him so much that I tried to keep any further comments as respectful as possible.

Chris is Nigerian, and his indoctrination, although having some seriously comic elements (He told me that he had seen Jesus, and yet when I asked him what he looked like he could not describe him. Chris does his best to remain politically correct), is indicative of the grip that religion has on the African continent. I have two main bones of contention with this influence, the first is the stance of the Catholic Church on the use of contraception, especially as the Bible does not make any clear or specific comment on the subject.

Until the twentieth century all Christian religions were anti-contraception, but as attitudes became more liberal, (maybe enlightened is a better word), this stance was slackened, theologians deciding that it was best for their faithful to decide for themselves what was conscionable Christian behaviour, rather than maintain a dictatorial platform on the issue. The Catholic Church did not follow suit and insisted that like abortion, contraception was alien to the laws and power of God. They argued, and still do, that couples using contraception as a form of birth control were detracting from the power of the Divine, and only God should be able to decide whether a life should enter the world or not. (So, if a would-be mother was the victim of rape, or her life in danger from natal complications, abortion is still a sin, and religious edict must take precedent over the woman's psychological and physical well-being. How can the Vatican morally substantiate this as a firm party line? The mind boggles!)

This position is substantiated with a variety of dubious moral arguments, such as contraception leads to widespread sexual immorality, sex should only be performed between married couples and specifically for the purpose of procreation, contraception reduces the male respect for women (an argument that infers that women do not, or are not, supposed to enjoy sex, which was one of the main reasons that the Witchfinder atrocities of the 16th century took place, and why excision, as I shall mention shortly, is practised widely in Islam), it turns sex into a non-marital act, etc, etc., and yet no one is harmed by the use of contraception, the need for which is entirely positive.

What is being denied, is that the act of sex, or even masturbation, is not purely for procreation, and is a natural mammalian instinct that fulfils other physiological functions. It can be argued quite strongly that abstinence is the unnatural, or in religious terms, ungodly practice, leading to illness, frustration and warped manifestations of sexual desire.

If we look at the flip side of the coin, poverty, disease, and death would be cut drastically in Africa if the Church was to place logical morality above ill-conceived medieval philosophy. But it will not, and the latest Pontiff, Pope Benedict XVI, has underlined that this murderous doctrine must continue in its role as the divinely interpreted edict of the Christian supreme God.

I try to never to play the race card, even when white friends of mine suggested that I do so in my court case both before and after my incarceration, I did not view it as a sensible option simply because I did not feel that it was relevant. If I had been white I think my treatment and sentence would probably have been similar, but I have little doubt that if the people dying in Africa were Caucasian, the Catholic stance on contraception would have been relaxed long ago. Especially as it is an open secret that the laity of that church openly flout the anti-contra-ception edicts of the Vatican, particularly those that live in more developed countries. It is common sense.

The Catholic response that education and religious obser-vance are the answer to AIDS and morality problems does have some merit, the first part of their argument is sound reasoning, as, in the case of the HIV retrovirus the use of condoms without an enlightenment process could actually make a catastrophic situation even worse, the second part however has not worked for over a millennium, so one might suggest from this that a change of tack, considering human lives in a very real world are at stake, is in order. From a moral standpoint they stand on shaky ground, but once again, 'this myth of Christ hath served them well', and no doubt they will continue to leap behind it.

If it is a God that is deciding that the spiralling birth and infection rate in Africa is a good thing, then either he has abandoned them, or is also a racist. In a region where aids, poverty, and ignorance are rife, it is the responsibility of man to address these problems, and on this issue the hands of Catholicism are awash with blood. It is a given that 'causes' rather than 'symptoms' must be addressed in order to save lives, and no sensible person would deny that education is the major key to long term success, but it must be aided by pragmatism. The Band Aid banner should now become truly brave and bring the pressure of the masses to bear on the Vatican and its draconian policy. Religious reform, and notably not for the first time, can reduce the pain and suffering of millions, Catholicism must put aside its ego, and in the interests of humanity perform an about turn that will go a long way towards demonstrating that theirs is a God of love. Unfortunately I do not hold out much immediate hope on this matter.

The other plague of countries under the grip of religion is that of their cultural attitude towards women. In Islamic nations it is something of a paradox, as the Koran is arguably a less misogynistic text than either of its predecessors (or so my Muslim friends insist!). It does however consider the woman as a 'helpmeet', which is by many interpreted as 'a slave' for the man, a being created secondarily to him for that express purpose. A situation that women would be expected to continue in the afterlife, but other than that it does not encourage or blatantly promote mistreatment of women, and yet in Islamic society, private and social denigration, and violence towards females is rife.

Honour killings are performed on a regular basis, even when a woman has been raped, it is often successfully claimed that she was having an adulterous affair. She is then often likely to be either stoned to death in a tribal ritual, or murdered by her own family members in a bid to uphold their honour. The male perpetrator is rarely punished, and certainly not with the taking of his life, and the murderous and proud members of her own family are regarded as heroes. Staggering but true.

Just as horrendous is the barbaric practice performed on young girls known as excision. Technically it is described as female circumcision, (the removal of the clitoris), but in truth it is simply mutilation, a religio-cultural phenomenon commonly practised in African Muslim communities for non-medical reasons. Basically this is so women do not enjoy the sex act and will stay faithful to insecure and ignorant men as slaves, semen receptacles, and little else.

I find it difficult to pass objective comment on a matter which is so emotionally disturbing and sums up exactly how much progress needs to be made in Islam towards moral enlightenment. For those that argue that excision is merely a cultural problem I counter with the fact that religion runs the lives of those that take pride in such primitive behaviour and is their sole excuse to practice it. In such cases there can be no separation, religion and culture are inextricably linked.

This is the nature of theocracy, the rule of God by man, it is nothing other than politics, and as perfect as any philosophy might be, it is always open to interpretation, not that I am suggesting that Islam, or any religion for that matter is perfect. They certainly are not, and have proven not to be over the length of their existence. They are simply dictatorship in hidden form, and always will be until their Gods appear out of the sky to take over the helm personally. Until then, the rules of religion in so-called theocratic states must be imposed by men, and so far none of them, regardless of what their holy books state have been able to stamp out the barbaric attitude and treatment that exists towards women in their societies. In fact, in many instances, they have encouraged it.

The Muslim guys that I talked to on this subject seemed to be fairly evenly split in their attitudes. Some seemed keen to treat their partners as equals, as any reasonable and intelligent person might, and others were insistent, in indignant and ignorant fashion, that their partners would be treated well so long as they knew their place. That attitude in itself is a contra-diction to any promise of reasonable behaviour and by their body language and voice inflection I got the picture, women were beneath them. Period. I do my best to keep my cool in discussion, especially as I view the raising of one's voice as a sure sign of weak argument, however, when faced with this attitude, I found it difficult, and once or twice resorted to obscenities to register my disgust. I figured that if these guys were born and raised in the West and had such an aggressive stance on the matter, then how bad must it be in some Islamic states?

Once again, just as in the issue of the Catholic position on contraception, the obligation to effect cultural change in this topic, lies with the religious leaders of the Islamic faith. The problem in both cases, is that we are dealing with politically run religions, and these leaders will always place the political by-product of their policies ahead of the moral one. Their God has nothing to do with it.

As I write this is it is now September 2006, and it was with a smile that I noted the official, although non-governmental meeting attended by activists from 11 Arab countries in June of this year to establish a law on domestic violence. In the Arab world no such legislation currently exists and the meeting yielded the following statement:

Arab societies are still dominated by patriarchal authoritative systems that give privileges to male dominance over all aspects of life.

The national constitutions of all Arab countries state that women and men are considered equal in front of the law. In spite of that, none of the countries are working to attain this equality. None of the states have abided by the international human right treaties that they have signed, especially the CEDAW convention (Convention on the Elimination of all forms of Discrimination Against Women). Besides, the vast majority put reservations on this treaty, while some did not sign it yet.

Women in Arab countries are still suffering from violations to their basic human rights, especially from acts of violence perpetrated on them which, in some cases, lead to their death.

Until now, the vast majority of Arab countries did not take any measure to confront these acts of violence. Instead, some of these acts are legalized or even considered as "holistic", especially those inflicted, directly or indirectly, by the personal status codes. Women "femicide" under the pretext of "honor crimes" are flagrant examples.

Arab governments are still captured by the traditional culture which consider the family as a private property of men, giving them the privilege of being the "head of the family' and wide space of freedom to violate the basic human rights of family members, including women and children. Under the pretext of "home privacy", or "intimate relationship", governments remain standstill towards any human right violation of the family members.

In consideration of all the above, the participants in the regional meeting agreed on:

1. Calling upon all government who signed and ratified the international human rights treaties, including the CEDAW and its optional protocols, to lift the reservations on the CEDAW and act to amend their national laws according to those treaties.

2. Calling upon all governments to confront the multi faceted forms of violence against women, especially those that take place within the family. VAW (Violence Against Women) is one of the main obstacles that deprive women from attaining their basic human rights, and one of the flagrant violations to those rights.

3. Confronting violence against women necessitates from the governments their acknowledgment of its existence as a societal problem that hinders the development process. Consequently, it is a necessity to reconsider the legislative system in each Arab country, to ensure that the law plays a preventive role against acts of violence against women within the family.

4. Calling upon governments to set special legislations for protecting women against family violence, due to the fact that domestic violence against women is the most widespread form of violence against women, while at the same time it is still privatized and kept within family boundaries.

5. Enhancing the work on both the regional and local levels in order to establish special legislations on family violence, and continuing the coordination among each other, until this special law is adopted by the Arab governments.

6. Calling upon civil society organizations and official entities to help in elaborating a special legislation on family violence that would fulfill the ambitions and hopes of women in Arab countries.

Sometimes our heads will drop, but we should remain optimistic. There is hope yet.

13

I had been inside over two years by now and had worryingly become used to the fact that I hardly saw my children. The thought of release into the outside world was not even a consideration, try as I might, it was so far removed from my mind I just couldn't picture it. I still maintained myself physically in terms of health, fitness, and hygiene, although I only gave my aesthetic appearance any thought when I had a visit. Other than that, so long as I was clean I couldn't care less what my clothing looked like. That was not the same for everyone though as there were some real fashionistas in the jail who even wore expensive dress rings and designer watches on a daily basis. I could understand their reasoning, they were simply maintaining their self-worth, even though I thought it unnecessarily risky. After all we were in jail and it's not as if there was a shortage of thieves.

On the psychological front and with my heavy daily schedules I never considered that I was in any way institutionalised, but on reflection, to some extent I certainly was, everybody was. Prison life had become the norm, which is not 'normal' by any standards, even so, I felt strongly that I would have no problems readjusting to life when eventually released.

This issue regularly crossed my mind and was an interesting topic of conversation due to the number of long serving inmates who historically could not adjust to the thought of outside life, they were understandably fearful of the new situations and responsibilities that awaited them. The pattern of their behaviour was always the same. They would go through the routine of attaining open prison status, and within a few months of being allowed to go out on their own for a day into the local town, they would abscond. This was an offence punishable by an extra thirty days jail, a mild sentence only because it is not technically an escape, you have to be in closed conditions to do that, and the punishment then is obviously harsher. When inevitably picked up at their family home or some other obvious location, the absconder would then be returned to closed conditions. Severely institutionalised inmates repeat this process until the day they die.

This mindset may seem odd, but you have to consider that these are people who have not had to pay a bill, prepare a meal, or earn a crust for years, who would now also have the added burden of being stigmatised by society. In many cases their thought processes had been dulled to the point of inertness because in jail you are told what to do and when to do it on a daily basis. You do not even have to calculate what time to get out of bed, or why, you just do as you are told, and it was clear why some long-termers were fearful of release as they struggled to keep clean or decorate their tiny cells so how would they handle the larger accommodation that they would be released to?

For a variety of reasons there were also those that would not be afforded the privilege of gradual release via the open prison route, where you could at least get to dip your toes into the outside world. They would be released after years of incarceration straight back onto the street with the heavy thud of the main prison door behind them and hardly a penny in their pockets.

The prison service runs token courses to help prepare such convicts for outside life but how can that be enough to resettle inmates that have served a lengthy sentence? It is alarmingly clear much of the prison release process makes little sense.

Open prisons are full of prisoners that have received

sentences of less than a year, and with parole they only have to serve half of that or less. Many of them are repeat offenders, and therefore used to social absence, and others would be away for a period so short that the consequence on their lives, although traumatic, is containable. It can never be logically argued that they need the resettlement process more than a long serving inmate, even one that has an horrendous record, for even in that instance they are still being considered for release into society, and so it is even more vital to allow and monitor the process and guide them in a calculated manner back onto the streets.

I saw many guys released directly into society from B category prisons, because they were considered too much of a risk to be granted open prison status. Does such an assessment make any sense? And I have witnessed that this too often results in re-offending or some even more tragic event. This back to front situation raises some interesting, and alarming questions.

One of the most burgeoning businesses in the western world is imprisonment. It is a dream opportunity for big business, as in simple economic terms demand seemingly far outstrips supply. If we were to delve into every reason why this phenomena is so widespread and increasing then this book would double in size. The questions, and indeed the answers, are many and complex, but one thing is for sure, the prison system is not as successful in producing rehabilitated offenders as it is in providing a revolving door for its regular clients.

It has the latent power to ensure that inmates improve in every area of life, whether this is in academics, reasoning, self-discipline, or the ability to financially support themselves and their loved ones in a legal manner. But it fails miserably. It does not need to be a boot camp, as systems of reward can be as effective as ones that merely punish, and it is clear that a mix of tough love, mandatory achievement targets, and support are required. This will not happen though, because more HMP Rye Hills are on the way. Prisoners are profitable clients, and it may sound cynical, but if they rehabilitate in droves, big business will lose out on a nice little number. The system makes sure that this will not happen by one very simple method. Issuing longer sentences.

The issue of justice in the USA and Great Britain is not about punishment, rehabilitation, or balance, it is about business and retribution hence the draconian and vindictive nature of their courts.

In the United States the crime rate has been falling steadily since 1991 and yet the prison population has increased by more than 50 per cent. The British situation is equally as paradoxical and alarming, the prison population is now at a crisis level with figures increasing from 42,000 in 1991 to 82,000 in 2008.

The Blair and Bush administrations promised to get 'tough on crime and tough on the causes of crime', a fey political state-ment that if correctly initiated could indeed be effective, but you need to fulfil both ends of the promise. They have only got tough on crime by the handing out of longer sentences and squeezing cons for financial reparation, a primitive reaction which historically has been proven not to work.

British statistics reveal that the legal system now sends approximately 64% of convicted adults to jail in comparison to the 45% figure of 1991, average sentences have increased from five months to two years and two months in a ten year period, a huge jump, with equally huge social reverberations. In 1993 53% of prisoners were found guilty of another offence within two years of release, by the year 2000 this had risen to 59%. The revolving door is on increasing and continual spin.

This makes it clear that the simplistic approach of merely being tough on crime has done little to reduce the problem itself and may well be feeding it. The causes of crime are in urgent need of attention and I have witnessed first-hand that they have only been paid lip service. It would be difficult to convince me that the patchwork solution of building more jails and continu-ing to imprison a greater proportion of offending men and women for longer periods of time is not preferred because it is more lucrative. In such a situation the taxpayer foots the bill as the 'jobs for the boys', i.e. Barristers, Judges, Politicians, and the Penal businesses become more profitable and secure. It may sound cynical but they would be even harder pressed to convince me that they do not view taxes as 'free money'.

I have lost count of the number of inmates that asked me to write letters for them, and this simply because they did not possess the basic literacy skills to do it for themselves, at a guess I would say that such a problem afflicted between 65-80 per cent of inmates, and yet here they were in the perfect environment to be forced to address this issue. The situation is no secret so one can only conclude that it is being ignored intentionally.

I have already mentioned the problem of drug dependency in jail and how that has been mishandled, the problem is still rife and prison policy in this area needs urgent review. The courage to use a common-sense rather than a politically correct approach is the only solution as inmates have proven to be far more resourceful than prison officers, who are far fewer in number and have other priorities.

In Great Britain it costs approximately £36,000 per annum to keep one prisoner in jail, a cost which is in many cases avoidable as there are often alternatives other than imprisonment available. If the rehabilitation process was an effective, or indeed realistic one, then this might well be justifiable. But it is not. The mass of people in prison are either re-offenders, the socially excluded, the disadvantaged, or the inept. A statistic which the justice system does not seem to mind one iota, it keeps them well fed and they are expert in feeding themselves and their friends at the trough of human misery.

For example, Group Four, the European conglomerate that have the contract for HMP Rye Hill are the same company that fought for and won the right to build the Palestinian Wall that allegedly 'protects' Israel from Palestinian terrorist attacks, while at the same time impinging heavily on the human rights of many innocent people. Group Four are insensitive to such issues, they merely see themselves as fulfilling a function while getting richer at the same time. Their mindset is quite clear, the more people go to jail, or need to be incarcerated, the better for their business. One wonders how they would react if the prison system was to become what it is supposed to be, a successful correctional facility where offenders are assisted in the re-organisation of their lives and values to become positive members of society? At the moment it is a moot question, for no such agenda is on the cards.

It is no surprise then, that during my time inside I was asked to participate, by some very intelligent career criminals, in some very interesting projects, both drug and fraud related, that were elaborate, well networked, and potentially very lucrative. These deals usually included 'legitimate' businessmen who had operated in crime for years and had never been caught, and it was this fact that encouraged many inmates to focus their future hopes in criminal activity. They simply knew of too many examples where this had been performed successfully, and to be honest, so did I.

This did not sway me though, whenever I heard the usual talk that 'everything is covered and we will not be caught' I usually added 'not the same way you were last time you mean.' With all of the repeat offenders around how could I see things otherwise? To me the rationale seemed quite simple. If you had never previously been convicted, then the chances of you leading a successful criminal life were much higher than if you had been, as you were now on the police radar. As a known criminal the odds would surely be stacked against you in any future venture. My logic usually fell upon deaf ears, people want to hear what pleases them and the avenues I suggested of using the current time available to prepare a legitimate living must have seemed both boring and too much like hard work for a lot of guys.

The reasons why I was constantly approached to engage in illicit ventures were quite simple. I was well educated, knew a lot of people, and kept myself to myself, which are the basic requirements for successful criminal activity.

In one instance I was asked by some Columbians that I had befriended, older men that were clearly well-heeled and respected, to liaise with a business contact of theirs in Scotland after we had all been released. He received shipments of cocaine from them through his business and they felt that I would be an ideal distributor to add to their operation, even trusting me to work on a sale and return basis. In other words, with no financial risk whatsoever.

Similar offers to take part in cannabis distribution were ten a penny, and both English, Dutch, and Italian inmates that I either worked with for a period of time in industries, or were resident on my unit, came to my cell at various times because they wanted to initiate future business.

I cannot say that I was not tempted, my sentence had created a bitterness in me towards the system that took quite some time to subside, and the amount of easy money on offer was always substantial, but whenever I thought things through, my answer would always be no. If I were a single man with no children I am not so sure that I would have been quite so pensive. Money has a way of dulling the keenest of consciences and it seemed to me that if I had taken up the offer of working with some of the more efficient contacts in question the risk would have been minimal and the profits most certainly worthwhile. I always wonder how those guys are getting on and I admit quite readily that I liked many of them a great deal.

I did not however share the same affinity with everyone and it was during this period that I had my second run-in with an inmate in which I was prepared to regress to more primitive behaviour. Try as I might, it was impossible to get on with everybody, and on the whole I would merely avoid the people that my spirit did not take to. My instincts are not always correct and life has taught me that on occasion these are the very people that become lifelong friends and prove how poor a judge of character I can sometimes be. In this case however, my feelings were spot on, the guy in question was one prize prick. He had been within my proximity many a time in both industries and the gym and we had never uttered a word, shared a glance, or stayed in the same space any longer than necessary. The reason for this is not a mystery, he was a token tough guy who continually walked with a swagger, which got more pronounced as he approached guys that he did not know, not that this was any reason to dislike him, I like plenty of guys that swagger around, some of them are quite comical, but there was something nauseous about this numbskull. So imagine my surprise the very first time he spoke to me.

Over time my model behaviour had earned me certain privileges, and as I have stated one of them was that industries would release me from work early to go to the late afternoon gym session. As such I was allowed to make my way unescorted through the various security checks from the works building to my unit. The units were situated in blocks of two, and mine, Carling, named after the famous English Rugby player Will Carling, was adjoined to one known as Davis. I was admitted into the foyer that served both of these blocks and had to wait for an officer from Carling to come from the unit reception desk to let me in. As I passed the gate for Davis I was beckoned in a manner that I normally do not respond to, it was the phrase, *'Hey!'* I turned to see my caller, the wannabe superstar in question, who for some reason was not at work that afternoon, standing with his arm sticking through the metal bars of the Davis unit gate with a package in it, *'pass this to Roberts'*. That name softened me enough to respond so I asked him what was in the package, *'It's just some burn, pass it to Roberts'*. Burn is the standard prison term for tobacco. I liked Roberts, he was one of the young lads on the unit that I did not spend any time with, but he was pleasant, respectful and fun to observe as he got up to whatever mischief he could get away with.

They obviously had this rendezvous planned, as Roberts had spotted me and came to the Carling gate to see if I would pass the parcel over. I could see clearly through the bars that no officer had begun to make their way to open the gate for me so I asked Roberts sternly, *'What's in that parcel?'* He said plainly, *'I can't lie to you Brownie, its gear!'* 'Gear' is a colloquialism for heroin, a class 'A' drug that if you are caught dealing in prison can have some serious consequences. Loss of parole is a strong possibility, loss of visits, single cell facility, and gym, are guaranteed, with the added threat of movement, probably to another unit where you would have to start your climb up the prison reward system from scratch, or even transfer to another facility even further away from your family. I was livid. I did not even like this fool anyway and the first time he speaks to me is with a bare faced lie that could have destroyed all of the goodwill that I had built up in one foul swoop. On top of that the Davis unit gate was directly opposite the unit administration quarters which featured a one-way window. We could not see in, but the officers inside it could see out, so there was also the chance that we were being watched.

Nevertheless, I walked up to the Davis unit gate and told him in no uncertain terms what I thought of him, he responded by telling me that if he ever saw me outside that he would fuck me up properly and stab the shit out of me etc, etc. I told him not to worry, I was on the way to the gym right now, the same session he attended, and he could fuck me up within the hour. He shouted and cursed until I was let onto my unit and I don't think I've ever gotten ready for gym quite as quick as I did for that session. I raced back down into the queue to be let out, grateful that I was going to get the chance to have a more practical discussion with the moron. I can be so naïve. There was no sign of him.

I didn't sleep much that night as I could hardly wait to get to work, me like the idiot I can be, still thinking that I would get the chance away from prying eyes to enter into the dialogue I was now so eager for behind closed doors. 'Tough-guy' swaggered broadly while in my vicinity as everyone walked to industries that morning, he could, there were officers everywhere en route to the works building, but once inside he stayed away from me all day. I worked with two friends of his but he never came near them, I took that as a sign that a 'straightener' was out of the question, because if he had approached them he knew that I would have told him to meet me privately to settle our disagreement. As a result my anger subsided and I kept myself so busy that it was easy for me to ignore the issue so long as he kept his distance. So guess who got the last laugh? He did, and no sooner than the very next day.

Most of the workers in industries could not begin their

tasks until tools had been handed out, and likewise no one was allowed to leave, whether individually or en masse, until they had been collected, this for the obvious security reasons. Trusted inmates were sometimes allowed to assist in this process and I would often stand at the gate of the tool-holding cage to help out and speed matters up. The cage would normally be opened up early so we could get a full mornings activity as most of the guys were on piece-work and the whole process was usually quite frantic. We would greet friends from different units as well as pass out tools every morning and having been resident so long at Rye Hill I said *'morning'* to pals as they passed by or I handed them the tool they needed. One stream of guys walked past me to their stations and I said *'morning'* one by one to all of them as they crowded through. If you can imagine the scene, they greeted me, I greeted them, and so on, *'morning Howard'* I heard as a guy I could not make out on the outskirts of the crowd strode past, *'morning'* I responded before I looked up to acknowledge who it was. I could have kicked myself, it was Mr Swagger, and his greeting spoken in a manner as if we had been acquainted for years. Nice move I thought, there was no way that we would ever be friendly, but how could I think about a confrontation now with the psychological spanner that he had just thrown into my works? I was flummoxed. Still, it was just as well, violence only succeeds in breeding its usual offspring so I found it agreeable to let the matter rest.

My studying was by now well and truly in full flight, and I was pleased with the amount of original points that I was gleaning and able to prove in order to substantiate my writing. I was sure that I had spotted a vein within the biblical works in regard to the book's true stance on the practice of magic. The magic feats of ancient legend are of course entirely mythical in nature, but I have little doubt that humans do indeed possess special gifts that are under-rated, under-developed, and under-used.

We understand very little about the power of thought or

our abilities to draw upon inner strength. As a martial artist I have an acute insight into the latter and have personally witnessed feats that many have not believed when I related them, so I do not take much convincing of some apparently paranormal occurrences.

My Muay Thai-Boxing trainer, Master Thosaphon Sitiwatjana is a Buddhist and can stand amidst ankle high flames whilst crunching broken glass with his bare feet for minutes on end without enduring any physical injury whatsoever. I guarantee you this is not an illusion but a feat that I have watched him and other Thai-Boxing coaches, including his own brother, and Master Sken Kaewpadung, perform so many times that I do not even bother to watch any more. When I asked him how he did it he said it was the power of the mind. I never once entertained trying to learn it.

Likewise, much of the psychological hold of organised religion can be attributed to the mind-bolstering practice known as prayer, which as well as relying strongly on psychology and the power of positive mental attitude, also claims to have some capability as an external force. I am dubious about this and studies have shown that people being prayed for while gravely ill have poorer recovery rates than those that are not. I imagine the reason for this is psychological, because if you are in a sick-bed and spot people praying for you then you know you're in trouble.

One thing I am sure of though is that the citation of paranormal testimonials as proof of the authenticity of any particular belief system means nothing, every religion can provide extraordinary examples of such power that cannot be explained in a scientific light. They cannot all be the correct belief system, and certainly 'unexplainable' events do not provide endorsement of any particular mode of thought, especially when any variety of explanations can be equally applicable.

As far as the arcane arts are concerned the original party line of Christian doctrine stated that the attempted practice of magic was wrong and should be abhorred and avoided by devout followers, this included divination, magical healing, and fortune telling, which is a very clever way of stating that such practices really do work. The other upshot was that they were also classified as 'evil', a political necessity during the formation of the early church as rival belief systems, both near and far, were steeped in the practice of what became known as the 'dark arts'. That this stance was a political ploy becomes clear when you realise that rituals of healing or prophecy performed by characters sanctioned and featured in the Bible were not placed in this category but were seen as demonstrations of benevolence, divine love, retribution, or even the right to inflict death. Some of these tales not only have positions of prominence in the texts, but are also quite contradictory.

In the gospel nativity story we are told that three wise men travelled from the 'east' (heaven) to visit the new born god, Jesus, and worship him. To do this they followed a star which pinpointed his location, a tactic which is the essence of astrology, one of the allegedly taboo anti-Christian practices. The reference to the trio as 'three wise men' is an odd interpretation as the term used to describe them is 'magi', from which is derived the words 'magic' and 'magician'. Are we to assume then that the Bible is telling us that magicians are wise? It seems it is.

In a later New Testament tale, a character known as Elymas, falls foul of the Apostle Paul due to his use of arcane practices and is apparently punished for his transgression. The account, in the book of Acts, informs us that the name 'Elymas' means 'sorcerer' when it actually means 'wise', and what makes matters even more interesting is that the Hebrew name of this fellow was 'bar-Jesus' which translates 'son of Jesus', was this all a coincidence? And why would the account make a point of telling us his other name unless it was of some relevance to an otherwise very brief story? What also struck me as odd when reviewing this episode was that the 'punishment' Elymas received was the following, *'you shall be blind, not seeing the sun for a time'*. The length of 'time' is not specified, but I am willing to bet that his journey through darkness took 'three days' and I have very good reason for saying so which I will expound later.

Much of the book of Acts, as with other earlier stories, is devoted to the Christian battle to show that its magic was greater and more pure than that of its competitors, which sums up the essence of all of the holy books. They decry the practices of the earlier cultures from which they themselves were developed and yet continued with them in barely disguised form. As became clear to me time and time again, tricks of translation, such as that in the story of Elymas and others were constantly used to hide the true messages of the texts, but there is a tale that I mentioned earlier, a prolific Old Testament one, that is as revealing as the story of Noah and the Ark in showing that the Bible is clearly the Hebrew version of earlier culture belief.

In the story of Saul and the witch of Endor the practice of divination is featured as what it was, a staple of ancient Hebrew behaviour, they consulted with the gods and with the dead as much as anyone else. After his God, Yahweh, would not answer him, either in dreams or by other methods, in his plea for counsel in the face of a formidable enemy, Saul turned to a spirit medium in desperation.

In disguise and under the cloak of nightfall he visited the medium and asked her to raise up from the dead his former mentor, Samuel. The mistranslation that follows is one of the worst examples of deception in the biblical canon. Samuel rises up from the underworld and is described as a 'spirit', this when the Hebrew word used in the narrative is 'elohim' which does not mean spirit at all. The Hebrew word for spirit is 'nephesh', the term *elohim* means 'god' or 'gods' taking on either a singular or plural connotation dependent upon the context of the passage.

The detail of the story is unmistakable, the witch conjured a god up from the underworld, a purely Egyptian theology that was also heavily present in early Hebrew religion. To translate this section accurately would have opened up a very large can of worms for the Church, and so every single translation of this tale, in every version of the Bible, has rendered the word 'elohim' as 'spirit'. I do not know who is responsible for such a disgraceful ploy, but either they have immense influence, or later charlatans have merely followed suit. Even so, there are other questions to answer. What was one of God's good guys, Samuel, doing in hell anyway, and as this was the case, why was he so comfortable, his first words to his old friend upon his rising were, 'Why have you disturbed me by bringing me up?' This does not sound like a guy being incessantly tortured or burned, and let us not forget that the account makes it clear, whether organised religion wishes to dismiss the fact or not, that he was now also a god.

In a snapshot assessment of the latter examples, it could be strongly argued that the Bible presented magic as something to aspire to, but as a power reserved only for God's special people, that is, the priests, and not for the common man, who would be considered evil if they tried to use what was essentially the power of the woman in any way at all.

The hypocrisy of the situation is summed up perfectly in the Samuel account. Saul had previously banished all spirit mediums from the land under threat of death, but as soon as he felt a need for their much valued services what did he do? Run as fast as he could to consult one, yet if any of his subjects had done such a thing, they, and the medium, would have been severely punished. This 'do as I say but not as I do' attitude is rife in the holy books from beginning to end, and yet the mass of devout followers do not see through it. This does not mean to imply that they are stupid, for the brightest of minds can fall for the simplest of confidence tricks, especially when the emotion known as fear is brought into play, and history has shown us that the fear of a god is one of the most potent phobias in existence. It is the adult version of being scared of the dark, and belief is the teddy bear.

Religious apologists stress that such psychological comfort is not only necessary, as informal studies have apparently shown that believers, regardless of their faith, suffer less mental illness than those without one, but also proves there is a God. This latter argument is illogical unless Yahweh, Brahma, and Thor the Thunder God etc., all tolerably co-exist and look after their own. Fear however is once again the key, and the underlying threat remains, if you do not believe in God, then you are likely to go nuts.

In light of this acknowledgement, that the use of fear was and still is a predominant factor in world religion, not only did I have to continue research of numerous ancient texts, but also had to become familiar with the science of psychology.

I knew from the outset that I had set myself a daunting task, as its gamut was so far reaching, but fortunately I was receiving a lot of help. Many guys that I mixed with would go to the library and borrow books that they felt would be useful to me and drop them off at my cell. It was much valued assistance and although some of the material was poor in quality and augmentation, sometimes I would be delivered a real pearl. This was important as I could never write a book based solely upon opinion, my hypotheses had to be substantiated, so a reference book was the only way to go. I had to show my working and how I had arrived at the conclusions that I did, otherwise such a work, no matter how valid, would never be respected. I kept Archie's motto in mind all the time, which insisted that I should write and confirm so well that my conclusions could be rejected but not refuted.

Fortunately, prison is great for concentration, simply because it is so easy to shut yourself off from the real world, so my task was made easier in that respect, it was a blessing in disguise so to speak.

To fulfill any project successfully and simultaneously make it through a long period of incarceration the ability to mentally 'block yourself off' is an option that has to be taken, because if you do not, the frustration brought about by your inability to have any tangible impact on the lives of people you care for would drive you crazy. While I was away my sole wish was that those close to me on the outside would remain in good health and still be alive when I got out. For the most part I was fortunate. Four older people and two younger male friends died during my sentence and I was unable to pay my respects. In all six cases it was a bitter blow, a fact that made me even more insular and psychologically withdrawn. My best trick is that I never show it.

All of the elder people were close friends of my father, and I should have been there to represent him at their funerals. Shamefully, I could not, and the best I could do was send cards. Dad's friendship with two of them went back to what you might term the 'old days.'

Neither were flesh and blood relatives, my Aunt Dolly, was Dad's schoolmate from kindergarten back in Jamaica, and the other, Uncle Lloyd was a best friend that also fought through thick and thin to make something of himself as a property owner when they arrived in Britain. Once again, I was glad Dad was not present to give me that disapproving shake of his head or one of those disappointed looks of his. They cut to the bone, I preferred the licks.

There were those though whose losses made mine seem pale by comparison and there were three instances where I felt deeply for those concerned. Two of them involved inmates that died as soon as they tasted freedom, one was self-inflicted, and the other, a lesson in the tragedy of jail.

C-KO was at Rye Hill from the start and present when we had the run of the place to ourselves. He was also from Handsworth and very much a fun kind of guy, popular with both inmates and officers alike, so once again, just like with Yohanne, everyone was made up for him when his parole was granted and it was hugs and best wishes all around. (He was also a wicked cook and when he was allocated seniority in the kitchen and cooked a Jamaican meal for the prison menu, clean plates and second helpings were much in evidence, even the officers ate with us).

The same can be said, and perhaps even more so, for Mr Khan. I call him Mr Khan because I do not know his first name, it did not come into the equation to ask it as I would never have used it anyway. I feel uncomfortable calling my elders by their first names. Mr Khan was an Asian senior citizen, and one of those humble and understated men that you know has experienced every aspect of life. He automatically garnered respect from every inmate in the facility. I always wondered how any of the younger officers could have instructed him in a sentence review. I'm sure that he would have been humble and receptive throughout, nodding slowly when they were telling him how well he had behaved himself while in the facility. In spite of his predicament, he exuded an aura of wisdom that would have made any lecture seem redundant, let alone from some jumped-up ex-store assistant.

I remember one officer telling a group of inmates that he was leaving the service, and this after only a few short months. When pressed as to why, he said it was because he could not bring himself to lock the guys that he had become friendly with in their cells at night. I remembered reading of Nelson Mandela's warders being in a similar predicament after being in his presence for a while. In reality, someone has to do the job, I'm just glad that I was not the officer that had to turn the key on Mr Khan's cell. I swear I would pretend to lock it and leave it open every night.

The first of the shocks was when the news came back that C-KO was dead, and this barely two weeks after being released from an eight year sentence, some of the female officers and auxiliary staff wept openly in front of the inmates. The story as I heard it was that he was partying hard in celebration of his release before planning to knuckle down to employment. Unfortunately while in jail he had developed a heroin habit and swallowed a wrap of the drug when he thought he was about to be subjected to a police search after leaving a party. If found with this contraband, even though it was for personal use, (the legacy of an impractical prison system), he would have been in violation of parole and immediately sent back to finish the full term of his sentence. The wrap burst in his stomach leaving its contents free to poison his system. He died that very day. The irony? The police walked right past him to attend to a nearby situation, their presence on the street was a coincidence.

Mr Khan's case was equally tragic. As expected, because there would have been an outcry had it not been the case, he was granted 'D' category status almost as soon as he was eligible, which I for one was relieved to hear. Most de-classifications at Rye Hill are purposely delayed because it is a private jail and more profits are made from higher security graded felons, and I am not talking about by weeks or even a few months, I am talking a year to eighteen months in many cases. The excuses were usually bare-faced lies. 'We're waiting for this or that report, probation are late, it's the open prison facility dragging their heels!' etc, etc. Officers would be caught in a lie on a regular basis because they were either reluctantly following orders and eventually passed the buck, or were not bright enough to avoid contradicting themselves when forced into giving explanation. Exposure was par for the course. As a result, Rye Hill was labelled 'HMP Lie Hill', a name which is still popular with that institution to this day.

I know that Mr Khan was looking forward to spending lost time with his wife, his children, and his grandchildren. He had served his time impeccably and it was a joy to see him leave for open conditions. Within three months, less than a year short of his parole release, he was dead, a heart attack, suffered while in his room at the open facility. This tragedy was a stark reminder to anyone with a brain about how to serve time in jail. There is only one objective, serve it as wisely as possible and get out at the first available second allowed by the authorities. One day extra is one day too much.

I cannot name the person in the third example touched by the hand of death, for the grief that it caused him put him in a state of mind and path of action that would be hard to avoid. When a person feels that they have nothing to lose, anything goes.

While on day release from an open facility he accepted a lift from some friends in a transit van which was stopped by the police, as a result he was taken back into closed custody. The van contained multi-kilo parcels of cannabis. This was particularly bad news for him as he was currently serving time for a drug offence. Whether he was party to the transaction being perpetrated by the driver of the van is debatable as in the subsequent criminal case he was deemed not guilty and excused from the proceedings while the trial was in its infancy.

This mini-setback was bad enough but during his time in full-time lock up for that allegation, he was to endure an experience that he would never psychologically recover from. After a brief and unexpected illness his wife passed away. He was stricken with shock, grief, and guilt, and the charges from which he was subsequently absolved seemed trivial in comparison.

A few years had passed by the time I had met him and he was one of those characters that was liked and respected by everyone. He was of humble demeanour, quietly but firmly spoken, and like Mr Khan, well versed in life. He was another of the cons to approach me, for whatever reason he thought I was suitable, to conduct some 'business' upon our release.

I do not think I have ever met anyone so quietly and thoughtfully bitter with the authorities and it was clear that any thought of ever going straight upon release was as far from his mind as it could be. He was on a mission and made it plain to those that he trusted.

The last straw for him came when he was told that he would have to serve an extra eight months because the authorities believed that he had in excess of one hundred thousand pounds in criminal proceeds that he had not given them. It seems clear that very soon crimes of finance will routinely be sentenced more harshly than offences against the person. I remember the ruling that stated that the British serial rapist Iorworth Hoare would not have to compensate his victims one red cent after winning over six million pounds on the lottery. This because he won the money more than six years after the assault took place. I personally found this inconceivable. He was serving a life sentence that amounted to only 16 years behind bars after devastating the lives of several and in some cases retired women and yet was being given permission to live the life of a lord upon his release. He should have been ordered to hand over every penny to those women, in terms of morality the situation was a no-brainer and the grounds upon which the eventual decision was reached are unfathomable. (Just days before this book went to press the Law Lords unanimously ruled that this was unfair and any financial claims for reparation that exceed the six year time limit will now be considered upon individual merit. This includes the claim against Hoare although the amount of compensation is likely to be limited to approximately one hundred thousand pounds.)

This laxity however, does not apply to any criminal subject to a confiscation order ruling. I have been told with certainty by two barristers that if I ever win the lottery I would have to immediately turn the proceeds over to the Crown. When I asked what would happen if I became wealthy from legitimate enterprise I was told that the law was less clear but there were no guarantees! The serial rapist walks away a multi-millionaire because his was a crime of violence against a person but anyone convicted of a non-violent felony against the government is permanently under the screw. Go figure.

This type of imbalance breeds hostility and 'X' as I will now call him told me plainly that he would serve the extra eight months rather than give more money to the Crown. They had already confiscated his houses and the contents of his bank accounts, and had waited until the day prior to his parole to inform him of the extra time to be served. And this without consideration of the personal loss that he had suffered while away. When I say that the justice system is based upon vengeance and not justice I am not kidding. He was one very angry individual. He lives abroad now and sends shipments of various contraband, in very large amounts, to various contacts in the UK for distribution, and I know of two men still in jail as I write, that cannot wait to get out and work for him. It is that old 'nothing to lose' mindset that can make anyone very dangerous, and what was scary was that I knew that I had it in me to do exactly the same if subject to similar events. I consider myself fortunate that I did not have to find out.

14

There were many men and women, from both inside and outside the jail, that shaped a change in me during the years that I was locked away. Some by their actions, and others by their inaction, not only towards me, but also towards those that I cared about, namely Nia and the children. Some were considerate, selfless, and supportive, both morally and in some instances financially, and others, as expected were disappointingly apathetic on all fronts. Either way, I take it as a valuable lesson as it taught me the nature of people and their true colours, a sorting of the wheat from the chaff as it were, and one for which I am grateful. There were also the new relationship plusses which presented themselves in the many colourful characters that I was to meet, or indeed re-meet, if there is such a word. Some of whom it seems I am destined to have a lengthy relationship with.

It was to strike home early that it really is a small world and I am sure that the likelihood of anyone that gets sent to prison bumping into someone that they already know is quite high. Obviously I had a head start on most because of my martial arts career and of course my friendship with Tim. But there were other surprises in store.

Every week there would be a new intake of cons from other facilities, as profit is the main reason for Rye Hill's existence and business policy dictates that departed inmates are replaced on a one-for-one basis as quickly as possible. I came back from industries one afternoon to find some of the recent intakes bustling about their new cells as they made themselves comfortable. I passed one pad and experienced one of those double-take moments with the familiar face stood outside it and nodded to him as I continued to stride past, it was as I stepped onward that the penny dropped. It was Stan.

I had not seen Stan for some fifteen years, and even at that time only in passing for a quick chat. Even after all of the time that had elapsed since our escapades at the Silver Blades, some twenty-odd years, he was still easily recognisable, it was only the context of our meeting that had made it hard for me to realise it was him at first glance. The same was obviously true for Stan. It was a most pleasant surprise.

Stan had been on the police radar for years, in his youth he was a known villain and he reminded me that the last time I saw him I was telling him to quit crime as it is a mugs game. He laughed heartily on more than one occasion at the irony of my current situation. His comments reminded me quite quickly of what a sharp brain he has, both in terms of memory and astuteness, which was one of the reasons that I had given him such advice. I knew that he had the ability to turn his hand successfully to legitimate enterprises, he just did not fancy it.

His imprisonment on his current charge was the result of police frustration as they could not pin the committal of any suspected crime on him, and so, even though they are less keen to do so these days, they 'fitted him up'. Their logic being that you might not be guilty of 'this one' but you are guilty of plenty of others so all is fair in love and war. He is not the only villain that I know to have been the victim of 'dubiously acquired evidence' based on this tit-for-tat police philosophy, I know of one other who acquiesced peacefully and served the length of his sentence without being granted parole. The police planted a crowbar and stolen goods in the back of his car and then arrested him in a stop and search procedure. They told him that he was lucky as the crowbar could easily have been a shotgun in which case he would have been weighed off with much more than the eight year sentence that was handed down. Stan does not accept this approach one iota and states quite rightly that even villains should only be imprisoned for proven offences, otherwise they could never reform for fear of being framed by over-zealous and ambitious police officers at any stage in their life.

His appeal against conviction is going well and unlike Tim his chances of success seem quite high. If he is, as seems likely, exonerated of all guilt then I am quite sure that he will also press for corruption charges to be brought against the officers concerned. This of course is a double edged-sword and works for and against him in more ways than one. Influence brought to bear on the Court of Appeal could see his bid stopped in its tracks on a technicality before it became too hot to handle, and so the weight of his defensive evidence might work against him, much as it seems to be with Tim. Or, he could win hands down in every area of appeal and in the process make a formidable enemy for himself, the police. They have long memories, with many sons continuing the vendettas of their fathers, and officers of the law, like anyone that brings personal feeling into a domain where they have power, can be very effective in their vindictiveness.

Stan is non-plussed by the likelihood of such a situation and insists that he would use every legal avenue available to embarrass them if ever faced with such a predicament. Just to give you an insight into how sharp he is, he was the first person to make it known to me that it is within your rights not to be photographed by the police when arrested, charged, or convicted, and is proud of the fact that the police, in spite of several surreptitious attempts to gain it do not possess his mugshot. This was impressive but the legitimate business opportunity that he spotted and boxed off while inside was even more so.

Like myself, Stan is an avid reader, and came across a rare book on an ancient Greek system of fortune telling that is so accurate in its powers of prediction that it is uncanny. It consists of a series of statements based upon a coded numerical system and yields scarily concise answers to any question, or series of questions, that are asked of it. It proved a little too accurate for even someone as sceptical as me and so I gave it a wide berth. But there were many others who could not wait to get near it. I initially wrote it off as I believe most successful clairvoyance works because of self-fulfilling prophecy, but hand on heart, I am not so sure.

Stan, who is as strong-minded as anyone that I know, has no doubt about the book's occult ability and such was the respect and interest that it garnered that he registered for world-wide patent while we were at Rye Hill. He also purchased an internet domain and was having a website constructed so that all would be in readiness for its business launch on the internet upon his release. Stan was also to be of great assistance to me in my own project. He is one switched on cookie.

The surprise presence of old faces did not end with Stan's arrival. The physically strongest, and biggest person in the gym, was another lad from Handsworth, a gentle giant who went quite appropriately by the moniker 'Bigger' (not to be confused with the other 'Bigger', the Rastafarian). He had been at Rye Hill for some six months or so before we really spoke, initially he was housed on a different wing, but was moved over to Carling because of a dispute with another inmate. The other con had attacked him with a sock full of snooker balls, and had been rescued by several officers before retaliation began in fullness. Bigger was moved from that unit and his assailant transferred for his own safety. Although he will hate me writing this, if you have seen the Hollywood movie *The Green Mile*, starring Tom Hanks, then you will have some idea of Bigger's physique, it is identical to that of the character played by Michael Clarke Duncan. Bigger is solid muscle, and huge, weighing in at twenty-two stone. He put his arm around me once as we walked along the unit landing while discussing something in confidence. I swear I disappeared, it must have looked as if he was stooping and walking with three arms. The officers on the wing were grateful that he would often intervene when a fight broke out as he would simply pick up one of the protagonists, put him under his arm and carry him back to his cell. It is fortunate that he is not a violent man, and certainly not a bully. It was to become clear to me why, blood is indeed thicker than water.

Bigger and several inmates were sitting at a table in discussion one weekend when I stopped by for a brief chat. He took the opportunity to ask me if I knew a fellow by the name of Lawrence White. It was an unexpected question and immediately put me on my guard as I figured if Lawrence, whom I knew very well, was someone Bigger did not get on with then this would be a problem. I always back my friends up in such a situation and Bigger and I would have had to declare our differences as I like Lawrence a great deal. Imagine my shock, and my relief, when he stated quite bluntly, *'He's my brother!'*

I verbally attacked him for not revealing this sooner by stating that we had been in the same jail for so long and he had just now decided to mention something like that. He laughed and said that he had a feeling that I knew his elder brother but was not sure. Lawrence and I go way back. He was a world class kickboxer and like Bigger, the gentlest of giants.

It had been twenty years previously when Lawrence, myself, and several other martial artists that made up a British team travelled to Yugoslavia for an amateur international contest in the coastal resort of Split. We travelled from England on a combination coach and train journey and enjoyed a successful trip organised by a good friend of mine, the then Yugoslav World Heavyweight Kickboxing Champion and the country's Sports Personality of the Year, Branco Cikatic. We were well received and it was the first time that I had ever competed in an open-air tournament as the ring was placed alfresco due to the marvellous Mediterranean weather. It was a return match as I had promoted the first event in Birmingham, and we were equally successful this time with two of us winning by knockout and the others by points decisions. The return journey to England was equally memorable, and I would not be exaggerating in the slightest if I were to label it an adventure.

In a reverse of the outbound journey, we caught the train from Split to Zagreb where we were scheduled to rendezvous with the coach from England that would take us back to Victoria station in London. Two of us, Lawrence and myself planned to travel on in my car to Birmingham, Ronnie Green, the greatest exponent of Muay Thai Kickboxing ever produced by Great Britain was to catch the train to return to his home city of Manchester, and the fourth team member, Owen Comrie, would do likewise to Nottingham. Well, that was the plan.

We waited at the coach pick up point in Zagreb city centre for hours, and hours, and hours. No coach arrived. To add to our woes, without reserve we had all spent the bulk of our money on gifts for friends and family, we had finance for food, but very little for alternative travel back to Britain. As night began to fall and it became more and more apparent that we were in all probability stranded, the elation of our victories in Split dissipated in tandem with the daylight. We were worried, Yugoslavia to England is a long walk.

A generous boutique owner took pity on our plight and lent us some chairs to sleep on in the shelter of her shop entrance, a situation that bemused everyone that passed us during the night. When the city's call girls came out to work I am sure that we provided an interesting backdrop to Zagreb's night-time activity, and the local police took more than a passing interest in four young men splayed out on chairs as if sitting in a living room in the middle of their city. The ramifications of what that interest might yield if they decided to arrest us did not make for fun consideration.

In the morning we made our way to the train station and spent what was essentially the last of our money on tickets for Mestre, an Italian resort town near Venice which was one of the coach stop off points on our inward journey. It was not home but was a relieving step in the right direction and after several phone calls back to England we were told that the coach company had gone bankrupt while we were away and a substitute company would be picking us up the following day. In the meantime we had pooled enough money together to purchase a single fare ticket for one of us to head back to London and Ronnie Green was selected as our cavalryman. If all else failed it was his duty to spread news of our predicament and arrange our rescue if we encountered any further problems. The remainder of us spent that night sleeping outdoors at a beach in another nearby area, Jessolo, and it is an experience I do not want to repeat.

We collected a selection of deckchairs from the seafront and settled into them as best we could, but as the night drew in and the wind became colder, discomfort soon settled in, and hypothermia was most definitely on the cards if we did not take preventative action. We scavenged every table, dustbin, and shop that was still open to gather as many newspapers as we could and stuffed our clothes with them until we looked like scarecrows, but this was still not enough. The wind had turned from being very cold into an icy blast so we extended our hunt for string, rags, or any type of material that would bind the remaining sheets of newspaper to the exterior of our clothing and snuggled into our respective recliners as best we could. It is one of the longest and most uncomfortable nights that I have ever spent anywhere and gave me a newfound respect for vagrants in terms of their resilience and ingenuity. Sleeping rough is exactly that. Rough. Still, the three of us survived nature's onslaught and our spirits picked up as the morning approached. The only question was, would the new coach arrive as promised? Having spent the last of our funds on bread and jam for a hearty breakfast we were now totally destitute and without money for food, drink, or telephone. Thank goodness for collect calls.

The coach was scheduled to arrive in the late afternoon and so it was a long, hungry, and fretful day. When it came we had the usual language barrier problems as the driver did not speak English. Owen tried to ascertain whether he was headed for London, and the driver did his best to security check us with a myriad of broken-English confirmation questions. I lost my patience and simply boarded the bus, I wasn't in the mood to discuss which area of England it was destined for, the correct country was more than enough detail. Lawrence did the same, and we plumped ourselves into some empty seats leaving Owen out front as the United Nations Ambassador that he was meant to be. He soon got the picture and came and joined us too. We were on our way home at last.

At the outset of this incredible journey I had picked Lawrence up from his parent's home in Handsworth as the two of us were going to make our way to London together in my car. When I arrived, the house was abuzz with excitement and I waited in the hallway for him to come downstairs with his luggage. There were a myriad of children running around the place as they do on such occasions all the while wishing that they were going too. I asked Bigger if he was one of those kids that were so excited that day. 'Yes', he said, '*I was!*'. He wasn't a pesky little kid anymore though, and looking at him I threw my mind back in time, not so much trying to remember that particular day, but more in trying to get a grasp on how one of those brats could be this athletic giant that now stood before me. The fact that we were both also now in such an outlandish predicament made fate seem all the more bizarre. Who could have foreseen it? And yet there was more to come in a strange twist of fate that was to save the life of my nephew.

A month or two earlier a new batch of inmates had arrived and a week or so after this I settled in behind a group of them in the dinner queue. It was clear who the alpha-male was, as many inmates came to the unit door to ask for him and he was given a healthy respect by the others that were constantly in his company. He was tall, about six feet, with a huge upper back and comparatively thin legs, the classic boxer torso. So much so that he reminded me of the legendary pugilistic world champion, Thomas Hearns. He had an equally stern demeanour too and I figured that without a doubt he was someone to be taken pretty seriously, but as normal I was my usual jovial self when we caught each others gaze and I made a throwaway comment that he needed to work his legs more in the weights room to catch up with that impressive back. He wasn't offended, he just looked at me and said, *'Don't watch that my friend, they're stronger than they look'* then turned around to continue his conversation with his compatriots. I was impressed, normally you would get much vitriol with what could have easily been taken as a put down, although I certainly didn't mean it as one. It was pleasantly surprising and I felt it was clear that this was one self-confident young man.

It was a few nights later, while I was studying in my cell that he knocked my door, opened it and glanced in, he nodded his head as he took in the sight of me sitting bespectacled at my sideboard with several open-paged books before me, and umpteen others scattered behind me on my bed. I told him he was welcome to come in and he did so, still nodding in approval, *'So this is what everyone's talking about that's going on in here?'* Scanning the titles of some of my reading material he picked up one or two and flicked through their pages while I gave him a summary on their subject matter and we began to converse. I was surprised that he was not only open-minded and able to talk in a relaxed and confident manner about my specialist subject, but that he also chose to substantiate his comments with facts, dates, and figures. As usual I was re-learning that old lesson again, never judge a book by its cover. I eventually got around to asking him his name, Bones, is the one he gave me, another street name, to go along with the numerous others in the facility, Skippa, Matches, Cougar, Fire, Full-eye, Canada, Ranks, Ella, 'T', 'K', Jelly, Fathead, Popeye, Chubby, Crazy, Trog, Johnnie 'J', Predator, Joe-Dawg, et al and not to mention 13, Silk, and Bigger (twice), it didn't matter whether they were black, white, or Asian, aliases were cool. I'm sure they all had a meaningful origin but after a while you get too tired to ask. I was to discover that Bones was not called by that term because of his lean appearance.

As I stated earlier the formation of the Burger Bar Boys and the enmity that developed between them and the Johnson gang is so vague now as to be almost mythical, what is sure is that in the case of the Burgers' there were two main figures, one, referred to by the national newspapers as a 'shadowy figure', is

'S-1', the other, is Bones. As expected, they are older than most of the other members, and in criminal terms are wisdom figures to the young wannabes on the way up. This reverence is not without its tragedy, as so clearly emphasised by 13's death, for the more the leaders are admired, the more daring, brazen, and foolish newer recruits will be to impress them. This was not a point lost on Bones, and was one that I put to him early on in our relationship. He confided that he was concerned at how matters were escalating on the streets of Handsworth, especially since his imprisonment, stressing that even he could never condone violence for the sake of it. When atrocities had begun there were some very clear black-and-white beefs, followed by the subsequent recriminations, yet much of it now was mindless machismo that would raise its ugly head in the slightest shade of grey. Yet, even with his thoughtfulness and insight it is a life that Bones will do well to pull away from so long as hostilities continue, a fact that made itself clear within the walls of Rye Hill prison.

He began to borrow books from me the very first night that he came into my cell and would rapidly absorb them before bringing them back for exchange every few days or so. He became friends with Tim as well as myself and we enjoyed each others company immensely, so naturally, when I did not see him in the dinner queue and he did not visit my pad for a few days I sensed that there might be some sort of problem. This is not unusual in jail and I assumed that it might well be that he had a personal issue of some kind that he simply needed to meditate upon.

It turns out that my intuition was not only correct but it was worse than I thought, there was a powder keg brewing on Carling unit. The staff had inadvertently moved one of the Johnson Crew onto the wing. It was a young lad named Nathan who went by the street moniker of 'Lynx', who just as I had mentioned earlier, was as respectful a youth as you might wish to meet when in the presence of sensible company, and came from an admirably Christian household. The reason that I know this is because he was another of those many visitors to my cell who had heard about my literary enterprise and chatted to me with interest about my chosen subject matter, and again, as usual, I lent him reading material upon request. It really is a tragedy how endearing these guys are when dressed in their natural persona, but their need for street credibility makes their lycanthropic transformations almost impossible for them to shed and they have anger at finger-tip call twenty-four seven. It is because of this that my pleas for tolerance cut no ice with Bones.

'Are they trying to wind me up?' was the greeting I was met with when I entered his cell. His rhetorical questioning continued in the same vein as he sat on his bed, bespectacled, reading, and clearly, very, very, annoyed. I suggested that he keep doing the right thing, that is, stay in his cell, while I try to resolve the problem. As I walked out of his pad he said *'Howard, make sure they move that boy off this wing!'* It was my sole intention, but first I had to speak with Nathan.

He knew as soon as I asked permission to enter his cell why I was there and told me that he could not understand why he had been allocated to Carling unit as other members of the Johnsons at Rye Hill were on Farley and Hastings. I asked him how he would feel about moving as it was the most sensible option for all concerned, thankfully it was a point on which he readily agreed.

The current bone of contention was that before his transfer to Rye Hill, Nathan, (allegedly), and three other Johnson gang members had waylaid one of the Burger Bar Boys while on remand at The Green and stabbed him repeatedly with makeshift weapons. Unlike Rye Hill, such incidents are rare at Winson Green, that institution is on the ball with the politics of urban life and these two rival factions are even allocated separate gym sessions. Rye Hill was, and as I write still is, a work in progress, and they were clueless at the situation that they had created. In this day and age how hard could it be to set up a computer file to list gang-affiliation or other acquaintances of incoming felons? Such was their amateurishness that I wondered if the staff had even bothered to read the files of inmates that were resident within the prison walls.

I asked the unit reception desk to arrange a meeting with one of the other unit managers, Carling did not have one at that time because they were awaiting a replacement, and I was told that Michelle Hancock was on duty and presiding that evening. That suited me as Michelle was another ex-martial artist and was a former student of my old friend Ivan Riley, having trained up to Black-belt status under his tutelage. To ask for a unit manager on such an impromptu basis was a breaking of protocol, such a request was normally made by the filling out of forms and processed within a forty-eight hour framework, this situation could not tolerate such bureaucracy and without specifying detail I told the officers on duty that night that I needed to see Michelle on an urgent matter as soon as possible. I imagine that they were surprised to see me in such serious mood and passed the message to her without any further question.

She arrived within thirty minutes and expressed that she considered matters to be of some concern because the request had come from me. After outlining the situation the only name that I could give her was Nathan's, he was the one that was going to be moved and was serving a relatively short fixed-term sentence, this was pertinent as there was no way that Bone's, a two-strike lifer could have any mention of this enmity on his papers as it would without doubt have been a further hindrance to his chances of parole, she understood my reticence to be more specific and wisely took my comments on board anyway. Nathan was transferred to another unit the next morning. He and Bones later had a confrontation in the gym, (what does that tell you about the administration at Rye Hill?), but fortunately it did not amount to anything serious. For my part it was great to have Bones back to his usual self and it was not a moment too soon.

Nick, my eldest, was now in his early twenties and had left the family home to live at the old Brown family house where I was born in Handsworth. He had grown used to the independence that he enjoyed while away in residence at Bedford College, and now back in Birmingham had settled in well to life in the old neighbourhood of his father, uncles, and grandparents. He had also secured a decent evening job as manager in one of the bars on Broad Street, a premier location of Birmingham City Centre night life, and as a result was well known by many of the town's popular faces. Fortunately, one of these was S-1 and some of the younger Burger Boy and Johnson members. I was proud of the fact that he did not favour any of them over the other but dealt with them all as his business demanded, without prejudice.

His cousin, Julian, a relative on Nia's side, was staying with him at Boulton Road and unbeknown to Nick had just finished in a relationship with a girl that had begun dating one of the Burgers. With the usual vitriol of youth and spurned love, Julian apparently passed some unsavoury comments about his ex-girlfriend, and her new beau responded in Galahad fashion, Burger Bar style. I was informed of the seriousness of events when I phoned Nia one morning to check that all was well, she told me that her sister had been crying as some of the Burgers had threatened to kill her son. I contacted Nick immediately in the hope that his cousin was also at Boulton Road and that I would find out more detail about the situation but Julian had already left the property, and quite wisely too. The Burgers had been there twice to look for him. On the first occasion they had asked Nick if Julian was in the house and had left when he told them that he was not, on the second they barged past Nick while he stood at the front door and conducted a search of the premises. If Julian was there that evening one can only imagine what would have transpired.

I made my way to see Bones before going to work, told him that my nephew's life was in danger, and asked for his help. He assured me that by the time I came back from industries that evening all would be resolved. It actually took him a few days of constant telephone conversation to totally quash the hunt for Julian, but when he did he told me with no small measure of confidence that I could rest easy as without a doubt he had smoothed the issue over. I did not ask him what had been said or any other detail and I have never heard another word about the matter to this day. Thank goodness.

What Bones did mention however was that he wanted explanation of one of my throwaway incendiary devices during a debate with some Christian inmates. I had told them that not only was the name of their saviour Jesus not unique in the biblical canon, but in the gospel story of his crucifixion the church had intentionally hidden the fact that another of the major characters in that story was also named Jesus, and in more meaningful fashion than the one now recognised as the Christian figurehead. Bones would not let me leave his presence until I had explained my comment in detail.

The red-herring in question was not just a trick of translation, but also a deletion that has spurred much of the world's anti-Semitic feeling as was so readily propagated by the Roman Church. The story relates how when the Christian messiah was captured and taken for trial to the Roman procurator Pontius Pilate, the official, believing him to be innocent, was hesitant to pass any form of sentence, and was pressured into it by the Jewish religious hierarchy. The Jews did not want to execute Jesus under their own law, even though he was delivered to the Romans for claiming to be the 'King of the Jews'. That part of the story makes little sense, for if Jesus was a literal Jewish king, then it would have been the ruling Romans who would have been keen to execute him and not the Jews, who historically, and even in the gospel subtexts, were fed up with Roman tyranny.

In a bid to placate his own conscience Pontius Pilate took advantage of a supposedly Jewish practice that allowed for a prisoner to be released from captivity at the time of their Passover, and suggested that they choose between Jesus and one other. These particular Jews, who are painted as extremely pro-Roman made no bones about their preferred selection. They were given the choice of releasing a murderer who had taken part in rebellious activity, or the gospel hero. It is here that the Church has played one of its biggest deceptions.

The text tells us that the other prisoner was named Barabbas, which in itself is deceptive as like the earlier mentioned bar Jesus (Son of Jesus), his title is correctly rendered bar Abbas. The word Abba means 'Father' and so we have a character here called 'Son of the Father', the 'Father' in question is not specifically identified because there was no need, it is an alternative reference to the supreme Hebrew God. This was part of the deceit, the remainder is more sinister, the first name of Bar Abbas was initially included in the original version of the tale and was removed for two reasons, one, it would have negated the whole premise of Christianity, and two, because it would have absolved the Jews of any guilt for what was later to be deemed an evil choice. Bar Abbas' first name was also Jesus.

In the hidden detail of the story the Jews were faced with a situation where they had to decide who to release from captivity, Jesus, the self-proclaimed, King of the Jews, or Jesus 'the Son of God'. This is intimated in Pilate's words to them in the gospel book of Matthew when he asks the question, '*Whom do you want me to release to you? Barabbas, or this Jesus who is called Christ?*' The deletion seems clear and the entire translation should correctly read, '*Whom do you want me to release to you? Jesus the son of God, or this Jesus who is called Christ?*' The correct translation was bad news for fledgling Christianity even though it gave the tale greater maturity, depth, and intrigue, but alas, due to the subsequent religio-political spin of the early church this literary thought-provoker was denied to the masses.

A later gospel description of Bar Abbas helps to enlighten the Jewish decision even further. We are told in the book of John that he was in custody 'for a certain rebellion made in the city, and for murder', actions which were in keeping with the anticipated behaviour of a Jewish messiah. They were expecting a military leader in the mould of the legendary King David, who would tackle their oppressors, the Romans, head on, and restore their national independence under the laws of Moses. Jesus the King of the Jews did not even come close, whereas Jesus Bar Abbas, far from being the criminal as painted by the church, fitted the bill perfectly as the expected hero figure and symbol of hope.

In light of this, the popular choice made by the Jews was entirely plausible and we must ask which one would we have chosen for release had we been in their predicament? As we know, history, whether ancient or modern, informs us that in such volatile periods the public will always choose the warrior as their leader. The authenticity of the story is diminished even further in this respect as the Romans would never have allowed a character that fomented rebellion within their empire to be given freedom, let alone in exchange for a pacifist.

There is a reference in the New Testament book of Acts which intimates that Bar Abbas was even more than the gospels portray and it is one that made me wonder if the hidden homage paid to him by such a segment is an occult indication that it was he, whatever his real name was, and not his cruci-fied namesake that actually existed.

The later passage concerns the questioning of the apostle Paul by a Roman commander, who asks him, *'Can you speak Greek? Are you not the Egyptian who some time ago stirred up a rebellion and led the four thousand assassins out into the wilderness?'* The gospels tell us that Bar Abbas was released from custody and does not mention him any further yet my suspicions were aroused that this comment might well be in reference to him for two reasons.

The first was that I took the view that nothing was kept in these texts unless it had some significance, otherwise why mention something that in essence was totally irrelevant and would only serve to confuse the reader? Having read so much ancient material I knew that obscure information was usually very significant, and here, apart from this mysterious charac-ter's obvious link to Bar Abbas as someone committed to violent anti-Roman rebellion, there was something else about him, a detail which concerns another main gospel figure, John the Baptist. And it is that this noteworthy rebel was called 'the Egyptian'.

It is curious that the gospel prophet was known as John 'the' Baptist, and not John 'a' Baptist, which indicates that he was uniquely recognised in Judea for performing the ceremony of baptism, which was essentially the water purification rite of the Egyptian goddess Isis, and adopted by the Greeks and Romans before finding its way into Christianity. It was clearly not a Hebrew custom and is not mentioned at all in the Old Testament. With the respect given to John in the gospels it is safe to assume that he would have learned these rites first-hand from the Egyptian priests themselves. Which puts him in good company as almost every major character mentioned in the bible spent time in, or had links with Egypt, such as Abraham, Joseph (he of the many-coloured coat, who was also mummified), Moses, Solomon, and of course Jesus.

Having established that there could well be a connection between Bar Abbas and 'the Egyptian' mentioned in Acts, and the fact that he was one of two Jesus' being considered for crucifixion, called to mind a puzzling question that was asked by two messengers sent by John to find Jesus, or we should say, one of the Jesus'. They were told by John to ask the Hebrew messiah the following, *'Are You the Coming One, or do we look for another?'* Is it possible that this was because John, having been trained in Egypt knew of someone else from that land who was to act as a liberator for the Jewish people, who was also named Jesus, and was known as the 'Son of the Father'? Even within the biblical narratives Bar-Abbas fits the bill perfectly on all counts. All things considered it is not at all an outlandish hypothesis, especially as the gospels are laden with Egyptian dogma and esoteric imagery. It is food for thought.

When I had explained all to Bones, he had some choice words for me, *'Howard, be careful, you're going to upset a lot of people!'* Quite a few friends made similar comments, and some even felt that if *Rulers & Lies* was a success then my life would be in danger. Anything is possible and I am not naïve enough to think that fundamentalist nutcases will not take umbrage at my opus.

They will certainly have a tough time trying to discredit it and so I expect the standard reactions from them. The first will be to personally attack my character as a convicted criminal and imply that it has affected the integrity of my work, and the second may well be to threaten my person. If this is the case then it will mean only one thing, that what I have written has substance and is well presented. I do not think that I would have things any other way.

It is far from my intention to antagonise anyone but merely to give pause for thought, enlighten, and encourage positive debate, especially in the light of current world conflicts, too many of which are religiously charged. It would certainly not hurt to get a more sensible perspective on such matters.

In terms of causing offence I have made a conscious decision to use as inoffensive a style of writing as possible and in that respect believe that I have been as careful as I can be. Not completing my project because of such considerations was certainly out of the question, cowardice has never been my thing.

15

Desire is a funny business. I've had plenty of time during my period of excommunication to contemplate a host of psychological issues, such as human behaviour, emotion, and relationships, and it seems to me that the drive behind them is clearly primeval. Who can explain why some women are hot for murderers and rapists that they have never even met? I can understand to some extent that such feelings might be based on a lustful urge, because I'm convinced that at some point every woman likes the beast in her man, but normally this is allied to a sense of safety and control. Yet to take on a perfect stranger, which is a risk with the most law abiding of guys, let alone a convict, must be like playing Russian roulette. Still, such liaisons were enlightening and fun to observe.

One of the best friends and most magnetic men that I met while locked up was the son of a Ghanaian businessman who had fallen foul of the law while on a trip to England, and had done the tour of British prisons before finding his way to Rye Hill at the tail end of his sentence. Everyone called him 'K' and I liked him from the very first time we met.

An extraordinarily erudite and well rounded young man, he had three university degrees, all based around engineering, was a talented oil painter, and worked out in the gym like a monster. 'K' had muscles coming out of muscles and looked like an American wrestler, yet physically he carried himself as small as he could. I used to admire him walking along the narrow corridors on the upstairs landing of the unit, either squeezing by or halting as smaller inmates came the other way. 'K' is huge but tries to hide it, Bigger has much the same psychological make-up, a trait I find most impressive. In the gym they were the uncrowned kings of the weights room, and the bar would bend as they both dead-lifted well over seven hundred pounds in a bid to outdo each other. It was great to see their power unleashed, and with such good spirits too.

But nothing endeared me more to the big African than our debates, and boy would we argue. He was one of a select number of guys who could change my view on a topic, and anyone that knows me will tell you that is no mean feat. 'K' has a lot about him, and his physical appearance allied with his intellect made him more than a hit with the ladies as I will explain in a moment.

I must impress, I had no idea that prison was such a hotbed for romance. The amount of dates fixed up by inmates for other inmates was something to behold and an enigma that I could never figure out. Many of the girls had never previously met the blind date in question and yet were willing to commence a relationship, if one can use that term in such an instance, and wait for their new 'partners' to finish their sentence. I got used to that abnormality quite quickly and decided that there must be a certain type of woman that finds the allure of a man pitted against society quite appealing. I could think of no other reason why they would voluntarily put themselves through such torture. And indeed there were a few instances that were straight out of Hollywood.

One lad, Mark, had a medical condition that required him to be taken outside the facility for anaesthetic surgery, as a category 'C' prisoner this entailed him being handcuffed and escorted by two officers to and from the hospital grounds. The procedure to remedy his ailment required that he stay on ward overnight, and he was handcuffed to his sick bed throughout the entire pre and post operation procedure, with one member of prison staff permanently at his side. It was a pleasant surprise to hear that he enjoyed celebrity status at the hospital as the sight of him being led around in his handcuffed state brought onlookers to a standstill. Children that were misbehaving straightened up in his presence and the reaction from adults was also quite remarkable. Mark told me that the bulk of people that he came across offered him words of encouragement and were quite polite, and some, feeling that such a display of restraints were unnecessary, were openly antagonistic to the accompanying officers. One old lady even berated them and made it plain that they should be ashamed of themselves for what they were doing to him. What he enjoyed even more was that the nurses made much fuss of him, smiling, chatting, and clearing his path while ushering him through to the allocated doctor with zero delay. Clearly there is an aphrodisiac quality in the notion of the caged animal. He lapped it up.

To top all this, his story of the pretty attendant nurse that took his prison details and promised to write to him, made great dinner time chat and boy did he get quizzed. Guys can be such lechers, working their way from questions about her personality and hair colour to the size of her breasts in surgical fashion. When he received the promised letter and photographs it was the icing on the cake, and our new star had to prepare a fresh round of after-dinner speeches, and all this within two days of being back at Rye Hill. He showed his mementoes off with pride to all his inner circle and I have to say she was a very attractive girl. I sometimes wonder if the allure faded after his release and he became a 'regular guy'. I hope not, from his stories and later correspondence I got the impression that she was as keen on him as he was on her. Maybe it was not a match made in heaven, but who can tell? It would be a great anecdote when entertaining close friends, and very hard to top that's for sure.

This kind of unforeseen attraction was not an isolated incident and one of the interludes that 'K' was involved in was equally intriguing, reminding me of the old Trevor Howard and Celia Johnson ill-fated romance in the classic British movie *Brief Encounter*.

'K' continued to study hard while incarcerated and did most of it, as well as honing his oil painting and sketching skills, during the jail's most quiet period, night. His cell light would remain on throughout the early hours and he would often lock his door after tea to sleep until about 10pm before burning the midnight oil. Lock down was at 8.30pm and the night shift staff would take over for duty by about 9pm. Many of these officers worked permanent nights and so were not known to the majority of inmates, not unless you were awake when they did their hourly rounds and opened our door flaps to check we were not sawing through the bars.

Until they got used to those of us that were regular night-owls, it was a cause for alarm to night staff when an inmate was awake at all hours as it could be due to sickness, a drug habit, or some other reason that might cause a security problem. They all became used to 'K' quite quickly, his intelligence, determination, and talent, were evident in equal measures, notwithstanding his good looks and Herculean physique, which I must assume, to the female officers was worthy of note. Quite a few of them would ask him to hold up some of his work and chat to him to pass the time in-between their rounds, and it brought a smile to my face, on the occasions that I was still awake studying myself, to hear them stop at his door and begin whispered conversation.

One of them, who quizzed him about his endeavours every time she was on duty, told him one night that she had put in a transfer application for re-allocation to another unit and so it would be their last chat together. When 'K' asked her why she had done this she said it was because of him, a statement that left him more than a little bemused, as he had been nothing but polite and respectful to her, as well as to the other sleeping inmates by being as quiet as he could both while working and during their conversations. She was at first reluctant to elaborate on her statement and it took him some pressing for her to confess that she had fallen in love with him and it was in her own best interests to move on. 'K' was flabbergasted, and having enjoyed their relationship in an inspiring fashion asked her to reconsider. It was a pointless request, she had made her mind up, and after that night he never laid eyes on her again.

When he told me what had transpired I wondered why he was so surprised, for even with his current predicament he was still quite a catch. I asked him if he had told her about his upbringing during their conversations, that he came from a middle-class family and that his father, a successful business-man, had launched his own African television station that same year. I was bursting with pride myself when I saw the newspa-per reports that had been sent over from Ghana, so how must a working class night-shift worker have felt when faced with this friendly and interesting young guy? 'K' was still at a loss with the whole situation and continually pointed out that their chatter had never stepped over the boundaries of an officer-inmate relationship. It occurred to me at that point that I was not the only person slow on the uptake with regard to the thinking patterns of women.

These types of relationships were so rife that I could reel off a string of them, some were entertaining, and others quite tragic, as a percentage of these girls were coerced by their new suitors to bring drugs into the prison for them, and I felt genuine pity for those that were caught. The penalty for bring-ing even a small amount of contraband into one of Her Majesty's Prisons is an automatic custodial sentence, and so these girls would become victims in more ways than one. Not only had they fallen under the spell of truly incorrigible men who could never love them as much as they loved themselves, but they had also now dramatically lessened their own worth in the scales of human society. I loathed selfish behaviour and made it clear to the inmates that encouraged such a risk, that they should be ashamed of themselves, even those that I had become friendly with. No one ever argued back.

On the topic of merely being an observer of romantic inter-ludes I was soon to get knocked off my perch of being respected as the least easily swayed of all inmates. And to be honest, I did not see it coming.

We all checked the post board everyday. It's a habit you develop quickly in prison as receiving mail, aside from visits and using the telephone, is the next port of call for keeping in touch with the outside world. I regularly received post from friends and relatives but was struck one day by the fact that my correspondence was marked as having entered via the jail's internal section. I thought this odd as I was not resident at that time on any rehabilitation courses or anything else that required Rye Hill administration or any other jail to make contact with me.

My letter was in actual fact a form from the Prison Location Service, the government unit that informs those interested in the whereabouts of persons in custody. Its contents froze me on the spot. 'K' walked by as I stood transfixed, and concerned about my well-being asked what was the matter. I didn't answer, I just kept lowering then raising that mesmerizing piece of paper to and from my face, I was a world away.

I was being asked a very simple question. Would I give my permission for a Elle Evans to be given the details of my whereabouts? At first I thought it was a prank, being perpetrated by Nia to discover whether I had rekindled my affair with Elle during our marriage, and I seriously thought about not authorising the request. I took the form up to my cell to digest it more calmly and had barely sat down on my bed when 'K' entered to see what had invoked my so obvious trauma. When I explained my background with Elle as an old flame that I had not seen for twenty years and that she had rejected my later attempts to contact her, he was in no doubt that I should return the form in the affirmative without delay. It was what I wanted to hear.

Now came the sleepless nights, as I waited and checked for post more diligently than I had ever done. I wondered whether she even knew where I was, and contemplated the possibility that the form might have been sent by an agency, who would inform her to her horror that I was now a convicted criminal. To my mind this would explain why I received no reply in the week that followed. The week following that one began in the same pattern, I was sure now that I was right. She had been scared off. I told you, I know very little about women.

It was almost two weeks before I received Elle's letter and my diary entry for that day read thus: '*At last, got Elle's letter, maybe I can get some sleep now. She sounds glad to have located me. I'm hoping I get to see her soon. Wrote to Elle tonight, told her about the children and an outline of my situation. I'm looking forward to getting her reply. I didn't do any work tonight. Read some more Chomsky.*' I've kept diaries of every single day that I spent behind bars in the hope that one day they will make interesting reading for my offspring. After logging events that night I slept like a baby.

While I waited for the reply to my missive I ordered a prison location map from reception in readiness for insertion with the visiting order that I felt sure she would request in her reply. I was right, she did, and she also informed me of her own family details and new married name, she had used her former surname to ensure that I knew it was her. It was the information that I had waited almost two decades to hear. Now all I had to do was wait patiently for her visit, it seemed like the longest three weeks of my life.

The night before the visit was one of those when you check the clock every ten minutes in the hope that an hour has passed. I felt like a school-kid the night before a coach trip, I was so excited I didn't sleep a wink. I watched the clock all morning thinking it would be just my luck for there to be some last minute hiccup and Elle could not turn up. When I eventually received the call from visits to make my way through to the meeting hall, it meant for sure that a twenty year wait was over.

When I saw her it seemed as if I had last seen her just the week before, such was the natural connection between us, it certainly did not seem like twenty years. As I expected she looked sensational, she had aged a little, as had I, but likewise had done it well, looking much younger than her years, and very glamorous too. I was smitten, and I hate to admit, over the moon to hear that she had also recently become divorced and was renewing old acquaintances, she made it clear though that she was not looking for a relationship and was enjoying her new found freedom, but that was more than enough for me and certainly more than I could have hoped for in my wildest dreams. The two hour visit flew by as we tried to pack twenty years worth of chatter, opinion, and restrained emotion into such a short session. She told me how she had never forgotten the call that I had made a few years after we had finished, and even though she was still furious with me at that point, it later touched a nerve as the years passed. I for my part told her how I had told many people about her whenever the topic of broken hearts reared its head, and had even mentioned the depth of our relationship to Tim when he arrived at Rye Hill. Earlier in my sentence I often wondered whether she would come to hear of my plight, and maybe even take action to visit me but quickly dismissed such a notion as fantasy. Just like my old friend Mark Page, the prison officer at the Green, she must be telepathic.

Elle had gone through quite a mill to locate me. In the first instance she had contacted some very well known people in the martial arts world, all of whom told her that they did not know where I was. They all did know but out of respect for me would not tell her. At that point she thought that their guarded behaviour was because I had passed away and they did not have the heart to pass on such news. She told me she had cursed me if that had been the case. When she eventually got through to an old student of mine, who was now the head of his own kickboxing group, she pressed him to tell her if that was indeed the case. Was I dead? *'Oh no'*, he said, *'He's not dead.'* She was flabbergasted when he reluctantly told her of my fate. How could Mr Nice Guy come to such a pass? Still, this information did not dampen her resolve and at last she had something concrete to go on. Her only reservation was would it be me now that did not want to re-establish contact? I told her about my receipt of the form from the prison location service and my initial reaction. I guess she knew it would knock my socks off.

It's difficult to put into words how that visit felt, short of to say that in the annals of my life it was historical, and it was fun. I came out walking on air and when I got back to my cell, I locked the door and lay down on my bed, chilled, happy, and emotionally exhausted. 'K' walked by as soon as he came back from industries, and after trying to open my door peeked through my door-flap and burst out laughing. I never lock my cell door. I was a mere mortal after all.

In terms of our social standing Elle and I were now poles apart, she was employed in a management position with a national-sized company, earned an executive salary and drove a luxury car. She had two children, and lived in a luxurious house in the most prestigious area of Nottingham. I was so proud of how well her life had turned out that it was my turn to become prison storyteller and I enjoyed it to the max. I took it as a mark of respect that no one dared to ask any lecherous questions.

On her next visit Elle told me that I should not be afraid to ask her for any help if I needed it. I did not need any money, in prison most things are free, and I had a decent amount of savings from my work in industries, but her words were still music to my ears. I get very excited when I discover a book that I need and the process of ordering reading material through the prison system can take over a month, which to me was most inconvenient as I needed access to research material on a constant basis.

Stan had found a book in the library entitled 'Battle for the Mind' by an author named William Marshall, a leading physician in psychological maladies, who in this work had analysed the contributions to psychiatric medicine of the Russian neurophysiologist Ivan Petrov Pavlov. Having read some of their work in my mind there is no doubt, these were two very brilliant men. It was no surprise that it took someone as bright as Stan to realise that this tome would be invaluable to my project. I asked Elle to get me my own copy as soon as she could. She jumped at it and pulled out all the stops as the book had been discontinued, and got me an almost brand new copy via the internet. I was falling in love all over again.

The reason that I was so interested in this book was because it addressed the reaction of the brain to traumatic stress. This included the psychological and physiological pressures that can be induced by both internal and external forces, and for me it answered some important questions.

Why is it that intelligent adults become convinced that age old stories of paranormal events are true, and against all logic and evidence defend them to the hilt? I remember telling a Muslim acquaintance in jail, who also happened to be a university educated man, that the story of Noah was not original to the Hebrew religion and was adopted from the metaphorically based belief system from the land of Sumer. He responded that even though what I said made sense, and could even be proven academically, he would continue to believe that the biblical version was both literal and correct simply because 'he had to'. And this from a man that had an outstanding education, so how would the less literate fare under such indoctrination? Out of respect for his belief I left the topic alone, but had to smile when he requested a copy of my book upon publication. I assured him that I would get one to him and it is a promise that I will keep. This was a prime example of what I call intellect battling faith, and I noted that faith usually won. The question is, why?

One explanation can clearly be attributed to the information passed on to us as children by our parents, we trust them unerringly during the fledgling stage of our life, and have to rely upon them for everything, food, shelter, protection, education, and entertainment. This naturally entails a great level of trust, and the belief that what they tell us is good for us becomes entrenched in our psyche. So, whatever beliefs they have, whether political, moral, or religious, we adopt, and keep, certainly until we learn to take responsibility for our own pyramid of needs. It is a fact that less than ten per cent of children break away from their parents' religious beliefs, even in a liberal country like England, so you can imagine how much that figure is reduced in heavily indoctrinated countries such as those in South America, Africa, and the Islamic states.

But even with the trust imbued in the judgement of our parents, there is one over-riding factor, an ultimate mechanism that when all else fails guarantees obedience will be maintained, and it is a simple one, fear. Whether it is a the threat of a spanking, confinement, the bogey-man, or the wrath of a God, the use of fear is effective in the government of behaviour providing the object of the perceived punishment believes that it will take place.

Thus the success of parental indoctrination is not surprising, and eighty to ninety per cent of belief can be ascribed to the traditional influence that falls under the psychological heading of behavioural conditioning, which is extremely hard to break, as evidenced by the example of my Muslim friend at Rye Hill. But what of the remainder, where a person changes dramatically to a completely different way of life or stringently takes on a belief system to which they had no previous affinity? Some even changing so drastically as to embrace beliefs that were not only alien to their upbringing, but in direct contrast.

Pavlov's work illustrated that such psychological conversion could be monitored and analysed under experimental conditions, taking it out of the realm of theory and enabling the results to be assessed and utilised in a practical manner. As ground-breaking as this was, William Sargant's further study made it clear that the methodology Pavlov examined was not new, and had been used for millennia in the realms of religious and political indoctrination.

One of the most intriguing questions surrounding this topic is succinctly posed by Sargant in *Battle For The Mind*, and it is a simple one, 'How can people be induced to believe in what may contradict obvious fact?'

If we consider that billions of people on the planet believe that a giant and invisible super-being created humans, conversed with them, engaged in their national affairs, then voluntarily made himself redundant until an unpredictable future period when he would return to take vengeance on all who did not believe he existed, and add to this that believers choose to ignore the fact that he is brazenly documented as ultra-violent, hot-tempered, vengeful, control-seeking, puerile, and xenophobic, and we have some insight into the power of indoctrination. From an objective viewpoint it is staggering that this mythical history is accepted by so many with no evidence whatsoever, but this is not so surprising if we consider their belief is based upon and fuelled by phobia.

It occurred to me that humans find it very difficult to deal with two things, change, and loss. We are creatures of mammalian habit and attachment, which is why many of us find it so difficult to make what in essence are the simplest of decisions. Moving to a new school, house, job, or partner, especially at an unexpected time, is a monumental task for many. It is generally accepted that moving house is the second most traumatic experience of someone's life after losing a loved one. It seems clear that this is because we build up attachments, associate them with safety, and settle into psychological burrows where we feel secure. It is our natural extinct to avoid fear like the plague, and we are not the only creatures to do this.

Even after his death in 1936 Pavlov's work was largely ignored in the West for two reasons, one, because it was conducted under the auspices of the alienated Soviet Bloc, and two, because the base subjects for his experiments were not humans, but dogs.

In the religious view, experiments gauging the cerebral responses of dogs in reaction to varied physiological and psychological stimuli were of no relevance to the human model for one simple reason, they unlike people, were not considered to have souls. In effect, it was thought that any such comparison was an affront to God's ultimate creation, the human, and could not possibly yield any accurate results. Boy, were they wrong. In the advances of psychiatric treatment Pavlov's findings were invaluable.

His experiments on dogs were conducted under stringent laboratory conditions and are well respected simply because his methods were painstakingly diligent in their attention to detail. He also wisely insisted on comparisons with parallel control experiments conducted by collaborators working in separate laboratories or institutes.

Pavlov was awarded the Nobel Prize for his research on the physiology of digestion before commencing his study of the higher nervous activity of animals which he felt it was necessary to understand in order for him to progress his earlier findings. His logic was simple, the brain and nervous system controlled digestive functions, and so he felt that this was the natural area for the next phase of his research.

This led to over thirty years of work in which he accumulated a wealth of information on the workings of the canine psyche, and the Soviet Government readily made available any equipment and facility that he required when he informed them that he wanted to apply his findings to similar problems associated with human psychology. Their reasons for assisting him were not entirely philanthropic, and it seems clear that his findings influenced the techniques used by the Russian and Chinese Communist regimes in the eliciting of confessions, brain-washing, and the inducement of political conversions. Governments never miss a trick when there is a chance for turning discovery into a double-edged sword.

As much of experimental work on animals tends to be, Pavlov's opus was unsavoury, but he staunchly believed that practical evaluation, no matter how limited in range, could be repeatedly checked and verified, and should therefore take precedence over psychological speculation as was so prevalent in the Freudian school of thought. World War Two was to prove him right.

He had discovered that the reaction of dogs to applied stresses depended largely upon their basic temperament, and in this regard they could be divided into four categories, all displaying a predictably different response to various levels of trauma. Pavlov logged them all meticulously, including the subsequent treatments needed for cure, and even recorded the prescriptive amounts of sedatives needed to help the different categories of dogs to recover from nervous breakdown. The treatment would invariably depend upon the constitutional type of the dog that was afflicted. He learned to invoke neuroses in these animals and then cure them according to type. The application of his findings as a parallel to the human psychological condition became apparent in England during the time of the Normandy invasion of 1944, when doctors noticed that much of the responses which Pavlov had induced in his dogs corresponded all too closely to the war-inflicted neuroses being experienced at that time.

Word spread amongst the neuro-psychiatric physicians responsible for treating these ailments that the findings of Pavlov as recorded in his book *Conditioned Reflexes and Psychiatry* would be of immense assistance to them in their tasks. He had made significant headway into the drug assisted (usually Bromide) treatment of both physiological and psychologically induced trauma, the war had also forced further research, and achieved improved success, especially in the use of either barbiturates or ether, in repairing the same problems.

These drugs could be used to cause the patient to 'abreact' a term used to define the re-incurring of the emotions brought about by their traumatic experience, in an effort to allow them to confront and release the horror they had felt. For their condition to improve it was noted that the emotions that most needed to be revisited were those of fear and anger, Sargant noted that *'little could be done by making, say, a melancholic patient weep and become more depressed.'*

What was equally important, and applicable to the conversion of adults to a religious or political dogma that had not previously featured in their life, was the fact that trauma causes the mind to go into a state of 'protective inhibition', during which previously conditioned responses, as imposed during childhood, are temporarily discarded. This creates a blank slate, or window of opportunity, wherein new information, even data which the afflicted person might once have totally rejected, is now considered, and if the traumatic experience is extreme, it is the formerly abhorrent that now becomes the most acceptable. Pavlov's analysis of this phenomenon was ground-breaking.

Through controlled experiments he had implanted a set of conditioned responses in his dogs and created various stimuli to then gauge their reactions to the most basic of functions such as feeding. This conditioning was so fine-tuned that he showed that a dog could be made to salivate with the expectation of unseen food when a tone of 500 vibrations a minute was sounded, but would not respond at all if the tone was set at only 490. He was thus able to build up a wide range of responses within the dogs in demonstration of their nervous systems' ability to utilise powers of discrimination, and develop both positive and negative reactions to various signals. Humans do the same thing.

Much human behaviour is the result of conditioned processes, implanted either consciously or subconsciously within the brain from early childhood onwards. This is to the extent that certain tasks, when practised enough, become automatic, while others need us to switch on a different part of our brain to focus on them. This conditioning takes into account sight, sound, smell, and touch, and many words also invoke a conditioned response although we may not consciously be aware of it. As children we may for example, build up positive responses to words such as 'sweets', 'play', 'Christmas' etc., and negative ones to 'vegetables', 'homework', and 'bedtime.' The same model can be applied to adulthood where emotional responses also become both positively and negatively charged, so the word 'payday' may automatically incur the opposite sensation to the word 'taxes', and so on. The discovery that severe trauma can in certain cases turn such conditioned responses on their head was entirely accidental.

While being held in their cages in Leningrad during the 1924 flood in that city, water seeped into a low level laboratory holding some of Pavlov's dog's, this was to such an extent that they were left swimming around in fear with their heads at the top of their cages. They were saved from death at the last moment by a laboratory assistant who pulled them down through the water and guided them to safety. The effect on them varied in extent. The dogs that exhibited a marginal amount of fear at the prospect of being drowned were found to retain the conditioned behavioural patterns that Pavlov had induced, while others were so scared that their brains imposed upon them what Pavlov described as 'transmarginal protective inhibition'. This is a condition akin to a nervous breakdown where the brain shuts down to whatever point it needs to in order to protect itself.

There are three stages to this inhibition, the first is described as 'equivalent' and is comparatively mild, showing itself in humans that have suffered such stresses as lack of sleep, a continuously heavy workload, self-inflicted pressure such as seriously contemplating the meaning of their lives, or grief. The result of this phase is that the brain's response to both mild and strong stimuli is the same, and the afflicted person would give the same reaction to someone striking a match to light a cigarette as they would to a building burning down. This stage is usually a temporary affliction and normally cured by a period of rest, but again presents itself as a window of opportunity for the acceptance of new thought.

If the external stresses are intensified then the next phase of inhibition is known as 'paradoxical', where the sufferer responds positively to mild stimuli, while showing little response to strong ones. This is common amongst people who have been subject to extreme fright, in which case they involuntarily respond poorly to direct commands, especially when they try to focus on what they have been ordered to do, conversely, they are able to unwittingly perform the required act once they take their mind off it, in other words when there has been no direct request or stimuli.

The third stage is the one experienced by sufferers of severe trauma, it has been labelled 'ultra-paradoxical', because victims respond by loving what they formerly hated and loathing what they once loved. In the cases of the dogs trapped in the Leningrad flood, those afflicted with this phase became aggressive and snarling towards their regular keepers, and affectionate towards the keepers that had previously been unable to handle them.

Pavlov's meticulous note-taking and study of these responses and his further experiments based upon them were invaluable in the progress made in the treatment of psychologically disturbed victims of the Second World War. It was found that the response to trauma of the human brain was similar to that of Pavlov's dogs, and that successful treatment was largely based upon abreaction, i.e. forcing them to relive the event that had frightened them so much. The dogs would invariably need to be treated with drugs, whereas in milder cases, usually the first transmarginal phase, humans could be forced to revisit and confront their fears by 'talking them out', a technique practised efficiently by Breuer and Freud in their early studies of the treatment of hysteria.

The relationship between these findings and the 'sudden' conversion towards a new political or religious mindset was explored in depth by William Sargant who found that in many cases, both historical and modern, individual and group indoctrination could be incited by peer pressure and other more extreme devices that stirred the emotions, and it was these techniques, especially the incitement of fear, that brought success.

The use of music, chanting, fasting, dancing, prayer, lighting, the propagation of a fear of God, and eternal damnation, are tools that even today have proved so effective that very few religious groups would consider dispensing with them. Fear is the ultimate tool of faith, which is the reason that intellect will normally lose out when it faces this foe in battle.

Having considered this mechanistic treatise on brain function and tallied it with my own experiences and numerous discussions about religion, politics, and the history of morals, I am in no doubt that religion will never die, churches will rise and fall, and belief systems will grudgingly change with the times, but they exist because they are required.

The childhood necessity for answers to the unknown in a bid to stymie our fears never leaves us, from a religious point of view there is much irony in this, as the answers presented are based upon fear anyway. And so, if mythical tales, and their subsequent belief systems are implanted at a young enough age, or even in later life, during a window of opportunity presented by even mild transmarginal inhibition, then it will stay firm even in the onslaught of contrary factual evidence.

To suggest that intelligence, or academic ability alone can prevent this is to show a limited understanding of the human brain and psyche. It is worth noting that some very well educated men of science are devotedly religious, a paradox that flies in the face of their everyday vocation, making it clear that even if we are aware of the aforementioned breakdown processes and the effectiveness of childhood programming, this knowledge in itself does not protect us from inhibition or the indoctrination that might follow. It is a natural defensive function that operates once emotions reach a certain level, be they anger, fear, or guilt, all of which affect our rationale and judgement, and make our minds suggestible to ideas that we would never otherwise consider.

By the time I had finished digesting the bulk of this information a lot of things began to make sense, and it became clear why all major religions insist that where possible their creed be instilled from childhood, and the younger the child, the better. The formulators of the 'holy' texts knew well that this was by far the most successful type of indoctrination and that if done well the child would almost certainly never break free from it, no matter how absurd the doctrine. In this way it would be absorbed at every psychological level, both consciously and subconsciously, and become so awe-inspiring that it would give myth an edge over literal fact. In this manner, their dogma would be perpetuated from generation to generation, for centuries. They were well aware that if they waited to attack the fully developed adult mind their task would be considerably more difficult.

The latter is a point that reminds me of a conversation I had with one of the lads that I met while in Rye Hill, a Columbian named George, who also happened to be a national standard middle distance runner and a black-belt in Tae kwon do, so we had a lot in common. He told me that when he was first imprisoned, like many others he too sought to draw some strength from the Bible and began reading the Old Testament. When he was halfway through it he said to himself in reference to the Hebrew supreme God, 'This is a good guy? He's mad!' and decided to draw his strength from elsewhere. But such objectivity is a rare quality for fear normally rules the day. The facts speak for themselves, remember, ninety per cent of children will adhere to the religion of their parents throughout their entire life.

Still, I certainly feel no need to talk people out of their religious beliefs, it is indeed arguable that in many cases, a belief system, followed as a moralistic creed at a personal level, can be a good thing. It is also true however, that this needs to be tempered with a degree of reality, humility, and tolerance, for there is truly no such thing as 'the true religion', from factual, philosophical, and logical standpoints, all are anorexic when subjected to the glare of objective examination. It is in light of this I stress again that religious arrogance should be actively battled, wars of ideas based upon religious belief are a political nonsense perpetrated by the corrupt in a bid to manipulate the blinkered masses, and worse still, they cost lives.

HOWARD BROWN

16

I had long decided that HMP Hewell Grange was the open prison for me. Based in the town of Redditch on the outskirts of Birmingham it was a mere twenty minutes drive from my now former family home. Not only was this convenient for visits from my children, but the Grange was also a well-run facility with the added bonus of inmate day-release employment schemes. I had some months earlier turned down the chance of transfer there because the timing of the offer was inconvenient. Bearing this in mind, the Rye Hill senior staff that I had built up a relationship with over the years assured me that I would be transferred to Hewell Grange with minimum delay upon request.

The reasons for my procrastination were simple enough, I had not finished my research on *Rulers & Lies* and had well over a year left to serve of the minimum five years of imprisonment required before my first application for release could be granted. No inmate is allowed to find an outside job with more than twelve months left to their earliest parole date, and if I had moved to Hewell Grange earlier I would have been stuck in a dormitory in the presence of six or seven other noisy guys trying to complete my work. Open prisons are generally not as comfortable, or as clean, as long term jails, because they are geared towards short-term accommodation. So no flashy single-cells and personal toilets, but instead the chance of release during working hours into the outside world, and if you worked it right this was attainable every day of the week. This is a most appetising prospect when you have been locked away for so long. I therefore decided to dovetail my transfer so that I would be eligible for outside work detail as soon as I arrived. But first I had to get out of 'Lie Hill'.

During the months leading up to my plans for transfer there had been some dramatic changes in the middle-management staff and several officers that were extremely supportive of me had been moved on to posts elsewhere. Just my luck. When I submitted my official transfer request I experienced the same incompetence and lies that many before me had endured. My application was mislaid! Hewell Grange had not replied to the requests for a space! Hewell Grange were not answering the telephone! It was laughable, the transparently fabricated excuses just kept coming and coming. Calm as I naturally am, I found myself becoming stir crazy, and it was only the guilt of certain officers at this obvious fiasco that gave me any sense of relief. It was therefore suggested and agreed that I could apply for monthly town visits where I would be allowed to go unescorted into the town of Rugby and be trusted to return to Rye Hill under my own volition. I thought I'll believe it when I see it.

In all fairness I was soon presented with the necessary forms for completion and it became clear that an official process had genuinely been started. There were obviously conditions attached to the proposed privilege and the main one was that I was not allowed to see my children during my excursions. This was because Nia and I were divorced and the presiding home office controller was concerned that emotionally charged scenarios might present a breach of security, especially if Nia was also present on these outings. Even though there was zero chance of any histrionics, I could appreciate the logic behind his decision and agreed to abide by it quite willingly. I told Elle of my still as yet to be seen good fortune and asked her if she would mind meeting me for my first meal on the outside in almost four years. You can imagine my elation when she said that she could tie it in with her work and also pick me up on the allocated day. Sleepless nights were once again much in evidence.

As expected, the official sanction of my town visit came the afternoon before my day out, meaning that not only was I left on tenterhooks, but so was Elle in the arrangement of her working day. It's a good thing that I was prepared for such sloppiness and had primed her in the way that things might unfold.

When the day came my six hours outside flew by. Elle picked me up in the prison car park and took me for a slap up breakfast, on reflection, it must have been embarrassing the way I wolfed it down, but this was nothing compared to the treat that she had prepared for me later in the day.

When we were an item all those years ago we would regularly go for picnics in the countryside, it was a habit that Elle introduced me to and that I enjoyed a great deal. How fitting it was that she had arranged a sumptuous reminder for my first day out. The countryside was out of the question as it was outside the boundaries that had been set for my travel by the jail, but there are plenty of quiet local parks in and around Rugby town centre, and to top it all, the weather was terrific.

Elle outdid herself and expertly presented an array of lobster, king prawns, crab, beef, chicken, freshly baked bread, and other assorted goodies, topped off by a couple of bottles of expensive non-alcoholic wine. When she had laid everything out I wondered how I could ever face prison food again, it was culinary heaven and this time I distinctly took things more slowly.

Unsurprisingly I arrived back at Rye Hill on cloud nine, and began the thirty day countdown to my next sanctioned day-trip as soon as Elle dropped me off. But my excitement for the day however did not end there.

I had withdrawn fifty pounds from my prison spending account to pay my way on the day. Elle would hear none of it and so I returned to Rye Hill with the same notes that I left with that morning, and guess which officer was on reception duty? Mr Hater. As usual, to me anyway, he was courteous and polite and after the required searches and security checks were conducted I handed him the money to be re-deposited into my account. He took it and told me that there were no receipt forms on hand and that he would bring one to me later in the evening. The night came and went and I saw neither hair nor hide of him.

I informed several officers for days on end that I needed to see him with no success and when I received my weekly bank statement was more than a little alarmed that my fifty pounds was not listed as an entry. I felt that I had detected an air of sheepishness from the attendant officers when making my last few requests to see him and when I was told that one of the jail directors wanted a meeting with me about the matter it was clear that controversy was in the air. I was ready for a battle but did not get it though. I was merely asked to outline the nature of my enquiry and the amount of money that I had brought back to the facility. I was further assured that it would be put back into my account within twenty-four hours. You guessed it. Mr Hater was a petty thief.

In his post as admissions officer he had been subject to complaints from inmates about missing property on such a constant basis that higher ranking officers had laid several traps to catch him in the act. He fell for them hook, line, and sinker. He had stolen jewellery, music tapes, compact discs, clothes, and money on a regular basis for years, and this from almost every consignment that came in during his shift. What rankled me was that he did not face criminal charges but was merely fired from his job. I guess Group Four and Rye Hill did not need the bad press, but they could at least have officially reduced him to the same social standing as the people that he treated with such disdain.

Still, it was no skin off my nose and I quickly put the episode behind me, especially as I had not lost out, and put my mind back onto the most important issue for me at the time, my transfer. My days out were terrific but make no mistake, as welcome as they were, these perks were a stop-gap, I wanted what I had been promised and felt that I had earned.

It took three months for Rye Hill to finally decide that they had made enough money out of me and that I could be replaced in my capacity as both a supervisor in industries and as a model inmate. It was also agreed that I could make my way to Hewell Grange under my own steam. I phoned Elle to tell her the good news and asked if she was going my way any time soon with her work commitments. It just so happened that she was and I was happy to hitch a lift.

There were many people to say goodbye to, both inmates and staff, and I also had the task of finding enough boxes to pack the numerous books that I had bought over the years and needed to take with me. It was as I was doing all of this that it dawned on me, I was not just leaving one cell for another, I had been at Rye Hill for three and a half years, and it had become my home. I could hardly believe that I had developed an emotional attachment to a prison. But I had. What was especially touching were the amount of officers that specifically came to the unit to bid farewell and wish me well in my future, I was particularly proud of the fact that none of them were condescending enough to advise me to keep out of trouble, which was the usual kindly advice dispensed to leaving inmates. I must have done something right throughout my stay.

But nothing was more affective than the inmates that took time out to visit my cell, I will not name them, but I am talking hardened men, who felt they had to tell me that I had changed their lives. I did not ask them what they meant, but I think I know, and if *Rulers & Lies* is written and digested in the manner that I intend then I believe that many of its readers will feel the same way. Psychological liberation is truly something to be valued.

The journey to Hewell Grange was quicker than I would have hoped, Elle was under a heavy schedule so we moved post-haste, but we made enough time to stop off and grab lunch which was a valued treat. No matter how much less restrictions are promised, no one wants to rush to jail. Fortunately Redditch is not a complicated town and its prisons are well sign-posted, which is just as well, because if I had arrived later than the time specified on my travel licence my security level would have been downgraded. This would have been a disastrous start considering the trust I had built up over the last four years.

When we pulled up at the imposing frontage of the former stately home I must admit that I was impressed by its grandeur, that was until I stepped through the Great Hall and made my way to admissions. The buildings historical façade soon gave way to a prison visage as dark and dingy as a medieval dungeon, that was depressing enough, but not as bad as the news that met me. Even though I had already proved myself trustworthy by having flawlessly completed three unescorted town visits while at Rye Hill, I still had to go through the standard security processes as a newcomer to the Grange before I would be allowed out again. I had been told the opposite by Rye Hill staff before my departure, but they were wrong, that part of my record cut no ice, I would not be allowed outside Hewell Grange prison gates for at least six weeks. I remember placating myself by thinking things could be worse, I could still have been in Rugby.

At least the admissions process was less painstaking than normal, especially as I was the sole newcomer to the facility that day. Mr Keys, the admitting officer was both courteous and clear in his instructions, and I felt relieved that I was now back in the custody of government professionals, lines were once again clear cut. I was to discover later, that Mr Keys and a handful of other officers at the Grange were seasoned martial artists, and well aware of my achievements before I even stepped through the door. It made no difference though, I had to toe the line like everybody else.

New entrants are all allocated dormitories on the top floor of the three storey building which is quite a pain when you have heavy boxes to carry. I chose to view it as an exercise session, which is what it turned out to be as I trundled up and down those stairs for about an hour. After a brief rest I took a tour of the building just so that I knew where to eat, sleep, pick up my post, and attend official requests. I also met a few guys that had transferred out from Rye Hill a month or so before me, they were quick to prime me on the realities of what to expect at my new home.

After dinner I slumped on top of my bed and fell asleep fully clothed, when I awoke the dormitory was in darkness and my new pad-mates were all comatose under their covers. I figured they must have had a tough day. I got changed and slipped under my covers too. I was glad that this new regime was not going to last three and a half years.

The next morning I was informed of the induction process and it was apparent that until I had made my choices for in-house work detail I would have some time to kill. I was happy to hear it and found myself a bright little spot on the mid-level landing, a table and chair, and began re-editing *Rulers & Lies*. I also managed to wangle myself a gym session and an enjoyable day was rounded off by the fact that I could now use the phone twenty-fours a day. I spoke to Elle first thing to make sure that she had got back to Nottingham safely the previous day and to tell her that I would call her later. I also spoke to Nia and Kelis after school-time. The best call though was the one I made to Elle in the evening, it was after eight o'clock, well after eight o'clock, and I made it that late just because I could.

There were a variety of jobs on offer including cleaning, gardening, or even working on the prison farm. I opted for the education programme, it was an easy choice to make as I had been promised during induction that if I took part in the timetabled lessons then I would be allowed to work on my own material during unscheduled periods. It was a deal that I thought was too good to be true. The next week I asked permission to post the updated preface of my work to some publishing houses to see if I could initiate some early interest and get feedback on the quality of my writing. The education staff read the pages that I wanted to submit and kindly offered to pay the postage and package for me, they also informed the governor, or to be politically correct, governess, of my intention.

She visited the education unit on the day that I was sending my work out and read my preface. I got the impression that she was not overly impressed, a feeling that was enforced one week later when education informed us that personal projects were no longer allowed in the education block. The guys present on the class looked at me, pointed, and laughed. They had all noticed that the governess was not keen on my subject matter, but like me, thought the manner and pettiness of her reaction was pretty sad. A few of them asked me if I knew that she was a devoted Christian. I did not, and it would not have made any difference if I had, my work was not a personal attack on anyone, what rankled though was her apparent abandon of any form of professional ethics. Of course it just might be that we were all paranoid and the timing of the new edict was coincidental, but it is hard not to believe that if I were writing a treatise proving the existence of God my work would have been lauded and free study lessons granted as the norm. So much for Christian tolerance.

As it was, the replies from the publishing houses that I wrote to yielded nothing solid, except to confirm that my writing was of a professional standard. I sent the extract to twenty different publishers and received fifteen replies. The bulk of them were impressed and told me that although the topic seemed interesting they did not publish work on the theme I had chosen. Four informed me that they did not accept any unsolicited material and advised me to contact a literary agent in the first instance. There were also two replies that stood out from the others because they were noticeably brief and very curt and I had no doubt that I had caused offence. I figured that I should prepare myself for similar responses down the road.

Even though my avenues for private study were blocked I remained in education so that I could become more computer literate and obtain some extra qualifications to bulk up my curriculum vitae. After exiting prison I knew that I would need every advantage possible in order to secure meaningful employment. It was also an enjoyable and worthwhile way to pass the time while I waited for my first town visit.

I phoned Nick and Chris and told them that I wanted to surprise Kelis on our first day out together in four years, my children are all practical jokers, and they readily agreed to the ruse. Unlike Rye Hill town visits, days out at the Grange, with the exception of special circumstances, are taken on either a Saturday or Sunday, and on the first Sunday allowed, Nick picked me up and drove to Birmingham city centre where we lay in wait for Chris and Kelis. Chris had told his sister that he was taking her shopping and that they would also be meeting Nick, they did this regularly enough so poor Kelis did not suspect a thing.

When I stepped out from hiding and hugged my baby girl it was one of the most enjoyable moments of my life. Poor Kelis was shell-shocked. I could virtually see her brain ticking over as she tried to work out how this was possible, to her such a moment should not have occurred for the best part of a year, but there I was, in the flesh and as free as a bird. She hardly uttered a word for about half an hour as we walked around the much changed town centre and they all did their best to renew my sense of direction. They needed to, I was lost. Not only had the city's much vaunted rebuilding plan, which had been on the agenda for many years, been completed, but due to the migration of asylum seekers, migrant workers, and refugees from Eastern Europe and North Africa, the city had now taken on a new cosmopolitan feel. It was another of those moments that rammed home just how much my life had changed, but with my children stood around me, healthy and so attentive, Elle back in contact, and the progress I had made with my project, I considered that it might well be for the better.

We had a memorable day. First we went to a new ten-pin bowling alley on the outskirts of the city centre, I came last. Big surprise there as I'm as blind as a bat. This was followed by a slap-up meal at a popular restaurant, which just happened to be around the corner from Nia's mother so we sprung a similar surprise on her. The children entered her apartment first while I hid in the wings and slowly snuck in the front door which they had artfully left open. I paid the price though when she berated me for not keeping in touch more often. I took my medicine then gave her a big hug. This was followed by the piéce de la resistance of the day when the children and I went swimming, to the very same baths that Kelis and I used to visit all those years previously. We played my favourite swimming pool game, 'stuck in the water', a tag game where once tagged you have to stand stock-still with legs splayed until an untagged player 'frees' you by swimming through them. By the time the children took me back to captivity and dropped me off in the Grange car park I was ready for bed. Once again, emotionally drained, but extremely happy. My only hope was that they felt the same.

I had cleared most of the hurdles that had been put in front of me in the run-up to the commencement of my parole application but I still had a few more to jump. The first was to be security cleared by the prison 'working out' board for outside employment. This was no rubber stamp process as even though my own security record was flawless, the company that you apply to work for also has to undergo quite rigorous examination, not just in terms of their stability and the legitimacy of their set-up, but the nature of the work that you are being seconded to do must also fit in with your prison profile. Fortunately I experienced little delay in this area as the prison football team centre-forward, already worked for the company I had in mind, so it only remained for the nature of my job to be found suitable, my own security status was never an issue.

The job itself was tailor-made for me, I had to record and process outgoing goods for a protective clothing warehouse that had installed a new computer system and wanted someone reliable to get to grips with it. I enjoyed almost everything about my new vocation, the freedom, the new conversation and social environment, and especially my mobile phone. William, the prison centre-forward, had left the company before I began work leaving me as the sole prisoner from Hewell Grange present at the warehouse. In such a situation convicts are allowed to have a cell phone in case there is ever any crisis such as illness or delayed travel. What a perk! I sent text messages and phoned Elle, the children, close friends, and relatives, as often as I could and enjoyed what I considered to be the first dipping of my toes into my future life. It was total paradise compared to what I had become used to, things were not perfect though and there was one aspect of my new employment that I absolutely detested, it was so damn cold.

The dead of English winter arrived with a vengeance within a few weeks of me starting work and no matter how many pairs of gloves or socks I put on it made little difference. Typing on the computer keyboard was like tapping a block of ice and the only thing that kept me going was the thought that it was either this or being stuck in the prison. I happily settled for working in arctic conditions.

My other problem during this period was the probation service, they wanted me to attend an evening rehabilitation course called 'Think First' which focused on the ability to consider the consequences of one's actions in advance and then tailor your behaviour accordingly. I couldn't believe they were asking me to attend it as a condition of my parole application, and to make it worse I was told that I also had to attend a precursor 'Black Awareness' session beforehand. Attending the main body of the course would be torturous enough but I felt that this appendage was ridiculous and borne out of political correctness rather than a real desire for progress. I made it known that I possess a mirror and know exactly what I look like. My protests cut no ice.

What particularly irked me was that I was now in with a real chance of losing my job as I would have to leave early on two days a week to attend the course. I was not at all happy. Fortunately the main manager at the warehouse practised the same style of martial art that I originally trained in, Shotokan Karate, and used to chat to me about the subject on a regular basis. He sanctioned my early departure for the twelve week length of the course without a second thought. Nevertheless, I was very agitated by the situation and decided to press matters further.

The deputy governor at the jail, Miss Alison Wing, had secured a reputation with inmates as being firm but fair, and the first time that I saw her I thought she looked very familiar, reminding me a lot of Miss Adams who was on the governor fast-track training course when I was at the Green all those years ago. I decided to ask for her help in removing me from these silly courses and purely by chance bumped into her at the prison gatehouse on my return from work one evening. I told her of my situation and argued that the Black Awareness course was insulting, ill-conceived, and discriminatory. She listened to me intently and asked, *'Were you resident at HMP Winson Green about 4 years ago?'* The penny dropped. She said I reminded her of an unassuming and polite guy that she used to enjoy talking to. I retorted that when I first saw her at the Grange I asked an inmate standing next to me if her name was Miss Adams, but when he said her surname was Wing I dismissed the notion as coincidence. I did not ask but assumed that she and Neil Adams, as is the way of things, had separated, a thought that had never previously crossed my simple mind. We chatted for quite a while. She agreed with me in principle on the politics of the impending black awareness course and I noted that her manner, in spite of her promotion, had not changed one iota. Some people are meant to handle power, I hope she gets a lot more. After our conversation I felt confident that I could easily have taken my objections further but on reflection that night I thought what the hell, decided to stop protesting and attend the course anyway. I'm glad that I did.

I was given permission to make my own way from the warehouse to the allocated probation centre which was a train and a bus ride away, a journey which I enjoyed more than I expected. After the course I was collected by the prison minibus which did a round robin trip of picking up inmates out on rehabilitation courses at various locations.

As anticipated the Black Awareness course was farcical. It was poorly designed and did nothing to address the underlying issues of why people of colour seem more likely to commit crime in inner city areas than Caucasians, or even why sport, entertainment, and prison are the only arenas where blacks are over-proportionately represented in western countries. I knew I was in for a long evening though when one of the course tutors held up photographs of Martin Luther King, Mahatma Gandhi, and Muhammad Ali, and asked the twelve or so of us present if we recognised them. I'm amazed that I stayed seated, did not put my bag on my shoulder and immediately start heading back to the jail. On the plus side, the tutors were very pleasant and respectful and well aware that they were poorly supported in an ill-conceived project. I felt for them and engaged myself in the evening as much as I could.

By the time December came the incessant cold had become too much to bear and I was eager to leave my job. Ironically, I applied for another one that I could also have started at the same time that I commenced the warehouse post but had declined because it meant working outside. What a mistake that was as it could never have been any colder than the one indoors. It entailed valeting cars for a showroom and vehicle service centre which would at least have meant that I would constantly have been on the move and not stood stock still for hours on end. The only hiccup in the job transfer process was that regulations at the Grange restricted movement of an inmate from his first employment for three months after commencement so I had to hang on in there. At least the Christmas period helped to make it seem shorter.

During the yuletide all working inmates were back in the unusual position of spending their days within the prison grounds. I found the break quite relaxing, especially as I could do some heavy catch up with my research, but for many, it was just plain boring especially without the luxury of being able to receive and make phone calls on their mobile phones. This was annoying as more than a few guys came to bother me while I was trying to work, its funny how they pretended that they were doing me a favour, and this no matter how many one word answers I gave them. Still, I managed to make the most of my extra time.

My academic resolve had created some interest amongst some of the officers, as it was clear to them from our conversations that I was well versed in my subject matter and could corroborate any points that I made in a lucid manner. It was during such a conversation that I was asked, or more pointedly 'accused', of being 'on the square'. This was not the first time I had been asked this question since my incarceration, but it was the first time that it had come from an officer.

It was more than ten years earlier when I had indeed been invited to become a Freemason at one of the most prestigious lodges in Birmingham, but I had declined because of the commitment that was required. I felt that I did not have the spare time available to do myself justice. At that time I was involved in the mortgage industry and some of my colleagues and their friends were Masons and came from families that had been members for generations. It was during this period that I learnt much about this secret group of men and I was intrigued by the many misconceptions held by the public about their activities.

As a world-wide charitable unit it is quite possible that they cannot be rivalled which is quite at odds with the devil-worshipping, world-dominating agenda that they are accused of planning as some sort of Machiavellian sub-plot by numerous conspiracy theorists. The truth is that they, like many other well-meant groups, have amongst their numbers a small minority of unscrupulous and power-hungry men who grab the headlines when their less than benevolent activities are brought to light. Nevertheless, to state that the majority of Freemasons, even very powerful and influential ones, are routinely implicit in insidious schemes is a nonsense. While the adage that 'power corrupts and absolute power corrupts absolutely' has some truth, it is my opinion that the balance of the 'greater good' in Freemasonry will always keep the corrupt in check and I have my reasons for saying this.

The essence of Freemasonry is based upon the principles of ancient Egypt where truth, justice, law, order, and charity were held in their highest regard. This is well reflected in biblical tales for whenever any major figure was in dire straits or danger they headed for Egypt, a land where food and shelter were practically guaranteed. The exploits of Abraham, Moses, Joseph, and Jesus, are the most prominent examples.

The essence of these moral principles were personified in the figure of a goddess known as *Ma'at* (Pronounced 'muh-aht'), from which, as I stated earlier, we derive the words maternal and mother. The fact that such etymology has been hidden from the masses may have more to do with the traditional need for secrecy within Freemasonry and earlier secret societies than any hostile plans for world domination. The ethics embodied by this ancient goddess were the precursor to the Ten Commandments of the Old Testament. Ma'at was the figure of universal law, order, balance, rule, truth, integrity, uprightness, and justice, hence her modern representation outside western courts as Lady Justice, wielding the scales of balance and equity.

If Freemasonry were to unilaterally attempt to impose any form of malevolent scheme, even by top secret cabals within its own structure, such actions would be diametrically opposed to the principles of this ancient goddess. This is not to say that certain members would never try to manipulate events and legislation in their favour, whether this be for ego, monetary, or political gain, for they certainly already have, but they will always meet with opposition from more conscientious and equally powerful men within their own ranks.

The other saving grace is that secret societies are brotherhoods and many have traditionally been rivals for centuries, and as such stand-offs also bring a sense of balance. The Catholic version of Freemasonry, the Society of Jesus, has been an on-and-off enemy of its better known version for seven hundred years and also has some of the most prominent and powerful men in the world among its members.

These groups have followed the trends of popular society and politics throughout their heritage and have been known, or rather their members have, to be both racist and misogynist in the most blatant fashion. But times are changing and as the world becomes smaller and tolerance must be taught by example, tradition is evolving to accommodate this.

In response to allegations of racism, masonry boasts a shining example to the contrary, Prince Hall is a premier lodge for blacks that was founded in America and gained its charter from the Grand Lodge of England in 1784 and today has 4,500 lodges under its name with 300,000 plus members world-wide. This is not to say however that many influential blacks have not been, and still are, members of English based Lodges throughout the USA and Europe, a fact that defenders of Freemasonry are quick to point out to counter allegations of segregation.

Unfortunately female masons are still not sanctioned by traditional Freemasonry, even though female and mixed sex lodges do exist and seem to be thriving. It is admirable that women continue to strive for equality within this traditional concept, although from a feminist standpoint they quite puzzlingly accept being referred to as 'Grand Masters' and 'Brothers' as a privileged achievement. Still, it is only tradition as adhered to by obstinate men, that in this day and age could maintain that the attainment of the principles of Ma'at, be restricted to a strictly male organisation, and apart from the fact that such lofty ideals are universal, the situation takes an even more bizarre twist when you consider that Ma'at has always been personified as female anyway. Tradition often makes little sense.

I was not interested in the rites of secret societies just because of old acquaintances however, there was another topic that caught my eye, one shared by every secret society and every religion, which was noticeably important to them all, the 'light'.

In the Masonic initiation ceremony the 'candidate' is blindfolded to represent his existence in a state of darkness, with symbolic emphasis placed during the ritual on the number 'three', he is then asked the question, *'Having been in a state of darkness, what is the predominant wish of your heart?'* The answer is then whispered to him, *'Light'*. It occurred to me that these same elements were repeatedly evident within the biblical canon and I had a good idea why. The journey from the darkness to the light was representative of inter-realm travel between the underworld and heaven which symbolically took 'three' days, an esoteric statement from the texts of the elder cultures that is also rife in both the Old and New Testaments.

Simply put, the lower domain was one of darkness, and heaven was one of enduring light, a situation that existed in ancient lore from the day that these two realms were 'separated'. Travelling from one realm to another was not a physical journey, but metaphorical, one of either moving from a state of ignorance to one of illumination, or conversely, falling from grace to potential oblivion.

Illumination is a powerful theme in the Egyptian, Hebrew, and Greek texts and is the cornerstone of the secret schools. The God Osiris is the earliest illuminated God and is featured as entering a mountain (heaven) and exiting it with a 'shining face', the Old Testament book of Exodus repeats the process with Moses entering a mountain and coming out with his face so bright that he has to wear a veil so as not to harm onlookers. The gospels continue the theme with Jesus becoming illuminated on a 'mountain' and shining with radiance 'like the sun'. All of these gods had the power to shine their light on others if they so wished, and of course it follows that anyone that became illuminated through contact with these shining characters was of course living in a state of darkness beforehand.

The literal 'light of the world', as Jesus is so often referred to in the New Testament, was the Sun, and symbolically speaking it is this object that successful initiates 'see' upon their exit from the darkness of the underworld. It was at this point in my studies that I remembered the New Testament story of the 'magician' Elymas who did not see the sun for a 'period of time', which it now seemed clear was informing the reader that he had been initiated into the secret society of Christianity after his journey through darkness, especially as it was one of the main mystery schools of that time. Why else would the account have taken pains to tell us that he was also known as the 'son of Jesus'? If anyone is in doubt that this kind of coding exists within the biblical texts then they only need to consider the events and final words of the Christian messiah during his execution.

During a total eclipse of the sun that lasted a symbolic 'three' hours Jesus uttered the phrase '*My God, My God, why* have You forsaken me?' According to the gospel of Matthew this rendition is the translation of the words 'Eli, Eli, lama sabachthani?' The gospel of Mark renders it slightly differently as 'Eloi, Eloi, lama sabachthani?' The difference here lies in the spelling of the words 'Eli' and 'Eloi', which apparently mean 'My God', and in a sense, as I will explain, they do. Our attention is further drawn to this term by the story itself as onlookers present at the scene think that Jesus was calling for assistance from an Old Testament prophet named Elijah, throwing even more doubt upon what was said.

The authors of the *The Templar Revelation*, Lynn Picknett and Clive Prince comment on this discrepancy and point out that in the Aramaic language the term for 'My God' is actually 'ilahi', if we add to this that the word used in the Matthew version 'eli' means 'ascended' or 'gone up' then matters become even more confusing. Clearly, the use of the word 'eli' in Jesus' valediction makes no sense whatsoever, making it obvious that the passage is indeed telling us something other than the apparent. It was upon reading the extant books of the New Testament, the ones that the church concluded were not fit to be included in the accepted canon, that I became sure of the scenes occulted significance and the message that was really being conveyed.

The book of Nicodemus renders the enigmatic phrase as 'Hely, Hely, lama zabachthani?' with the spelling of 'Hely' taking us closer to a hidden meaning which is laid bare in the 'lost' Gospel according to Peter which informs us that Jesus' words were 'My power, my power, thou hast forsaken me.' As I already knew from etymological examination of the word 'Holy', like its predecessors 'Helios' and 'Hely', it meant 'sun'. Correctly translated the statement should read, '(My) Sun, (my) Sun, why hast thou forsaken me', and for Jesus to make this statement during a 'three' hour total eclipse not only made perfect sense, it could also only mean one thing, he was being prepared for the necessary plunge into darkness, a descent into the underworld in readiness for his return to heaven. The book of Nicodemus goes on to state quite plainly that this is what happened.

This story, like the bulk of the gospels, continued to relay Egyptian theology, and it was the 'most high' god of the ancient trinity, the 'Aten', that Jesus was indeed referring to as the eclipse took place. This was the occulted message being relayed by the gospel writers and why they continuously drew the attention of the more enlightened reader to the word 'eli', for it was too profound not to. In the most important New Testament story of them all 'eli' and 'hely' meant the same thing, 'sun'.

I had more detail to consider in confirming this hypothesis, such as the fact that in Egyptian lore for a dying sun-god to return to heaven it was indeed a prerequisite that he would first have to descend into the lower realm in order to commence his journey. The passage not only points out that Jesus, like earlier archetypes, was a sun-god, but that he was intentionally pictured as following the ascribed and ancient route that many had travelled before him. I noted with some interest that this story had been updated with huge success in a popular modern day fable.

The comic book hero Superman, like Jesus, was sent to earth by his father from an exploded planet, Krypton, to assist mankind. This is relevant because the ancients had assumed, because of meteorite activity, that heaven had exploded and fallen to earth and that the gods had entered the underworld as a result of that catastrophe, it seems likely that the writers of the Superman story were aware of this detail.

The Sumerian texts and the Koran tell us that this was later rectified with a separation of the heavens and the earth by the gods. Unsurprisingly there are also other similarities, Superman, like Jesus, was born in a small town. Jesus was born in the 'little' town of Bethlehem and Superman was born in 'Smallville'. The American superhero was also meek and mild unless fighting injustice, could defy gravity, and had the title of a god. I found this quite intriguing as his name is *Kal-el*, and his father's is *Jor-el*, that is 'K'-god, (Kristos), and 'J'-god, (Jehovah), as the word 'el' in Hebrew translates as 'god', thus we have here the same divine father and son relationship of the

New Testament. But most notably of all, Superman, like Jesus drew his powers from the earth's sun, and so was also a sun-god in the most obvious fashion.

It is difficult for me to believe that the inventors of this character were not privy to secret society information which they, for whatever reason, chose to disclose in the usual occulted manner. The story fulfilled its function in helping to boost morale during the depression and that of American troops in the later war effort with early comics featuring the all-American hero battling Nazi villains as part of the US propaganda machine. It is fitting and true to his messianic roots that he had come to earth to favour one nation above all others. This reworking of an age old tale was in no way expected to be as politically successful as the story of the Christ had been for the Roman Empire but it was a leaf worth borrowing from a well-worn book.

My comments on topics such as the latter used to engage the inmates and staff that questioned me at Hewell Grange just as they had at Rye Hill. I don't know whether they thought that I was a weirdo or a sage, the fact is I hoped I was neither, I just wanted to do something worthwhile and positive and salvage what I could of my reputation and respect for the sake of my children.

I was sure of one thing though, the Masons would never accept me now, not with a criminal record, but I sometimes wonder whether I would even have been arrested had I joined them all those years ago, for although membership is clearly not as exclusive as it was in decades prior, I would have been welcomed with open arms by a clique of very respectable and well-connected men. Still, it's a good thing I do not deliberate too much on such matters as I am of the firm belief that everything happens for a reason, it's just so damn tough sometimes trying to figure out what it is.

17

The New Year had come, just as fast as the others, and here I was, still alive, full of beans, and potentially into the last eight months of my sentence, yet I was nowhere near as elated at the prospect as I would have hoped. I had a feeling of dread that just kept nagging away, as if I had forgotten to do something but just could not remember what it was. My prospects were certainly clear cut enough. If I were to be successful in my parole application then I would have to serve exactly half of my ten year sentence. If the application failed then I would have to endure the full term of two-thirds, which was six years and eight months. At this point I knew two things, one, that the next eight months would seem as long as the four years plus that I had already served, and two, that there would be even more unwelcome surprises in store for me. I wasn't wrong.

On the social side of things there is no doubt that when you receive a lengthy custodial sentence the word 'custodial' can be substituted for 'death'. I say this because people talk and act as if you are never coming out, and when I entered my parole year, I decided there and then that I was going to revamp my life and social circles. The world is a big place with lots of interesting places to visit and people to meet, and so, with the exception of those closest to me and a few long-term trusted friends, it seemed quite pragmatic for me to decide to start my societal life from scratch. I found the prospect pretty exciting but mentally did what I thought was the sensible thing and prepared myself for the long haul, the prospect of parole had to be considered more of a hope than a reality.

There was also something else that needed resolution, the situation concerning my confiscation order. The courts had originally written asking for details of my financial circumstances and asked me to pay them a sum of fifteen thousand pounds or risk another year in jail. I had completed the accompanying defence application in the presence of a senior officer at Rye Hill whose job it was to pass the affidavit on to the court. That was a couple of years ago, and as I had not heard anything from Birmingham Magistrates I assumed, more out of wishful thinking to be honest than any sensible assessment, that the matter had been put to bed and my defensive statement had been accepted.

In a bid to make sure, I wrote a letter to the courts upon arriving at Hewell Grange asking for clarification of my position, this so that I could put all of my energy into my parole application without fear of distraction. The New Year had barely started when I received my reply. There was no reference to the correspondence that had been passed on by Rye Hill, in fact it seemed that I had been a forgotten case until I had initiated contact. I was told that unless I sent payment of fifteen thousand pounds plus interest at eight per cent per annum for the four years plus that I had spent in jail, then I would have to serve an extra twelve months. Added to this there would be no remission, the twelve months would have to be served in full, even though I had originally been told that if the decision stood, then like my main sentence, I would only have to serve half of it. I have to admit, I was not too surprised, but dreaded to think of the effect this new dilemma would have on my parole application. I wrote a string of legal letters and waited for replies.

Fortunately I had plenty to occupy my mind throughout this period and ploughed myself into work, gym, and writing with my usual gusto. With the pre-course Black Awareness session out of the way I was now attending the main twice-weekly *Think First* programme that probation had ordered, which to my mind was merely for the sake of bureaucracy.

I continued to make my usual way to the venue by train and bus every Tuesday and Thursday evening and I have to say that for the three months that it lasted it was quite enlightening. The content was sensible and well-presented but not ground-breaking, what broadened my experience were my encounters in a confessional format with youngsters who were a hairs breadth away from jail. The only person in custody on the classes was me, the others were mostly offenders who had been sentenced to community orders by the courts and ordered to attend the course as a means of avoiding imprisonment. It made me realise how much some people can struggle to make the most simple and logical of decisions in their lives, and need help and good counsel on a constant basis. Obviously I was well respected on the class because of my current status, and so decided to set as good an example with my comments, behaviour, and attitude as I could. It certainly made attending more enjoyable.

The other saving grace was that the course tutors were three attractive and professional young ladies, Sonia, Laura, and Nicky, and you can imagine the amount of cons that wanted to transfer to this session when word got out. No matter how much I protested to acquaintances at the Grange, in their eyes this proved their theories that I was most definitely a Freemason as I had somehow manoeuvred myself as the sole inmate from the facility onto the most 'attractive' course on offer. I wish I had such power.

I can see why they had their suspicions though, as about six weeks into the course I had a most unexpected night. The Grange forgot to send transport to pick me up. I can imagine that many of the lads would have made much capital out of such a situation, but that is probably why they would never find themselves in such a predicament.

I stood outside the probation centre and waited for about an hour thinking that there must have been a lot more inmates to collect than usual from other evening courses and this is what made the minibus late. Sonia, Laura, and Nicky, passed me with some concern as they made their own way home and were less than impressed that the prison bus could be so late.

I assured them that I would be ok and that I would walk back to the prison if I had to, little did I know how right I could have been. When more than half an hour later there was still no sign of transport I phoned the prison gatehouse from my mobile, *'Hello, its Brown here, can someone come and collect me?'*, when the reply came back *'Why, where are you?'* What else could I do but laugh? I could hear the expletives in the background about how the officers on earlier duty had neglected to put me on the pick up list. I wondered whether a friendly officer was trying to do me a favour or if I was being tested somehow to see if I would abscond or breach some lesser rule. If it was a test it certainly did not make any sense, only a fool would put a foot wrong at this stage of such a long sentence.

It took almost an hour for a car to arrive, yet even though I was tired, and damn cold, I thought the whole episode was pretty amusing. My tutors on the course did not share my view and the next week told me they were intent on filing a detailed report. I managed to persuade them otherwise by citing that the main victim of such a complaint would be me. If any of the officers at the Grange were disciplined then I would almost certainly be victim to any backlash. I asked them to forget about it as there was no harm done. I'm glad they saw my point of view. I also had an ulterior motive, I was waiting for an answer to my request for job transfer and allowing the boat to be rocked with me in it might not be such a good idea.

When the move came I was cock-a-hoop, I certainly preferred to be mobile on a car pitch forecourt washing cars with warm water than being frozen to death standing in the same spot for hours in a fridge-cum-warehouse. This job had other advantages too, it was in Redditch, only three miles or so away from the jail so I had more free time to myself during the period we were allocated for travel, and none of the regular employees at the site, which was a sizeable complex, had any idea that myself and four or five of the other car valeters were convicts. There were mechanics, salesmen, management staff, and secretaries, all employed by two national car companies that probably thought we were working class guys who had simply failed to make the grade in life. If they did, I suppose they were right, but they would have been hard pressed to guess why.

One thing is for sure, I would rather have been washing the cars than selling them. Second hand car salesmen are not known for their scruples and when some punters turned up to buy the vehicles that I had prepped for them I felt like yelling 'Run! Get away, and don't sign anything!' The salesmen made far more money on buyers that took out loans than cash payers simply because their company relished fleecing the desperate with horrendous interest rates and early settlement penalties. It was sickening to watch them rip off those that could least afford it while dressed in the ultimate tool of deception, the suit and tie. They were mercenary, and to be honest there were one or two of them that I would have relished giving a hearty punch in the stomach. I really do have to shake off this violence thing.

Back at the ranch the main topic of conversation was the recent Boxing Day Tsunami that devastated coastal areas in the Indian Ocean and took over two hundred thousand lives. Countries affected included Indonesia, Sri Lanka, India, and Thailand, in what has been recorded as the fourth most powerful earthquake since the 1900's and one of the ten worst in known history. There were many factors why it took so many lives, one is that a high proportion of its victims were children who were less able to defend themselves against the surging waters than adults, another is that tsunamis are hard to detect and the Indian Ocean, unlike the Pacific has no early warning system, this mainly because the Pacific suffers them more regularly, and then of course there is the usual reason, ignorance, or to be more accurate, lack of foresight.

People resident in the Pacific Islands know that preceding a tsunami strike the sea often recedes and begins to bubble on its surface and at this point they head for higher ground. The opposite occurred in the Indian Ocean as onlookers, especially children, were induced by these same signs to visit the exposed beaches and collect stranded fish. It is a monumental tragedy that such innocent curiosity sealed their doom.

Thanks to local folklore the villagers on the Indonesian island of Simeulue knew better as their stories included details of the earthquake suffered there in 1907 and they took safe flight to the hills during the initial shaking which preceded the arrival of the waters. They were not the only ones whose knowledge saved them.

A ten year old British girl, Tilly Smith, had learned of the tell-tale signs in a geography lesson two weeks before going on holiday with her parents to Phuket in Thailand. When she saw the receding tide and frothing bubbles she told her parents, they warned others, and the beach was quickly evacuated. John Chroston, a Scottish biology teacher, was also on holiday at a nearby Thai beach and after spotting the early warning signs promptly took a busload of holidaymakers to safety.

These episodes highlight the fact that education is often crucial in life-or-death situations and reminded me of an incident during a First Aid course that I attended a decade or so prior at Birmingham University, it was with candidates vying for qualification to become aerobics instructors. During a session that covered resuscitation techniques one of the women inexplicably stood up and fled the lecture room in tears. It transpired that had she attended this course just a few months earlier she could likely have saved the life of her own mother. Why such training is not made compulsory on a yearly basis as part of the British school curriculum I will never know.

The bulk of discussion concerning the tsunami tragedy at the Grange was largely quite base and I found myself in a situation experiencing the type of primitive arguments that actually encourage ignorance as several Christian inmates were convinced that the tsunami was the result of the 'wrath of God' and that the heathens, as many of the tsunami's victims were not Christians, were being punished. Ironically, and just as ridiculous was that the prison Imam was teaching the same nonsense, that the disaster was part of Allah's run-up to

Judgement Day as predicted in the Koran. I didn't bother to argue too much, ignorance is bliss, and such is the rarity of tsunamis that the whole world was in shock.

The fact that such conclusions were being drawn by educated people in the twenty-first century only made it more clear to me how the natural disasters of ancient times must have heavily assisted the origin and development of religious belief. They must have all been ascribed to divine vengeance.

I remember discussing the tsunami with a friend who made what I consider to be a very pertinent point, *'Howard, why hasn't anyone in the news mentioned the fact that India regularly conducts underwater nuclear testing in the Indian Ocean?'* Indeed they do, and Lila Rajiva, a US based free-lance journalist, compiled a list of facts about the effects of such testing on the earth's tectonic plates as well as the creation of underwater landslides which can also be responsible for such tidal waves.

It is not as if governments do not know about the possibility of artificially induced tidal wave devastation. During certain World War Two experiments, the details of which have now been declassified, a project to develop a 'tsunami bomb' by using underwater detonations was undertaken off the coast of New Zealand and succeeded in causing tidal waves in 1944 and 1945. Project Seal, as it was known, was never completed simply because the war came to an end.

In view of this it cannot be discounted that a large explosion, not necessarily in the Indian Ocean itself, (such is the immensity of some tectonic plates and the domino effect of disrupting them), may well have indirectly triggered the first of the Boxing Day quakes, but because research into the fall-out of nuclear testing is highly classified we may have to wait another fifty years for official confirmation.

It is surely relevant that in 1995 a legal case was brought against the French government due to a major underwater landslide caused in Tahiti in 1979 when a nuclear device exploded after getting jammed in its shaft and disrupted at least one million cubic metres of coral and rock creating a cavity estimated at 140 metres wide. This in turn triggered a major tidal wave in an area that was already geologically unstable due to previous nuclear tests. The mini-tsunami spread throughout the Tuamotu Archipelago causing coastal damage, property destruction, and physical injury. Whoops! The French government quickly denied there had been any mishap and declared that the tsunami was of natural origin, a stance that was altered some years later when in 1985 official documentation referred to *'the accident of 25 July 1979'*. The visible carnage caused by such a mishap is bad enough, but let us not forget to add the corresponding release of radioactive material into the sea and the long-term effect on the food chain of such contamination. It may eventually affect us all.

It is such clandestine official policy that rankles with an ever more intelligent and socially aware world public while at the same time providing ample fuel for conspiracy theorists. These cover-up stories have become so expected and common-place that it seems no controversial public figure can die of natural causes without some rumour, substantiated by soon to become 'factual' hearsay, that they were assassinated by the government, practised black magic, or are still alive and living in seclusion at a secret location. In prison these theories are rife, simply because jail is a breeding ground for gossip as plenty of cons have little to do and plenty of time to do it in.

Criticism of the government is obviously high on the agenda and I was not too amazed when informed of an insidious plot between the Freemasons of the leading western governments and their allies within the world's wealthiest families to gain world domination. In all seriousness the theory runs along the lines that they are being advised behind the scenes by extra-terrestrials who intend to enslave mankind and battle for the earth. And where do the bulk of these aliens live? At the heart of world domination, the US presidential residence, The White House! To be honest that part is probably the most believable. This popular fiction encouraged me to research a question that is more topical than ever, are aliens among us?

Although it may be debateable due to the ambiguous nature of ancient myths, the nineteenth century science fiction novel by H. G. Wells, *War of the Worlds*, was perhaps the first to alter the form of extra-terrestrials from gods to humanoid creatures whose physical structure was based upon our phobias of earth's amphibian life. To my mind the novel seemed to be a social commentary as well as entertainment, and included a critique of the uselessness of the upper middle-classes for whom it seems Wells had a particular loathing, and also demonstrated how social issues can be solved using common sense and simplicity instead of the complex political structures that are often more hindrances than solutions. This stance should also be of no surprise as Wells was a staunch socialist.

His work also touched upon an age old curiosity of our place in the universe, and the question of whether we are alone in it or not, and it is quite natural that with the advent of modern science the genre continued to gain in popularity throughout the twentieth century. But it was the aftermath of a global event that caused the alien question to grow to such an extent that it now rivals traditional religious belief in the minds of millions of people.

Nothing accelerates the enterprise and progress made in technological and medicinal development like war. The need for victory puts the 'no expense spared' stamp on many experimental projects that would never otherwise have seen the light of day. World War Two was no exception and proved to be a nip and tuck affair not just in terms of strategic military ability and force of numbers, but also in regard to scientific invention.

Prior to this most famous of international conflicts, sightings of unidentified flying objects could on the whole be explained as the result of atmospheric electromagnetic activity, after it they became something far more tangible, flying saucers. Further developments led to sightings of humanoid creatures that were credited with piloting these crafts, who like H. G. Wells fictional Martians had an amphibious appearance. Much of the evolution of the latter can probably be attributed to World War Two and its subsequent influence on world affairs, but it is very difficult to see the wood for the trees.

It is widely peddled that Adolf Hitler ploughed substantial resources into the development of a flying craft that did not need a runway, could both take off and land vertically from the ground, and could also deploy bombs while hovering directly above its intended target. The reason he made such an investment was because the theory for such a weapon had been in existence for years, and the manufacture of such a machine would have given Nazi Germany a significant advantage over the allied forces. Clearly he did not succeed in his efforts as he lost the war and there is no record of any weapon-laden unidentified flying objects in the much detailed annals of the conflict.

On the face of it the existence of flying saucer technology during this period seems to have no substantiation whatsoever, especially in light of the fact that the allied invasion of Berlin has been one of the most comprehensively covered episodes in human history. But curiously, it was just a few years later that UFO sightings actually began.

The period known as 'The Cold War' began in the aftermath of World War Two and was essentially a competition between the once allied forces of Russia, the USA, and Great Britain to access the advances made in technology by Nazi Germany. Hitler had assembled many of the world's leading scientists to help him develop the German military arsenal, and it is true that these men and their discoveries were very much in demand. It is also true that much progress had been made in many areas of experimentation and it is not beyond reason to assume that the flying saucer was among them.

As the saying goes 'a rumour is not a rumour that does not die' and it seems that this one has plenty of life. Sightings of UFO's have become more and more prominent, being witnessed worldwide by larger and larger groups of people. What I found particularly interesting was the fact that as our own technology has advanced so have reports of these 'alien' flying crafts, with descriptions becoming more and more specific.

They began as 'round' machines, with 'round' windows, or were cigar-shaped, then later became triangular with the ability to dissect themselves, and the capacity to travel much faster than the aircrafts of their time. Not only have these advances been reflected in the physical make-up of the flying machines themselves but also in that of their pilots.

The first extra-terrestrial humanoids on record were short, between four to five feet tall, had yellow skin, large slanted eyes, no apparent lingual skills, and were always spotted in America. Is it not odd that during the period of The Cold War, the main enemies of the USA were Russia and China? I found it too coincidental that these alien descriptions were so ideally synonymous with the Chinese stereotype for it to be mere chance, and felt that they were the result of schemes intended to politically manipulate the public psyche. To this effect the power of the media cannot be ruled out as Hollywood was a major player in this arena even conducting its own government-backed anti-communist purge during the 1950's as well as producing the sci-fi genre of 'B' movies that gained world-wide popularity during this time.

Now that The Cold War is over, these aliens, again with Hollywood assistance, have now become 'grey' in colour and are 'known' to be friendly. They are affectionately referred to because of their colour as 'greys' and have featured in numerous films and television series. In popular imagination hostile aliens are now featured as reptiles of a lizard-like nature that originally came to earth during mankind's fledgling period and assisted in our evolution because they wanted to use us as slaves. Several new-age groups have made many millions of dollars by revealing a history between the reptilians and the greys and describe in detail exactly what happened during this ancient period, and how when the enslaved humans had dug enough gold for the 'reptilians' these aliens recharged their crafts and headed back into the depths of outer space. Apparently they are set to return at some point and once again wreak havoc so we had all better watch out.

There are now far more versions of how and why humanoid aliens are among us today and nearly all allege that these far older and technologically superior species are concerned for our welfare and the damage that modern man is causing to the earth.

What amazes me is why they do not show themselves. If they are so physically and scientifically advanced what have they to fear? The best method of whipping us into shape would be to approach the leaders of the world, take advantage of our satellites and media, and tell us point blank to get our act together.

Having digested a wealth of information on this topic and its profusion of lies, half-truths, and government led obscuration, I became sure that human research, construction, and testing of man-made flying crafts was responsible for many of the sightings of UFO's that have been attributed to extra-terrestrial activity and that a proportion of these were carried out and then denied by official sources so that public opinion could be moulded for political advantage.

The legend of Roswell is a good case in point as we now know for certain that alien craft did not land in the US military desert region in Nevada known as Area 51, but that the whole affair was an elaborate scheme based on both military and public misconception. It is the same strategy of misinformation and implanting of myth that has lead governments to test manned and unmanned prototype flying crafts and then deny they had done so. The mystique is exacerbated by the 'need-to-know-basis' secrecy that government departments pride themselves on so that one agency truly has no idea what another is up to. Hence the recorded cases where a denial comes from one department of a 'paranormal event', while another 'admits' such an occurrence, saying that something mysterious did indeed 'show up on their radar'. Let us bear in mind that the technology for the Hovercraft, Jump-Jet, and Stealth Plane must have undergone stringent testing somewhere, this notwithstanding other continued experiments to expand our technology.

If the answer to the evolution of the extra-terrestrial myth does not lie within the development of our own sciences and unusual natural phenomena then we must assume it to be true that aliens did indeed start to visit earth in the 1940's, focused their attention on Middle America, and for some reason, after travelling many millions of light years, decided to stay hidden even though we do not pose much of a threat to them. I imagine there must be some mysterious logic to this popular assumption and am waiting to have it explained.

Not surprisingly these stories have taken on a life of their own as once again the unscrupulous and plain-crazy have made the subject their domain, while quite notably making sure the main ingredients are identical to those of the ancient myths. They run the usual gamut. The aliens came from outer space, there is no concrete evidence that they exist, they either created us or assisted in our evolution, they are wiser and more powerful than us, some of them are 'good' guys and some 'bad' (it seems a given, as usual, that even in outer space males are socially dominant!), they only reveal themselves to the chosen few, they have threatened to return to earth to forcefully teach us how to conduct ourselves, and they have always monitored our existence. Add to this the plethora of messiah figures, prophets, the reward of immortality for obeying secretly inspired codes of ethics, and parallel lines become paths of convergence.

There is also an unsavoury element to some of these tales in that several New Age groups propagate myths of racial superiority dating back to man's origin, and dependent upon which group, or I should say, very wealthy group, that you subscribe to, the dominant race can be either Caucasian or Negro. Well, nothing fleeces the aimless like telling them what they want to hear. The essence of these new tales is exactly the same as the old ones simply because their inventors are not stupid, proving that 'if it is not broke do not fix it', just put some new clothes on the emperor, especially when there is money, control, and power to be gained. The truth remains the same though, he really is buck naked.

On more mundane issues things were now very different for me at work because I was now in the company of people that were in the same situation as myself. This was the opposite of my previous experience at the warehouse, and the stresses and strains of some of the other prisoner's mood swings and inability to stick to sensible routines was often a pain. How it was not guessed that we were cons I will never know.

No one was aware that we were serving sentences and yet we were all itching to tell them. Only strict instruction at the risk of losing our jobs kept us from revealing the truth to all and sundry. When I was back at the warehouse I was the only inmate, and everyone there, the warehouse lads, the office and sales staff, and the ladies in the accounts department all knew that I was out of jail on day release and all credit to them as they treated me exceptionally well. If anything I was the object of much curiosity and enjoyed being quizzed about jail, the effect on my family life, and incarcerations other psychological influences. I told them all that in terms of relationships jail was more effective than any marriage guidance counsellor could ever be and I noted that both men and women paid particular attention when I stressed that side of prison life.

If you do not learn to appreciate your partner and the value of their company there is no doubt a spell in the slammer would be the short, sharp shock that would teach you quickly to appreciate the nuances of life. Most guys inside would give their right arm to be able to spend just one evening in the company of their loved ones, the things that seem so insignificant, like holding hands, a walk in the park, or just being able to sit on the same sofa, become luxuries. But when you are on the outside they can get taken for granted. I know because I was often so guilty of being too busy for that kind of thing. To my shame, much too often. It is not a mistake that I will make again.

There was one other area of freedom that prisoners nearing the end of their sentences were allowed to enjoy, and I was looking forward to it as much as anyone else. We were allowed to bring our cars into the jail and use them for travel to and from work and town visits. I had given Nick my car when I was sentenced and so had to buy a new one. I wanted something economical and reliable and was keeping my eyes open for one of the bargains that were periodically on offer at work. I had already missed two as the managers at the site get first refusal and was biding my time when a friend told me that he knew someone personally who had a rarely used Nissan Micra that they wanted to get rid of and that he could vouch for the validity of its mileage and service record himself. I told him to tell them I would buy it on the strength of his recommendation and arranged to pay for it by cheque from my prison bank account.

I enjoyed the whole process of arranging the insurance, providing the prison office with the details of my drivers licence and other relevant documentation, and was especially excited about collecting that little old motor and driving it to the prison, but the best was yet to come. I told Chris that I would be getting a lift from a friend to see him and Kelis that weekend, it was a little white lie that was necessary just so that I could see the looks on their faces when I picked them up from his flat and took them for a spin. Sure enough they smiled their heads off when they saw me pull up, it was another sign that dad was regaining his manhood and that pretty soon the nightmare might be over. It was one of the best town visits that I ever had.

18

Many of the staff and inmates thought it quite eccentric how Eddie Hill would bring his golf clubs to work to practise swinging technique during his lunchtime. I didn't, watching him honing his skills out there on the prison football pitch struck me as a pretty cool way to relax. I guess the fact that he drove a Porsche convertible and wore an expensive wristwatch did not help and gave the impression to some that he did not take his job as seriously as he might have. I thought that type of argument displayed little logic and reeked of more than a little jealousy, and that if anything the opposite was true. There are usually other reasons why such talk becomes popular and there was a simple one in Eddie's case, he was the prison probation officer.

Perhaps the most important reference in a convict's parole file is the probation officer report and if a prisoner gets a bad one then in all probability they face an uphill battle to get any other boxes ticked to sanction an early release. If Eddie highlighted security concerns in anyone's file, they knew they were in trouble and spat his name with some venom, either he did not take his job seriously, had a secret loathing for cons, or had some other similarly unprofessional axe to grind, every excuse would be forthcoming except that just maybe he had a point. After the length of time that I had spent inside I always took such rumours with a pinch of salt, and when the time came for my own parole report to be compiled I found that my reservations were well founded.

I eagerly anticipated our appointment and was not too surprised that Eddie had done his homework, he was aware of my exemplary disciplinary record, knew what courses I had completed, and had a good idea of what type of future I intended to construct for myself. He quizzed me in detail for almost two hours, I assume this was to make sure that I was sincere about my ambitions, we also talked at length about philosophical issues concerning both life and business. I enjoyed our conversation as much as I did the ones I had with Alison Wing, such was the length and breadth of the subjects we covered, and some time later I told him that I would like to keep in touch upon my release. I found it encouraging that he welcomed my suggestion. Needless to say, he gave me an honest and glowing report. In spite of this if I could not get the confiscation order issue resolved I was not going anywhere.

By this time Bones had also been transferred from Rye Hill and was one of the few from that establishment to join me at the Grange. We spent much of our free time together, either working out in the gym, or relaxing on one of the landings or a dormitory, discussing what we considered to be serious issues. His main concern was one born of fear, that his young son would follow him into the spiralling life of violence and repercussions that he saw so many other youngsters aspire to, (who were getting younger by the day), and he was apprehensive of the fact that his lad did not call him 'Dad', but by his street name. Bones was right. It was a cause for concern. His planned solution is admirable and like me he is working to re-invent himself. I came into jail a kickboxer, but am determined to become respected as a credible author upon my exit. Bones has something similar up his sleeve and is working towards it in a manner that is to be admired. The power of love, fatherly love in our cases, is not to be underestimated, and it is one of Bones' ambitions that his son progresses through school to university. He is well on course to lead by example.

They say that you do not find books, but that they find you, a little like the search for a partner where the man chases the woman until she catches him, and I should not be surprised that of all the material I had on philosophy Bones was attracted to the works of Friedrich Nietzsche more than any other. He soaked up the legendary German's work like a sponge. Although this did concern me as it is hard to get a handle on Nietzsche's opinions because they are so extreme, and can come across as anti-social and unfeeling, and no disrespect to my friend, but he is not known for being in touch with his gentler side. The philosopher's work certainly gets the grey matter working though, a point Bones often made clear with some very lucid arguments during our discussions.

I suppose I liked Nietzsche because mentally I had travelled a similar journey. It became apparent to me that belief could be imposed as fact if it was popular enough and had longevity, it was also clear that it is a double-edged sword that can also be used to inflict as much damage as it can to give counsel and solace. To my mind that risk alone made it an unnecessary social tool. I also became wary of the false morality of the Bible, a prime example is that it has been directly responsible for the justification of slavery which is accepted as normal within its pages, and even Jesus is not shown to condemn this abominable concept. (On this basis is it not truly an irony that the African nations and those of their heritage hold this book in such high esteem?) What is also overlooked is the fact that Christianity, like modern Islam, is essentially a suicide cult. Its namesake intentionally sacrificed his life, a feat which has become endemic within the Christian set of values and is seen as good and heroic when suffered for the sake of upholding biblical philosophy.

I found it quite agreeable that Nietzsche criticised both the slave morality and unnecessary guilt imposed by religious belief, waiting to go to heaven to experience a decent quality of life has never sat well with me, and the gospel words of Jesus that *'it is harder for a rich man to enter the kingdom of heaven than for a camel to pass through the eye of a needle'* were clearly a ploy to keep the masses in their place. Let us not forget that nearly all of the heroes of the Old Testament became wealthy men. The esoteric value aside, this was because the plight of the ancient Hebrew people demanded the aspiration and independence that wealth could bring.

The New Testament was a home to different times and the ruling Roman government needed subjects that were willing not only to pay taxes but would also settle for harsh conditions and the promise of future luxury. The lines *'Give unto Caesar what is Caesar's!'* and *'The meek shall inherit the earth'* were inserted for these very reasons. This realisation brings to mind the old adage 'a promise is only comfort to a fool', and that the New Testament was a text sponsored by the Roman Empire is as clear as the living daylights, which is why I found Nietzsche's words so appealing: *'Every tradition grows ever more venerable – the more remote its origin, the more confused that origin is. The reverence due to it increases from generation to generation. The tradition finally becomes holy and inspires awe'.* It would be hard to define religious history more succinctly.

Just as they had been at Rye Hill my opinions were also sought out on a regular basis at the Grange, this as usual for the sake of bolstering arguments, and I admit I would often be guilty of causing verbal conflict with flip comments, forgetting that I might be within earshot of the easy to offend. As far as such disagreements are concerned I have always enjoyed the company of people that are beyond petty dispute and are able to conduct an amiable relationship even though opinions differ, and in the final dormitory that I was moved to I was faced with just that situation.

I became friendly with a family of five Irish brothers that were as feisty as you can imagine, I got on well with all of them as they were keen boxing fans and we would notify each other when the big fights were screened in the main television room and exchange pre and post-fight opinions. They were at the Grange because of an altercation with other members of their family, winning the battle but losing the war so to speak as their own cousins testified against them and they were subsequently incarcerated. I shared lodgings with the last two brothers to be released, Isaac and Alec, and the company of another outlandish figure, Happy Gill, before achieving single room status in the prison hostel. My time in that dormitory was never uneventful.

During the papal election following the death of Pope John Paul II the candidates for his succession were featured on international television on a daily basis and of course I could not resist making my usual quips, in truth I was merely thinking out aloud, when I stated that there is no way they were going to let a 'brother' be a Pope, there would sooner be a black president of the United States before that would happen again. There have apparently been three black Popes in the early history of the Church but for the last fifteen hundred years the Pope has nearly always been an Italian, a tradition that has been broken only once in the last four hundred years with the election of Pope John Paul II who was from Poland. To think that the Church would choose a black man as its next leader in yet another historic shift was nonsense and a step too far. I pressed on that if successful the African candidate would be one Holy Father that would not survive the bullet and how he would have no choice but to say his prayers zealously night and day.

This of course was in reference to the Nigerian Cardinal Francis Arinze, an extremely intelligent and well-educated man who one would like to think is bringing pressure to bear on the Roman Church for their stance on the use of condoms. As I stated earlier and is common knowledge, many followers of the Roman Church in countries seriously afflicted with HIV are dying needlessly due to ignorance and unrealistic moral ideals. I stress again, Catholics in the western world tend to be more enlightened, a pattern to which the institution turns a blind eye and frankly it is abominable that this common sense revolt is not reflected in the international policy of the religion.

Still, once again, I digress, our dormitory was on the third floor of the building so it might have been wise of me to remember that the brothers are staunch Roman Catholics and take their belief seriously. With my running commentaries I envisaged Isaac and Alec hanging me out of the dormitory bay window by my ankles until I confessed my sins. They tore into me verbally but I mimed over them with what I pretended would be the actions of Arinze, if successfully installed in the papal hot seat, making the sign of the cross while dodging snipers bullets. They had to laugh, and why, the best comedy is based on truth. That difference aside, Alec and I became quite close, and until I bought my own vehicle he would drive me to and from work in his car as we both worked at the same location.

The other dorm member, 'Happy' Gill, was something of an anomaly, born of East Indian stock, but raised in the north of England, you could never picture him if you heard his voice before you saw him. Happy has as broad an English Geordie accent as you can imagine. Our meeting, let alone sharing the same living quarters proved once again just how small the world we live in actually is. Happy is a well trained kickboxer and was schooled in the art of Muay Thai Boxing by an old friend and sparring partner of mine, Barry Norman. So common were these coincidences becoming that when I asked Happy who his instructor was I already had a strong feeling who he was going to name.

Inevitably we began working out together in the gym and would supervise each other when on the boxing punch bag. He was amazed that I punched away for a solid hour so I taught him how to do it too. It's all about breathing, relaxation, and strength of mind, and of course, if you do not believe that you can do it, you cannot. Happy is a good listener and got up to the forty-five minute mark before we parted company.

Because of his heritage I knew it was likely that he was a Sikh by religion, a fact given away by the silver bangles he wore around his wrist, and he too was fascinated by the breadth of knowledge that I had acquired on the subject. I told him that Sikhism, originally a hybrid version of Hinduism and Islam, but now accepted as a stand alone faith, like other major religions has a lineage that can be traced back to North Africa, a fact attested to by the presence of baptism, and the halo, within its tenets.

As Hinduism is the oldest of the East Indian faiths its

followers argue strongly that the Sikh belief system is clearly based upon their own. There are many differences between them but the similarities are also strong and it seems to me that the Hindus have a point. But that is the nature of religion, no matter where in the world they exist they will split, change format, and create separate factions, all claiming to be the most divine, yet in the final analysis their schisms can always be traced to political factors. What was the famous question that Nietzsche posed, *'Was man a blunder of God, or God a blunder of man?'* it certainly is food for thought because these so called cults of love have always done well at fostering divisions of hate.

The truth is that Sikhism is the politically correct child of a fierce religio-political rivalry and was born when its founder became fed up with the ensuing bigotry and loathing that this contention fostered. The 15th century Guru, Nanak Dev, went to a river to bathe and meditate, and disappeared for a short period of time, when he came back he was a changed man, and enlightened by his experience declared, *'There is no Hindu, there is no Muslim.'* The period of time that he was gone? You've guessed it, three days. (A secret society member? It's always a possibility!)

It was clear that to achieve unity between the vastly different philosophies of Hinduism and Islam was an impossibility, and so Sikhism took the middle ground, acknowledging the existence of the 'one God' that could be found in the hearts of all men, while also nobly fostering the ethos of divine equality in all people regardless of race, gender, or caste. Guru Nanak shunned the idea of exclusiveness or the uniqueness of any particular prophet or God and warned that the performance of rituals and outward observance in other religions had their downside, *'Humans are led astray by the reading of words; performers of ritual are vain and proud'*. I think he was being overly diplomatic on that point, most religious leaders are revered like superstars, and have egos to match.

On the subject of Eastern religions I particularly like the stance of Hinduism on evangelism. Hindu's make little or no effort to convert anyone to their belief system. Their opinion is that any religion is an individual's path to God, and to change direction is an unnecessary disruption. Christianity and Islam, who are still hell-bent on their age old quest for global domination, have much to learn from such a tolerant attitude and the world would be much the better if they did.

On the whole I think that Guru Nanak developed a system that had many advantages over its contemporaries, and although far from perfect, (the despicable caste system permeated Sikhism as well as every other religion in India), he embarrassed his competitors in the areas where their teachings were deficient. With philosophies that appealed to the compassionate and moral side of human nature he secured many devotees from both Hinduism and Islam among his converts. This of course is an age old solution, and was almost exactly the same path taken to alleviate the rivalries between Judaism, Christianity, and Arabian paganism by the formation of Islam.

The Hindu caste system was, and still is, even though it is technically outlawed, abominably rife, and is segregation at its worst. The fact that Hindu's make up approximately 80 per cent of India's estimated one billion population, and that 80 per cent of them live in the countryside where the older traditions are more strictly adhered to, gives some idea of the scope of human denigration that is perpetrated in its name.

It cannot be hidden that the caste system is vehemently racist, and the Sanskrit term that the practice of *jäti* is derived from literally means 'race'. The fact that the lower castes tend to be more dark-skinned in complexion than the almost European looking higher castes is strikingly noticeable. Colour prejudice amongst the same ethnic groups is a world-wide phenomenon and one that tells us a lot about the baseness of human nature. What is even worse is that inter-caste marriages are a strict no-no, with violence, and often death considered suitable punishment for any that dare step out of line. Hitler must have found it quite inspiring.

Still, such bigotry had no place in our dorm at the Grange which was as cosmopolitan a mix as you're going to get and Happy, Alec, myself, and the other guys that shared space with us had some fun moments during our months together.

As for renewing old friendships during my weekend moments of freedom I had no difficulty sticking to my decision to leave the past behind and start all over again. The only other person apart from my children that I saw on my visits out was Elle who would occasionally pick me up and treat me to a Sunday meal and the cinema. Our relationship was blossoming so well that I suggested that she meet my children on one of her visits. I was both nervous and happy when she agreed and the occasion itself was entirely spur of the moment. The children knew nothing of our friendship and it was one of those situations where I could easily have been damned if I did or damned if I did not tell them. They might have felt offended that I did not think they were mature enough to inform them sooner, especially Nick and Chris, and of course there was the even worse fear that Kelis might have rejected our liaison out of hand.

On the day in question Kelis was out at a barbecue with Nia and we did not see her on our trip into Birmingham, Elle did meet Nick and Chris however, and just as I suspected my eldest was quick to point out that I should have told him I had a close female friend sooner. He was quite right, at twenty-five years of age he was by anyone's measurement a man. I could have kicked myself but the issue came and went with no further mention. Chris presented no critique, he was just plain surprised, and I am glad to note, happy about the situation, as was Nick. That was the minor two hurdles down, just young lady to go.

The following weekend I planned to visit Chris and Kelis and spend the day relaxing at the flat that Chris shared with Gemma by watching movies on DVD and chilling out. When I arrived I told Chris that I was taking his sister to the DVD rental store to collect the selected films which I also felt would be the perfect opportunity to tell her about Elle. Some surprise, she already knew. Chris had told his mother who had passed the information on to her daughter. I asked Kelis how she felt about the situation to which she replied that she was glad and when could she meet Elle? The way she spoke and the smile on her face told me that her comment was genuine, it was a relief for me and a nice moment.

My main worry concerning my children was that Nia might have held a grudge and poisoned their minds about Elle, but she clearly did not and all credit to her for being so mature about the situation. I know of plenty of women who would have acted in the opposite manner. Elle and I were still not an item yet, but she was the closest friend that I had on the outside, I not only relished her company but trusted her implicitly.

There were three reasons why I wanted to tell the children about our friendship, one was that I did not want them to feel sorry for the old man because he was on his own and yet mom had a new partner, it would not have made a scrap of difference to me but I felt that it might have been a concern to them, a point which Kelis' reaction to our relationship made clear. Two, was that I only had eyes for Elle but did not want to blow our friendship by stepping over the mark when she merely wanted to enjoy her freedom, so introducing her to my children was the biggest hint that I could drop about my intentions, and three, I was due for release in a matter of weeks.

For the Crown to keep me in custody they had to serve a document known as a Warrant of Commitment on Hewell Grange Prison and as far as I was aware this had not been done. When I raised the issue with my supervising officers they told me the current situation was that I would be released if parole was granted. When I pressed as to what would happen if the warrant for extra custody was served they were unsure whether I would be able to remain at the Grange or would have to be returned to closed conditions. I was well aware that such matters are often left until the morning the inmate is due to depart when he or she is re-arrested at the gate while making their way home, it's the Crown Prosecution Service version of a practical joke. To add to this technique of psychological torture I still had not received any written confirmation that my parole had been granted either. Mentally I prepared myself for the worst.

I took the precaution of asking Elle to assist me in arranging accommodation in the possible event of release and used my lunch break from work to arrange two new bank accounts, one for the money that I had saved while in prison and the other to start up a keep fit business that I intended to launch to boost my income. I was also determined to find regular daytime employment in a nine to five job doing whatever I could, I had a lot of ground to make up and intended to do it quickly. The truth is however that I dislike being employed by other people, but I remember well the favourite saying of my dearly departed ex-father-in-law 'Mr P', *'Take what you get until you get what you want!'* It was an appropriate maxim for my situation.

I did not have to wait too long to get clarity on my situation and as expected it was bitter-sweet. Within the space of a few days I was informed that I had been successful in my parole application, and also that the Warrant of Commitment that had been ordered unbeknown to me all those years ago by Birmingham Magistrates Court had at long last been served on the prison and unless I could get it revoked, I was going nowhere. My solicitors, the same firm that I had used throughout my ordeal had come up against a brick wall and despite impassioned pleas that my defence was a genuine one the London based confiscation order office stood their ground. The whole issue was one big mess.

The basis of the legal argument against my release was that I should have applied to stop enforcement proceedings of the warrant at the time it was ordered. That would have been a neat trick as I was not informed of the order. My right to appeal against it was now outside the allowable timescales which blew my chances of filing for the one document that would make the issue go away, a Certificate of Inadequacy. This piece of paper was issued to subjects of a confiscation order who could prove that it was impossible to pay the set amount from the moment that it was sanctioned. I could do that in spades, well, if the law was that simple I could, unfortunately it isn't. I asked my solicitors to ensure that my file was up to date as I was coming to collect it.

I drove from work to Birmingham, collected the file and took it back to the Grange so that I could glean what information from it that I could to construct a last ditch appeal to the courts.

The document that I prepared took me over four hours and was five pages long, it pointed out various legal discrepancies, logged dates and times of any relevant events, and I also attached the legal papers that had been served upon me in my bid to show that not only had I acted above board in my efforts to defend myself but also that the Crown was on shaky moral ground as they had given me, on several occasions, conflicting information on the penalties that could be imposed.

The Magistrates had originally informed me that there were a number of options available to them if I did not pay the order which included imposing a consecutive prison term in lieu of payment. The length of this term was measured against the amount of money that was requested and in my case was calculated to twelve months of which I would have to serve half. This seemed quite clear, either I pay the government fifteen thousand pounds or I face the possibility of serving an extra six months.

It was when I sought clarification of matters upon arrival at Hewell Grange that I was told that it was indeed still possible to obtain a Certificate of Inadequacy by making an ex-parte application to a Crown Court Judge as only someone of that stature had the power to overturn the original ruling as it was a Crown Court Judge, the one that presided over my case, that had set it. The Crown Prosecution Service had the option to oppose my application and pending their decision I was to be called to an oral hearing. I accepted this and was fully prepared to represent myself in court as legal aid was not available to cover Barristers fees. I felt confident enough to do this as my case was relatively straight forward and I had kept all of the necessary documents throughout the years as a matter of caution. It was at this point that the goalposts were moved.

My application was moved from the Crown Prosecution Service in Birmingham to the London office and I was told that there would no longer be an oral hearing and the matter would have to go to the High Court. At my request the CPS forwarded the necessary application forms and an instructional template for me to personally apply for the Certificate of Inadequacy. As if I was not already fighting an uphill battle the High Court was also in recess and would not re-open to deal with such cases until the winter, well after my release date.

It was points like these, and others, that I took pains to outline in my missive, and before going to work the next morning I drove straight into Birmingham town centre to hand over my written defence at the Magistrates Court along with the originals of all substantiating paperwork. I was careful to make photocopies of everything just in case my file went missing again.

The person that was liaising with my solicitors up until that point was a legal officer named Annette who worked in the court's Central Finance Unit. I had spoken to her several times on the telephone and it gave me a level of comfort that she had agreed to meet me that morning to collect my documentation. When she walked into the court lobby I knew that it was her immediately, she looked just as I had expected. She struck me as being quite prim and proper and had an air of legality about her that told me she was more than just a mere court clerk. She greeted me more warmly than I would have expected considering her officious appearance and took me to one side to inspect the paperwork that I had brought along. Our meeting made me smile quite a bit.

I suffer from astigmatism, an eyesight affliction where reading anything more than twelve inches away from my eyes without my glasses on is a huge strain. The dreadful strip lighting used in prison in addition to the amount of reading that I had done had worsened my condition even more and often words are just a blur unless I pull the text to within two or three inches from my face and squint like a pervert. Annette's eyesight was even worse than mine. She held those papers so close to her face that they were almost touching her glasses as she 'hummed' and 'ahhed' obviously scrutinizing every word that I had written. She reminded me of one of those eccentric day-saving lawyers in the old Hollywood movies. When she had finished she looked at me and said she was not promising anything but there was a chance she could arrange for the Warrant of Commitment to be set aside so that I could be released from prison on my due date of parole. I knew she had seen something in the points that I had mentioned that either provided the necessary escape route for my release to be sanctioned, or actually made it illegal for me to be detained. To this day I do not know what that point was.

Four days later Annette telephoned me at work on my mobile while I was busy washing a car. I do not normally keep my phone in my pocket due to radiation fears, but not wanting to miss a possible call I had done so since the day I had met with her. I threw my chamois leather into the bucket of water and raced to a quiet spot with my heart pumping like it used to before I entered the ring. The warrant had been successfully set aside and she was merely waiting to present it before a Judge in session for it to be rubber-stamped. I do not know how many times I asked her if she was sure, what would happen if the Judge did not agree, what would happen if there was not a Judge in session before my release date, what would happen if there was an earthquake, I just would not shut up. I know she was smiling on the other end of that phone as she waited patiently for my questions to subside before stating very clearly, *'Howard, stop worrying, you're going home.'*

All of this of course was as true to form as you might expect. My official release date was the very next day, but fortunately Elle had successfully helped me prepare for this eleventh hour outcome and I phoned her and my children as soon as I signed off from my conversation with Annette. When I told them the good news they were cock-a-hoop.

I informed both the management staff of the valeting company and the car dealership officials that I was leaving forthwith and said my goodbyes to the mechanics and salesmen that I had become friendly with. I have to say, I was back in that non-plussed territory again, far from being excited that I had at last gained my freedom and jumping for joy, I was as matter of fact about the situation as one could be. Shock again I guess.

On my drive back to Hewell Grange I imagined that I would have to convince the staff that they had to release me in the morning and mentally prepared myself for another battle. It was an ungrounded fear. Annette had faxed them with the necessary paperwork as soon the decision had been made. When I stepped into the post and administrations room I was met with the warm smiles of several officers, and Mr Bailey, a man who was as respectful as one human being could be to another from the first day I met him, took great pleasure in telling me, *'Howard, you're going home in the morning!'* It was a nice touch. It wasn't plain sailing yet though, I still had to pack! Those damn books again.

I took the ones that I had borrowed back to the prison library and then set about getting myself organised. It took all night and then some, to discard what I did not need, pack my belongings and clean every nook and cranny of my living quarters for its next occupant. Morning came all too quickly.

The final irony about jail was then pressed home by several officers who came to see how my departure was proceeding. They are quick to lock you behind a door, but once you don't officially belong there, they are even quicker to get you off the premises. Thankfully Bones got permission to help me transfer my boxes to my car as I was running so late that all the other inmates that had been released that morning were probably at home before I even got to the gate. Even Mr Ryan, the feared prison head of security and a really hard-edged man, ordered some other lads to assist in moving my belongings, anyone that knows him would be quick to tell you that I was getting some pretty special leeway.

Bones stayed in the car park when all the other helpers had left and we gave each other the usual farewell words of encouragement. He stopped and turned as he made his way back inside and said, *'Howard, I've got to tell you, I've never met anyone like you, you're a really different kind of guy!'* I was flattered, after all, he's not exactly run of the mill himself.

I watched that statuesque building shrink in my rear view mirror as I drove away and couldn't help but thinking about how another chapter in my life was now over, and I was about to begin a brand new one. It was an exciting thought. Maybe everything really is for a reason. Time will tell.

HOWARD BROWN

19

Five years, *il tempus fugit*! But no matter which way you look at it, I was a long time gone. I cannot ask the usual question, where did it all go? I know exactly where it went, I was counting every second and constantly analysing the consequences. On a personal level my absence from my family was a disaster and I accept that there is much that was lost that cannot be made up. Naturally, I refer in the main to my children.

Nick was an aspiring student when I came in and was now a fully-fledged adult, in fact I felt that he was not that far away from marriage. He had met Tina, a few years previously and even brought her to visit me a few times at Rye Hill. She is an attractive, ambitious, and respectful girl of East Indian heritage who it would be difficult not to approve of. I approve a great deal. Goodness knows what her parents, who against all cultural tradition have accepted my son as part of their family, will think when they find out his father is a convicted criminal? It is best they do not say too much about me at the moment.

Chris, barely a teenager upon my abduction, was now not only an impressively mature young man but could also be considered a parent, he stayed that close to and is that protective of his little sister. I am very proud of the way he handled the whole affair as it is arguable, because of the age he was when I was taken away, that he could have been affected the worst of all my children by my absence. He has also settled into a relationship with a very dependable girl, Gemma, who gets my vote all day long.

As for young lady, she barely reached my chest when I was sentenced and by the time of my release she was the same height, worryingly attractive, and still growing, it is that difference in her size by which I measure how much I have missed of my children's lives. In spite of and not because of me they have all grown even closer and thanks to Nia remain well grounded and disciplined. There is no making of any bones about it, I am an extremely fortunate individual. Things could easily have been a lot worse.

All other aspects of my life are still in the balance. I remain close to Elle and hope to become a successful author, whether I have the skills and have chosen the right material will become clear soon enough, the only thing I can be sure of is that unforeseen circumstance permitting I will see my projects through to their fruition. In this respect my incarceration was not long enough simply because of the size of the mission that I had set myself. It is a certainty that without being locked up I could never have dreamed of tackling such a venture. Due to the expansiveness of the subject matter and the amount of research and cross-referencing needed I knew from day one that I would be struggling to complete it before my time was up.

Naturally my writing skills have improved along the journey and I not only decided to write this autobiographical account as a pre-cursor but also rewrote *Rulers & Lies* from scratch again when I came out. If you are going to do a job then you might as well do it with patience and to the best of your ability.

Socially my life is totally different. I left Birmingham to live in a completely different town, have two jobs, and am enjoying the relative anonymity and fresh start. I even train at the local kickboxing/boxing club and have told them I am an ex-amateur boxer who everyone calls 'H'. I have been training there about a year and have not thrown a kick in anger and neither have I told the instructor, himself a world kickboxing champion, my full name as it would surely give the game away. One day I'll start putting kick and punch combinations together just to see the looks on their faces.

I remain in touch with a select few of the cons that I met during the years and those that I promised will receive copies of my work upon publication. Bones, Tim, Alec, Silk, and Jelly, and one or two others are probably the closest to me in terms of maintaining contact and I look forward to a reunion with them all when the time is right. But not now, I still have much work to do in terms of reorganising my life so that I can spend more time with Elle and my children.

Old habits die hard I guess, when I was competing I would train in seclusion and show my wares on the day of the fight which would be followed by a party and a few weeks of social activity before I went back into serious training. That's pretty much how I like my life, work first, express what I've been doing, then enjoy the success a little bit. It seems to me that the fighter and the writer are pretty similar animals, they are often required to travel roads of solitude, and their success depends largely upon the same principles, the foremost being self-discipline, with self-belief coming a close second.

There is little doubt in my mind that it is an eventful road ahead and I hope Elle will stand for the inconvenience of it all especially as living with me is no day at the beach, but as I said before, I do have some plus points.

My ethos on birthday and other event cards has always been that anyone can buy a card, sign their name and post it. To my mind that is quite mundane as I always want the person that receives one from me to know that not only was I thinking about them but that I also put time and energy into the thought. So I always make the effort to write poems in the cards I send to people that are close to me. As a result I've written numerous odes and ditties over the years and when Valentine's Day came around I felt it was time to take that extra leap and show my hand. Clearly I had to outdo myself with this one and then nervously sit back and wait for the hoped for reaction. I bought a fairly large card because I needed the space to pour my heart out. To tell the truth even I was surprised at how easily the words came and I have to say that I think it is one of the most poignant poems I have ever written:

Who could have dreamt my Valentine
That I'd be yours and your love mine
When I read the letter and saw your name
I couldn't dare to hope you'd feel the same
It knocked me senseless, near off my feet
Couldn't catch my breath, heart skipped a beat.

Then the memories came flooding through
Of the closeness, the fondness, that we both knew
I thought, second chance? You never know
Big difference this time, I won't let you go!

So if it's a dream, I'll stay asleep
This love's no fancy, it runs too deep
Too long it's been, yet worth the wait
It seems so clear now, we're locked by fate.

And for all those years that passed us by
I can't make up, but I'll surely try
I'll stroke you, kiss you, hold you tight
Love you every day from dawn 'til night
Neglect you, Never! Nor tell you lies
I'll show you true love never dies.

By no stretch of the imagination am I a player when it comes to the ladies, I'm a one woman man by nature and I meant every word on that card, but after letting Elle down so badly all those years ago I could not be sure that she would be ready to commit to a new relationship, especially so soon after her divorce. I posted the card anyway and waited anxiously to telephone her the next day.

Elle is quite the comedian and when I called she told me that she had just received the best card that she had ever had, but there was something else that she needed from me in spite of everything that I had told her. I was just hoping that it was not financial as I was not exactly flush at the time. She said not to worry as it was something that I should have to hand and would cost me nothing. She wanted to see my divorce absolute. I checked to see that document was in my files so fast my fingers caught fire. It was there alright and when I called her back and told her that I had found it she burst out laughing, she was only joking. When I got the chance I showed it to her anyway. Fun and games aside, it was clear that she was as serious about giving us a second chance as I was. As I said, I'm a very fortunate individual.

My children, mother, and siblings were all overjoyed about my release and particularly concerned that I would not be roped back into prison again, either for non-payment of the confiscation order, which with my mother's help was eventually paid in full with interest, or for some other unidentified problem that I had not told them about. They know me all too well.

I had been on the outside for less than a month when I received a totally unexpected phone call. It was a familiar voice, who when he heard me speak sounded concerned, relieved, and glad that I was receptive. I've always found the Dutch accent quite endearing, especially when it navigates its way around the English language, which was one of the main reasons why I got arrested in the first place. Listening to it now I could not help but laugh, and although I had not heard his pronounced tones for over five years, I found Breitling's voice as engaging as ever. Like myself he really is an upbeat kind of guy.

He wanted to know how I was doing and if he could do anything to assist me. I told him I was fine and simply glad to be a free man. Like many others he thought that the length of my sentence was ludicrous and stressed that if I lived in Holland I would probably have gotten the proverbial slap on the wrist compared to the substantial custodial sentence that was meted out. He also reminded me, with wistful reflection, how the whole affair started, which was simply because I agreed to introduce him to some friends of mine. It is funny how things can get out of hand, but as I have said, greed does have that strange habit of dulling your senses.

I had been travelling the world as an athlete for over twenty years, and as I mentioned earlier visited Amsterdam for the first time in 1978. During the fledgling days of kickboxing in the western world, the city's Edenhal Stadium was one of the sports most prominent venues and hosted many historic contests. There are many world champions and superbly skilled fighters in Holland and I have trained and broken bread with many of them. I did not think that such camaraderie would ever be a minus in my life.

I was asked, about eighteen months prior to my arrest, to supply some acquaintances with a contact in Amsterdam for them to import cannabis. Their old contact had dried up for whatever reason and they had pre-paid for a shipment of the drug which they needed to be brought back to England. I turned them down flat on more than one occasion over a period of weeks and stressed that my friends in Holland, although almost certainly able to assist them, (the fight game is surrounded by the criminal fraternity no matter where in the world), would never do so unless I introduced and vouched for them personally, something I was not prepared to do.

The pleading was incessant, and when they told me that if I made the introduction, for every kilo that they brought to England they would pay me one-hundred pounds without the need for me to have any further involvement, the seduction worked. They planned to import two hundred kilos a month. The sad part, I did not need the money.

Anyway, I was as good as my word and accompanied them to Amsterdam to make the introduction. After an initial test run they brought in a shipment of one hundred kilos, sold the contraband, and then gave me two and a half thousand pounds, a quarter of the fee agreed, claiming that expenses for the trip were exorbitant and they could not stick to their promise. This was hogwash of course, they just did not have the character to honour the original agreement. In fact, I estimated that in the following six months they cleared close to half a million pounds in profit. I should have walked away there and then, but for two reasons, greed and easy money. As business progressed their avarice manifested itself on the other side of the pond and my Dutch friends asked me to fly over as they were becoming so concerned with the business tactics of the lead figure in the English team that they intended to assassinate him. My trip was planned to coincide with a major Kickboxing promotion so that I could watch some old friends in action as well as dissuade them from their nonsense talk.

Of a similar nature to myself, Breitling was anti any form of violence, especially for the sake of money. They knew that I had been cheated on my own commission and made me an offer that I should have declined, but by now I had seen how easily this business operated and was also somehow of the mentality that it was practically legal. When you are around something or do it enough it soon becomes the norm and in my limited experience I believe that is often the reason why people get caught. They become nonchalant.

Breitling offered to ship consignments of cannabis to me in England and all I had to do was organise collection and distribution. He would arrange for someone to receive the money in various parts of the country and we agreed a reasonable figure for me to act as agent.

Like any other business, goodwill is of paramount importance, and I had no idea that I was so respected as a person until I got back to England. It must have been obvious that I was in Amsterdam with no official involvement in the kickboxing promotion, (I was long retired and had none of my own fighters on the card), as a result certain parties had noted who I was seated with and put two and two together, they easily came up with four. I had barely arrived home when my phone started ringing off the hook.

The amount of my Dutch acquaintances that asked me to fly back out to meet them was scandalous. As one of them said to me, *'Howard, is everyone stoned in England? Because that is where most of the cannabis from here goes and it is such a small place!'* He then pointed out that many Dutch drug gangs were looking for reliable English contacts to do business with, and preferably ones that they could trust. I was a known quantity but pointed out to all and sundry that I was already taken.

Over the next twelve months or so there were the usual ups and downs involved in the conducting of any type of business and it was on one of the trips that I had to make to Holland that I met Lex. Who could have figured that our fortunes were to take the same turn.

My stance on the use of cannabis is quite philosophical and I equate it to alcohol in many respects. In terms of the physiological harm it can cause and its effect on the psyche largely depends upon the tolerance of the user. It is less likely to make someone more aggressive, although I do know of cases where that actually does happen, but, by and large, 'ganja' smokers tend to chill out. There are of course the small percentage of people who have little resistance to its effects and in those cases it causes psychosis, I know this because I have witnessed it first hand with a member of my own family. If you smoke pot you had better make sure that you eat regularly, if not, the risk to your mental health is greatly increased.

I only have one problem with my own involvement with the drug, and for me it is a big one. I have never smoked a spliff in my life. There is no way on this planet that I would intentionally take smoke into my lungs, be it from tobacco, cannabis, or standing by a bonfire. I find the concept abominable. To be even more honest, for me, any type of drug is a last resort, again, as I said earlier I do not even take aspirins if I have a headache, I would rather do a headstand on my settee. The only saving grace in my hypocrisy is that I do like to drink some bubbly at weekends, and I believe that in terms of parity, if alcohol and tobacco are legal, then cannabis should be too, and subject to the same legal parameters. The only reason that it is not is because of the difficulty that governments would have in taxing it, for unlike cigarettes and alcohol, the cottage industry would be huge and too difficult to control.

So, even though I do not think that marijuana, especially in its natural form, should be illegal, there is no escaping the fact that for me, it should have been a no-go on personal moral grounds alone. Cannabis is not wrong, it was just wrong for me. Still, I'm not going to beat myself up about it, my mother will do that for me, I'm sure she will never let me hear the last of it.

To many people that I have talked to over the years there appears to them to be another paradox in my life which from their point of view is quite baffling and it concerns the question of life after death, for when asked if I believe whether there is an afterlife I diplomatically answer that I would be as remiss to say that there is not as I would to say that there is. Everyone expects me to say point blank that there is not. They misunderstand me. The holy books are as bogus, fraudulent, and transparent as you can get, and the stories of a supreme God, suspiciously of one gender, the male, that would lower himself to be interested in human affairs after providing us with everything that we need to progress our own survival are ludicrous. But whether death is the be-all-and-end-all of our existence is not a question any of us can answer. Not yet.

It is a given that we are the highest form of life on the planet but that in itself does not invest us with any claim to divinity, if it did what would be the argument for the presence of a hierarchy of intelligence within other life forms, for arguments sake, commencing with the dolphin, the dog, and the ape? Do they have their own set of divine rules? Their own lesser heaven and hell perhaps? Of course not, all such notions are invention. (Dolphins, like humans, even have sex for pleasure, while apes and other species with a neocortex masturbate whether there are females on offer or not, so one must assume that dolphin purgatory must be packed to the rafters, and many other mammalian groups are aflame in zoological hellfire!).

The distinction between humans and animals is not a spiritual one for one could easily argue that they are far more in tune with the balance required for life on earth than we are. The essential difference lies in our ability to reason and places a moral responsibility upon us in terms of behaviour. Spirituality has nothing to do with any belief system, it is simply the sum of our harmony with our surroundings, whether that be people, animals, nature, and just as importantly, our inner selves. Anything else is fluff and nonsense, belonging almost solely to the realms of the pious.

In fact, if we were to ask the question 'Would the concept of 'good and evil' exist if there were no humans?' The answer is a resounding No! If you were to equate the length of the planets existence to 24 hours we have been here for a mere seventy-seven seconds, where were 'good and evil' prior to this? Nowhere! There were only the natural occurrences of creation and destruction and the instinctive survival of the species, all else is the invention man felt necessary to govern groups of humans dwelling in harmony, or trying to. Our ideas on morals by the way have varied very widely throughout history and not always for the better.

With this in mind it seems obvious why our gift for logic developed the way it did and why it is more vital for Homo sapiens than any other creature. For openers, we are parasitical by nature and struggle to give anything meaningful back to the planet that we inhabit, a trait which is sheer madness as the Earth is in all probability the best house in the universe. Even at the risk to our own existence we will multiply, consume, and destroy every natural resource within our reach before we consider the consequences. Equilibrium is the over-riding rule of nature and we regularly upset its balance, other creatures do not have this problem, so it should be no real surprise that we possess a superior thought process. I would suggest that apart from safety, for we are woefully vulnerable physically, another of its purposes is to empower us to rectify the disturbance we cause, and why? Natural selection! Or to put it more bluntly, survival, for if we do not, the earth will get rid of us, ergo, 'We think, therefore we are.' We really should not neglect this point and need to be mindful that we inhabit a living entity which will be here long after we have gone. Ask the dinosaurs.

From an historic viewpoint it is unfortunate that religion has become synonymous with ethics and morals, fuelling the belief that without it mankind would live like wild-men in chaos and depravity. This is the biggest falsehood, religion was merely the traditional conduit used to organise social structures and educate the masses, and this long before the advent of Judaism, Christianity, and Islam. Modern man does not need to accept myths and legends as literal events in order to live a life of respect and decency, notwithstanding the fact that the holy books that purport these fantastic stories are both manipulative and deceptive. The role played by religion, can easily be filled by educated parenting and the school classroom.

Surely any sensible adult would agree that mythical scare-mongering is not only unnecessary, as young minds are brighter than we give them credit for, but children are also fragile and such falsehoods cause deep-rooted psychological damage. The biblical line that all humans are 'born in sin' is one of the most abhorrent and repressive doctrines of all time and many children have suffered both physical and mental abuse because of such nonsense. Religious absolutism that espouses what is unequivocally 'good' and what is unquestionably 'bad' limits the thought process, humanity, and consideration of other points of view. In many cases it is the real danger as 'good' and 'bad' are not always set in stone but often merely points of view.

So, if we accept that the need to be guided by fear and fantasy is passé then there is a gaping hole in the academic curriculums of the modern world that should be sensibly filled by the philosophical study of ethics and morals from kinder-garten upwards. There is no logical reason why this cannot be formulated in an inoffensive manner so that a mindset of toler-ance and consequential thought can be installed in young minds. It would be naïve to think that this would cure all social ills, as such matters are varied and complex, but it would do a lot to help.

Whether we live on in some other form of energy after our physical bodies perish is a terrific subject to explore and I think science should throw its hat into the ring and take a look at it. It won't though, it is just too tough a nut to crack. The irony there of course is that if science were to even hint at the existence of evidence of an afterlife religious belief would skyrocket to epic proportions. Once dwindling pews would be crammed and fear would return with a vengeance to shackle many that had escaped its clutches.

I imagine that the effects would be so far reaching as to permeate almost every stratum of the media and politics, and boy, would the unscrupulous have a field day, proclaiming loudly and with a less dubious validity that they have the only answers to the riddles of life and whatever follows it.

The same would apply to the mystery of our presence on the planet earth, even though the real answer to how we got here is glaringly obvious from the amount of argument on the subject, and it is indisputably simple, no one knows! It is not the answer that anyone wants to hear, but it is an unequivocal truth, and it is the existence of this vacuum that allows stories peddled by men so that they can control the lives of others to become taken as divine edict.

Life's riddle seems only partially answered by the Darwinian theory of evolution, yet thus far it is the only sensible explanation of how life began, and in contrast to the holy books the substantiating evidence for evolution by natural selection is overwhelming. Some of it does niggle me though. *It is a given that nearly all species have evolved within themselves but to believe that one species of being evolved into an entirely different one, no matter how much time passed, seems as groundless and specious as believing that a giant, omnipresent, and perfect invisible man is responsible for the solar system, the earth, and life upon it. Both theories are elaborate playground nonsense.

If I were a gambling man I would bet heavily that mankind will finish their existence on this planet and still never know the truth of life's greatest mystery, 'What conditions caused the

---

*(After reading Bill Bryson's brilliant 'A Short History of Nearly Everything' I must concede that species to species evolution is not as outlandish a proposition as it first appears, yet although I am willing to bow to a consensus of greater minds, due to the huge gaps in the fossil record I am still not totally sold).

initial spark of life?' Only science has a chance of discovering the real answer and it would be nice to think that the human race has long enough to find out. This of course, is unacceptable to many as we are all children at heart and feel the need to have the immediate answer to everything, a weakness that makes the masses followers of the corrupt rather than masters of their own destiny.

Still, if I were a true villain, I would start my own religion, it is money, power, tax-breaks, and control over others for old rope (actually, the oldest rope!), and you get respect instead of jail. The trouble is I just have too much conscience to pull off that particular scam. I must be stupid.

As far as my work goes, I already have another two books drafted and am currently researching them, both subjects are controversial which I do not think will surprise anyone, and they are just as challenging in literary terms as the ones that I have completed. I find the prospect of their publication exciting and am enjoying both the workload and my freedom. In an introspective analysis I imagine it is clear that by my very nature and life experiences I am a drama junkie, so it is pointless me trying to escape that fact. I just hope that the next episode runs a little more smoothly.

*Tact is the knack of making a point
without making an enemy.*

Howard W. Newton

HOWARD BROWN

HOWARD BROWN